Modern Critical Interpretations

Modern Critical Interpretations

Maya Angelou's
I Know Why the Caged Bird Sings

Edited and with an introduction by
Harold Bloom
Sterling Professor of the Humanities
Yale University

CHELSEA HOUSE PUBLISHERS
Philadelphia

© 1998 by Chelsea House Publishers, a subsidiary of
Haights Cross Communications.

Introduction © 1998 by Harold Bloom

Printed and bound in the United States of America

10 9 8 7 6 5 4 3

∞ The paper used in this publication meets the minimum
requirements of the American National Standard for
Permanence of Paper for Printed Library Materials,
Z39.48-1984

Library of Congress Cataloging-in-Publication Data

Maya Angelou's I know why the caged bird sings / edited and
    with an introduction by Harold Bloom.
        p.   cm.—(Modern critical interpretations)
    Includes bibliographical references and index.
    ISBN 0-7910-4773-3
    1. Angelou, Maya. I know why the caged bird sings.
2. Afro-American women authors—Biography—History
and criticism.   3. Women entertainers—Biography—
History and criticism.   4. Autobiography.
I. Bloom, Harold.   II. Series.
PS3551.N464Z77   1998
8128'.5409—dc21
    [b]   97-53105
                                                    CIP

Contents

Editor's Note

This volume contains a representative selection of the more useful criticism devoted to Maya Angelou's autobiography *I Know Why the Caged Bird Sings*. I am indebted to Tenley Williams for her devoted research on these essays, which are reprinted here in the chronological order of their initial publication.

My Introduction studies Angelou's autobiographical tone, with its skilled blend of intimacy and detachment. The chronological sequence of criticism commences with Sidonie Ann Smith's account of Angelou's "growing consciousness of self-worth and self-importance," after which George E. Kent locates Angelou within the African American autobiographical tradition.

For Myra K. McMurry, *Caged Bird*'s achievement is its transmutation of role-playing into "a humanizing of reality," while Liliane K. Arensberg centers upon Angelou's metaphoric transition from images of death to those of rebirth.

Christine Froula, in a very strongly argued essay, links Angelou and Alice Walker as chroniclers of women emerging from what Froula terms "the hysterical cultural text" supposedly imposed upon them by patriarchal canons. Somewhat less strenuously, Keneth Kinnamon attempts an intertextual connection between *Caged Bird* and Richard Wright's powerful memoir, *Black Boy*.

Joanne M. Braxton emphasizes that *Caged Bird*'s "song of transcendence" takes on the burden of the entire "black female experience" in the United States, after which Françoise Lionnet very usefully centers upon Angelou's problematic sense of her audience.

Angelou's status as pioneer is hailed by Fred Lee Hord, while Mary Vermillion broods on the representations of rape in slave narrative and in *Caged Bird*.

James Bertolino emphasizes Angelou's versatility as an author, seeing her as three-writers-in-one, after which Opal Moore defends the social importance of *Caged Bird*, particularly in regard to the issue of the kind of censorship the book sometimes provokes in school boards.

Introduction

African American autobiography is now a much-studied mode, as befits a tradition that includes such important works as Frederick Douglass' *Narrative* of 1845, Richard Wright's *Black Boy*, Alex Haley's *Autobiography of Malcolm X*, and the ongoing sequence of memoirs by Maya Angelou. Critics have agreed on the importance of the slave narrative and the African American church sermon as sources for this tradition, but I suspect that Angelou, in particular, is highly eclectic, and draws upon a very wide range of influences. The buoyant intensity of her tone, at once intimate and serene, is one of her principal virtues as an autobiographer, and her fictions of the self doubtless will maintain that attractive tone, which brings her an immense variety of readers.

Angelou tells us that she read widely as a child, saving her "young and loyal passion" for the African American poets Paul Laurence Dunbar, Langston Hughes, and James Weldon Johnson, all of whose voices can still be heard in her own poetry. Dunbar, whom she cites first, provided her with her most famous title, in the final stanza of his High Romantic lyric, "Sympathy," which still impresses me as a poignant and vital poem:

> I know what the caged bird feels, alas!
>   When the sun is bright on the upland slopes;
> When the wind stirs soft through the springing grass,
> And the river flows like a stream of glass;
>   When the first bird sings and the first bud opes,
> And the faint perfume from its chalice steals—
> I know what the caged bird feels!
>
> I know why the caged bird beats his wing
>   Till its blood is red on the cruel bars;
> For he must fly back to his perch and cling
> When he fain would be on the bough a-swing;

And a pain still throbs in the old, old scars
And they pulse again with a keener sting—
I know why he beats his wing!

I know why the caged bird sings, ah me,
    When his wing is bruised and his bosom sore,—
When he beats his bars and he would be free;
It is not a carol of joy or glee,
    But a prayer that he sends from his heart's deep core,
But a plea, that upward to Heaven he flings—
    I know why the caged bird sings!

I find it extraordinary that Angelou's *I Know Why the Caged Bird Sings* is finally more a carol than it is a prayer or a plea. The young Marguerite Johnson (as Angelou then was named) tells a story that would necessarily sink most of us without trace, were it our own. Yet she is a survivor, and the tale of her first sixteen years is a litany of successful endurances. Like all autobiographies, it doubtless has fictive elements, but whatever they may be, they evidently work to reinforce the book's engaging artfulness. The strong pattern of the narrative takes Angelou from public and private humiliations and deprivations through the terror of being raped at the age of eight. Trauma ensues, and yet the extraordinarily strong soul of Marguerite Johnson eventually goes beyond the trauma. At sixteen, she becomes an unmarried mother, through choice, a high school graduate, and a fully individuated consciousness, capable of sustaining all the hazards yet to arrive.

I return to the question of the achieved tone of *I Know Why the Caged Bird Sings*. Few of us, in our actual lives, can speak both intimately and serenely to others. Angelou, in her first memoir, provides us with a voice that we encounter very infrequently, whether in life or in literature. Sometimes I can hear a touch of Kipling's tone in that voice, and I suspect that Angelou has learned from Kipling's great tale, *Kim*, something of the knack of balancing closeness and detachment. Intimacy, in a woman autobiographer, necessarily has very different aspects than in a male storyteller, and yet Angelou, like Kipling, is very much a performer. Something in her, as in him, resembles a tale-spinner in a bazaar, directly confronting an audience. To accomplish the paradox of being there with the reader, and yet maintaining a reserve, both in regard to audience and to self, is a considerable achievement. I have doubts about Angelou's poetry, and do not find her other memoirs as compelling as her first, but *I Know Why the Caged Bird Sings* is likely to keep its vast readership for some years to come.

SIDONIE ANN SMITH

The Song of a Caged Bird:
Maya Angelou's Quest after Self-Acceptance

I know why the caged bird sings, ah me,
When his wing is bruised and his bosom sore,—
When he beats his bars and he would be free;
It is not a carol of joy or glee,
But a prayer that he sends from his heart's deep core,
But a plea, that upward to Heaven he flings—
I know why the caged bird sings!

"Sympathy"—Paul Laurence Dunbar

A young, awkward girl child dressed in a cut-down faded purple, too-long taffeta gown, stands nervously before an Easter congregation in Stamps, Arkansas, asking, "What you looking at me for?" The next lines refuse to escape forgetfulness, imprinting this one indelibly on the shamefilled silence. Finally the minister's wife offers her the forgotten lines. She grabs them, spills them into the congregation and then stumbles out of the watching church, "a green persimmon caught between [her] legs." Unable to control the pressure of her physical response, she urinated, then laughs "from the knowledge that [she] wouldn't die from a busted head."

But the cathartic laughter never even begins to mute, much less transcend, the real pain that is this experience, the palpable pain that pulses through her long trip down the aisle of that singing church as urine flows

From *Southern Humanities Review* 7:4. © 1973 by Auburn University.

mockingly down her grotesquely skinny, heavily dusted legs. "What you looking at me for?" The question's physical articulation is barely audible; its emotional articulation wails insufferably through the child's whole being, wails her self-consciousness, wails her diminished self-image: "What you looking at me for?"—"What you looking at *me* for?"—over and over until it becomes, "Is something *wrong* with me?" For this child too much is wrong.

The whole way she looks is wrong. She knows it too. That's why they are all looking at her. Earlier as she watches her grandmother make over the white woman's faded dress she revels for one infinitely delicious moment in fantasies of stardom. In a beautiful dress she would be transformed into a beautiful movie star: "I was going to look like one of the sweet little white girls who were everybody's dream of what was right with the world" (4). But between the taffeta insubstantiality of her ideal vision of herself and the raw (fleshy) edges of her substantiality stands the one-way mirror:

> Easter's early morning sun had shown the dress to be a plain ugly cut-down from a white woman's once-was-purple throwaway. It was old-lady-long too, but it didn't hide my skinny legs, which had been greased with Blue Seal Vaseline and powdered with the Arkansas red clay. The age-faded color made my skin look dirty like mud, and everyone in church was looking at my skinny legs. (4)

Wrong dress. Wrong legs. Wrong hair. Wrong face. Wrong color. Wrong. Wrong. Wrong. The child lives in a "black ugly dream," or rather night-mare. But since this life is only a dream, the child knows she will awaken soon into a rightened, a whitened reality.

> Wouldn't they be surprised when one day I woke out of my black ugly dream, and my real hair, which was long and blond, would take the place of the kinky mass that Momma wouldn't let me straighten? My light-blue eyes were going to hypnotize them, after all the things they said about "my daddy must of been a Chinaman" (I thought they meant made out of china, like a cup) because my eyes were so small and squinty. Then they would understand why I had never picked up a Southern accent, or spoke the common slang, and why I had to be forced to eat pigs' tails and snouts. Because I was really white and because a cruel fairy stepmother, who was understandably jealous of my beauty, had turned me into a too-big Negro girl, with nappy black hair, broad feet and a space

between her teeth that would hold a number-two pencil. (4–5)

In a society attuned to white standards of physical beauty, the black girl child cries herself to sleep at night to the tune of her own inadequacy. At least she can gain temporary respite in the impossible dreams of whiteness. Here in the darkened nights of the imagination, that refuge from society and the mirror, blossoms an ideal self. Yet even the imagination is sometimes not so much a refuge as it is a prison in which the dreamer becomes even more inescapably possessed by the nightmare since the very self she fantasizes conforms perfectly to society's prerequisites. The cage door jangles shut around the child's question: "What you looking at me for?"

In this primal scene of childhood which opens Maya Angelou's *I Know Why the Caged Bird Sings*, the black girl child testifies to her imprisonment in her bodily prison. She is a black ugly reality, not a whitened dream. And the attendant self-consciousness and diminished self-image throb through her bodily prison until the bladder can do nothing but explode in a parody of release (freedom).

In good autobiography the opening, whether a statement of act such as the circumstance of birth or ancestry or the recreation of a primal incident such as Maya Angelou's, defines the strategy of the narrative. The strategy itself is a function of the autobiographer's self-image at the moment of writing, for the nature of that self-image determines the nature of the pattern of self-actualization he discovers while attempting to shape his past experiences. Such a pattern must culminate in some sense of an ending, and it is this sense of an ending that informs certain earlier moments with significance and determines the choice of what experience he recreates, what he discards. In fact the earlier moments are fully understood only after that sense of an ending has imposed itself upon the material of the autobiographer's life. Ultimately, then, the opening moment assumes the end, the end the opening moment. Its centrality derives from its distillation of the environment of the self which generated the pattern of the writer's quest after self-actualization.

In Black American autobiography the opening almost invariably recreates the environment of enslavement from which the black self seeks escape. Such an environment was literal in the earliest form of black autobiography, the slave narrative, which traced the flight of the slave northward from slavery into full humanity. In later autobiography, however, the literal enslavement is replaced by more subtle forms of economic, historical, psychological, and spiritual imprisonment from which the black self still seeks an escape route to a "North." Maya Angelou's opening calls to mind the primal experience which opens Richard Wright's *Black Boy*. Young Richard, prevented from playing outside because of his sick, "white"-faced grandmother, puts fire to curtains and burns down the house. For this his mother beats him nearly to death. Richard's childhood needs for self-expression culminate in destruction, foreshadowing the dilemma the auto-biographer discovers in his subsequent experience. His needs for self-actualization when blocked eventuate in violence. But any attempt at self-actualization is inevitably blocked by society, black and white, which threatens him with harsh punishment, possibly even death. Finally Wright is forced to flee the South altogether with only the knowledge of the power of the word to carry with him. *Black Boy*'s opening scene of childhood rebellion against domestic oppression distills the essence of Wright's struggle to free himself from social oppression.

Maya Angelou's autobiography, like Wright's, opens with a primal childhood scene that brings into focus the nature of the imprisoning environment from which the self will seek escape. The black girl child is trapped within the cage of her own diminished self-image around which interlock the bars of natural and social forces. The oppression of natural forces, of physical appearance and processes, foists a self-consciousness on all young girls who must grow from children into women. Hair is too thin or stringy or mousy or nappy. Legs are too fat, too thin, too bony, the knees too bowed. Hips are too wide or not wide enough. Breasts grow too fast or not at all. The self-critical process is incessant, a driving demon. But in the black girl child's experience of these natural bars are reinforced with the rusty iron social bars of racial subordination and impotence. Being born black is itself a liability in a world ruled by white standards of beauty which imprison the child *a priori* in a cage of ugliness: "What you looking at me for?" This really isn't me. I'm white with long blond hair and blue eyes, with pretty pink skin and straight hair, with a delicate mouth. I'm my own mistake. I haven't dreamed myself hard enough. I'll try again. The black and blue bruises of the soul multiply and compound as the caged bird flings herself against these bars:

> The Black female is assaulted in her tender years by all those common forces of nature at the same time that she is caught in the tripartite crossfire of masculine prejudice, white illogical hate and Black lack of power. (265)

Within this imprisoning environment there is no place for this black girl child. She becomes a displaced person whose pain is intensified by her consciousness of that displacement:

> If growing up is painful for the Southern Black girl, being aware of her displacement is the rust on the razor that threatens the throat.
>
> It is an unnecessary insult. (6)

If the black man is denied his potency and his masculinity, if his autobiography narrates the quest of the black male after a "place" of full manhood, the black woman is denied her beauty and her quest is one after self-accepted black womanhood. Thus the discovered pattern of significant moments Maya Angelou superimposes on the experience of her life is a pattern of moments that race the quest of the black female after a "place," a place where a child no longer need ask self-consciously, "What you looking at me for?" but where a woman can declare confidently, "I am a beautiful, Black woman."

Two children, sent away to a strange place by estranging parents, cling to each other as they travel by train across the Southwestern United States— and cling to their tag: "To Whom It May Concern—that we were Marguerite and Bailey Johnson, Jr., from Long Beach, California, en route to Stamps, Arkansas, c/o Mrs. Annie Henderson" (6). The autobiography of Black America is haunted by these orphans, children beginning life or early finding themselves without parents, sometimes with no one but themselves. They travel through life desperately in search of a home, some place where they can escape the shadow of loneliness, of solitude, of outsiderness. Although Maya and Bailey are traveling toward the home of their grand-mother, more important, they are traveling away from the "home" of their parents. Such rejection a child internalizes and translates as a rejection of self: ultimately the loss of home occasions the loss of self-worth. "I'm being sent away because I'm not lovable." The quest for a home therefore is the quest for acceptance, for love, and for the resultant feeling of self-worth. Because Maya Angelou became conscious of her displacement early in life, she began her quest earlier than most of us. Like that of any orphan, that quest is intensely lonely, intensely solitary, making it all the more desperate, immediate, demanding, and making it, above all, an even more estranging process. For the "place" always recedes into the distance, moving with the horizon, and the searcher goes through life merely "passing through" to some place beyond, always beyond.

Stamps, Arkansas

> The town reacted to us as its inhabitants had reacted to all

things new before our coming. It regarded us a while without curiosity but with caution, and after we were seen to be harmless (and children) it closed in around us, as a real mother embraces a stranger's child. Warmly, but not too familiarly. (7)

Warmth but distance: displacement. The aura of personal displacement is counterpointed by the ambience of displacement within the larger black community. The black community of Stamps is itself caged in the social reality of racial subordination and impotence. The cotton pickers must face an empty bag every morning, an empty will every night, knowing all along that the season would end as it had begun—money-less, credit-less.

The undercurrent of social displacement, the fragility of the sense of belonging, are evidenced in the intrusion of white reality. Poor white trash humiliate Momma as she stands erect before them singing a hymn. Uncle Willie hides deep in the potato barrel the night the sheriff warns them that white men ride after black, any black. The white apparition haunts the life of Stamps, Arkansas, always present though not always visible.

Against this apparition the community shores itself up with a subdued hominess, a fundamental faith in fundamental religion, and resignation. The warmth mitigates the need to resist: or rather, the impossibility of resistance is sublimated in the bond of community.

The people of Stamps adapt in the best way they know: according to Momma Henderson—"realistically"—which is to say that they equate talking with whites with risking their lives. If the young girl stands before the church congregation asking, "What you looking at me for?", the whole black community might just as well be standing before the larger white community and asking that same question. Everything had to be low-key: the less looked at, the better, for the black in a white society. High physical visibility meant self-consciousness within the white community. To insure his own survival the black tried not to be looked at, tried to become invisible. Such a necessary response bred an overriding self-criticism and self-depreciation into the black experience. Maya Angelou's diminished sense of self reflected the entire black community's diminished self-image.

Nevertheless, there is a containedness in this environment called Stamps, a containedness which controls the girl child's sense of displacement, the containedness of a safe way of life, a hard way of life, but a known way of life. The child doesn't want to fit here, but it shapes her to it. And although she is lonely, although she suffers from her feelings of ugliness and abandonment, the strength of Momma's arms contains some of that loneliness.

Suddenly Stamps is left behind. Moving on, the promise of a place. Her mother, aunts, uncles, grandparents—St. Louis, a big city, an even bigger reality, a totally new reality. But even here displacement: St. Louis, with its strange sounds, its packaged food, its modern conveniences, remains a foreign country to the child who after only a few weeks understands that it is not to be her "home." For one moment only the illusion of being in place overwhelms the child. For that moment Mr. Freeman holds her pressed to him:

> He held me so softly that I wished he wouldn't ever let me go. I felt at home. From the way he was holding me I knew he'd never let me go or let anything bad ever happen to me. This was probably my real father and we had found each other at last. But then he rolled over, leaving me in a wet place and stood up. (71)

The orphan hopes, for that infinite moment, that she has been taken back home to her father. She feels loved, accepted. Ultimately Mr. Freeman's strength, his arms, are not succor: they are her seduction. The second time he holds her to him it is to rape her, and, in short minutes, the child becomes even more displaced. The child becomes a child-woman. In court, frightened, the child denies the first time. Mr. Freeman is found dead. The child knows it is because she has lied. What a worthless, unlovable, naughty child! What can she do but stop talking: "Just my breath, carrying my words out, might poison people and they'd curl up and die like the black fat slugs that only pretended. I had to stop talking" (85).

Now total solitude, total displacement, total self-condemnation. Back to Stamps, back to the place of grayness and barrenness, the place where nothing happened to people who, in spite of it all, felt contentment "based on the belief that nothing more was coming to them although a great deal more was due" (86). Her psychological and emotional devastation find a mirror in Stamps' social devastation. Stamps gives her back the familiarity and security of a well-known cage. She climbs back in happily, losing herself in her silent world, surrendering herself to her own worthlessness.

She lives alone in this world for one year until the afternoon when the lovely Mrs. Flowers walks into the store and becomes for Maya a kind of surrogate mother. Mrs. Flowers opens the door to the caged bird's silence with the key of acceptance. For the first time Maya is accepted as an individual rather than as a relation to someone else: "I was liked, and what a difference it made. I was respected not as Mrs. Henderson's grandchild or Bailey's sister but for just being Marguerite Johnson" (98). Such unqualified acceptance allows her to experience the incipient power of her own self-worth.

Inside her germinated this growing consciousness of self-worth and self-importance. Outside, in the life that revolved around her, sat the stagnant air of impotence and frustration. Of this lack of control the child gradually becomes conscious. The older narrator chooses to recreate those moments significant because of their dramatization of this lack of power: the fear attendant upon Bailey's being out late one evening; the church meeting during which the young girl comes to realize that her neighbors used religion as a way of "bask(ing) in the righteousness of the poor and the exclusiveness of the downtrodden" (110). Even the Joe Louis fight which sends a thrill of pride through a black community vicariously winning victory over a white man, becomes a grotesque counterpoint to the normal way of life. Then at the graduation ceremony, during which the exciting expectations of the young graduates and their families and friends are exploded casually by the words of an oblivious and insensitive white speaker, the young girl comes to know already the desperation of impotence:

> It was awful to be Negro and have no control over my life. It was brutal to be young and already trained to sit quietly and listen to charges brought against my color with no chance of defense. We should all be dead. (176)

After the humiliating trip to the white dentist's back door, the child can only compensate for such impotence by fantasizing potency and triumphant success.

One gesture, however, foreshadows Maya's eventual inability to "sit quietly" and is very much an expression of her growing acceptance of her own self-worth. For a short time she works in the house of Mrs. Viola Cullinan, but a short time only, for Mrs. Cullinan, with an easiness that comes from long tradition, assaults her ego by calling her Mary rather than Maya. Such an oversight offered so casually is a most devastating sign of the girl's invisibility. In failing to call her by her name, a symbol of identity and individuality, of uniqueness, Mrs. Cullinan fails to respect her humanity. Maya understands this perfectly and rebels by breaking Mrs. Cullinan's most cherished dish. The girl child is assuming the consciousness of rebellion as a stance necessary for preserving her individuality and affirming her self-worth. Such a stance insures displacement in Stamps, Arkansas.

But now there is yet another move. Once again the train, traveling westward to San Francisco in wartime. Here in this big city everything seems out of place.

The air of collective displacement, the impermanence of life in wartime and the gauche personalities of the more recent arrivals tended to dissipate my own sense of not belonging. In San Francisco, for the first time, I perceived myself as part of something. (205)

In Stamps the way of life remained rigid, in San Francisco it ran fluid. Maya had been on the move when she entered Stamps and thus could not settle into its rigid way of life. She chose to remain an outsider, and in so doing, chose not to allow her personality to become rigid. The fluidity of the new environment matched the fluidity of her emotional, physical, and psychological life. She could feel in place in an environment where everyone and everything seemed out-of-place.

Even more significant than the total displacement of San Francisco is Maya's trip to Mexico with her father. The older autobiographer, in giving form to her past experience, discovers that this "moment" was central to her process of growth. Maya accompanies her father to a small Mexican town where he proceeds to get obliviously drunk, leaving her with the responsibility of getting them back to Los Angeles. But she has never before driven a car. For the first time, Maya finds herself totally in control of her fate. Such total control contrasts vividly to her earlier recognition in Stamps that she as a Negro had no control over her fate. Here she is alone with that fate. And although the drive culminates in an accident, she triumphs.

This "moment" is succeeded by a month spent in a wrecked car lot scavenging with others like herself. Together these experiences provide her with a knowledge of self-determination and a confirmation of her self-worth. With the assumption of this affirmative knowledge and power, Maya is ready to challenge the unwritten, restrictive social codes of San Francisco. Mrs. Cullinan's broken dish prefigures the job on the streetcar. Stamps' acquiescence is left far behind in Arkansas as Maya assumes control over her own social destiny and engages in the struggle with life's forces. She has broken out of the rusted bars of her social cage.

But Maya must still break open the bars of her female sexuality: although she now feels power over her social identity, she feels insecurity about her sexual identity. She remains the embarrassed child who stands before the Easter congregation asking, "What you looking at me for?" The bars of her physical being close in on her, threatening her peace of mind. The lack of femininity in her small-breasted, straight-lined, and hairless physique and the heaviness of her voice become, in her imagination, symptomatic of latent lesbian tendencies. A gnawing self-consciousness still plagues her. Even after her mother's amused knowledge disperses her fears, the mere

fact of her being moved by a classmate's breasts undermines any confidence
that reassurance had provided. It was only brief respite. Now she knows,
knows in her heart, that she is a lesbian. There is only one remedy for such
a threatening reality: a man. But even making love with a casual male
acquaintance fails to quell her suspicions; the whole affair is such an unen-
joyable experience.

Only the pregnancy provides a climatic reassurance: if she can become
pregnant, she certainly cannot be a lesbian (certainly a specious argument in
terms of logic but a compelling one in terms of emotions and psychology).
The birth of the baby brings Maya something totally her own, but, more
important, brings her to a recognition of and acceptance of her full, instinctual womanhood. The child, father to the woman, opens the caged door and
allows the fully-developed woman to fly out. Now she feels the control of her
sexual identity as well as of her social identity. The girl child no longer need
ask, embarrassed, "What you looking at me for?" No longer need she fanta-
size any other reality than her own.

Maya Angelou's autobiography comes to a sense of an ending: the black
American girl child has succeeded in freeing herself from the natural and
social bars imprisoning her in the cage of her own diminished self-image by
assuming control of her life and fully accepting her black womanhood. The
displaced child has found a "place." With the birth of her child Maya is
herself born into a mature engagement with the forces of life. In welcoming
that struggle she refuses to live a death of quiet acquiescence:

> Few, if any, survive their teens. Most surrender to the vague
> but murderous pressure of adult conformity. It becomes easier to
> die and avoid conflicts than to maintain a constant battle with the
> superior forces of maturity. (231)

One final comment: one way of dying to life's struggle is to suppress its
inevitable pain by forgetting the past. Maya Angelou, who has since been a
student and teacher of dance, a correspondent in Africa, a northern coordinator for the Southern Christian Leadership Council, an actress, writer, and
director for the stage and film, had, like so many of us, successfully banished
many years of her past to the keeping of the unconscious where they lay
dormant and remained lost to her. To the extent that they were lost, so also a
part of her self was lost. Once she accepted the challenge of recovering the lost
years, she accepted the challenge of the process of self-discovery and recon-
firmed her commitment to life's struggle. By the time she, as autobiographer,
finished remembering the past and shaping it into a pattern of significant

moments, she has imposed some sense of an ending upon it. And in imposing that ending upon it she gave the experience distance and a context and thereby came to understand the past and ultimately to understand herself.

Moreover, she reaffirms her sense of self-worth by making the journey back through her past on its own terms, by immersing herself once again in the medium of her making. Stamps, Arkansas, imprinted its way of life on the child during her formative years: the lasting evidence of this imprint is the sound of it. Her genius as a writer is her ability to recapture the texture of the way of life in the texture of its idioms, its idiosyncratic vocabulary and especially in its process of image-making. The imagery hold the reality, giving it immediacy. That she chooses to recreate the past in its own sounds suggests to the reader that she accepts the past and recognizes its beauty and its ugliness, its assets and its liabilities, its strength and its weakness. Here we witness a return to and final acceptance of the past in the return to and full acceptance of its language, the language a symbolic construct of a way of life. Ultimately Maya Angelou's style testifies to her reaffirmation of self-acceptance, the self-acceptance she achieves within the pattern of the autobiography.

GEORGE E. KENT

Maya Angelou's I Know Why the Caged Bird Sings *and Black Autobiographical Tradition*

Maya Angelou, who spent much of her early life in Arkansas and grew up in California, is the author of three books: the autobiographies *I Know Why the Caged Bird Sings* (1969) and *Gather Together in My Name* (1974); and a volume of poetry, *Just Give Me a Cool Drink of Water 'Fore I Diie* (1971). My concern is with the autobiographies, with primary emphasis upon *I Know Why the Caged Bird Sings*.

I Know Why tells the story of a child's growing to maturity in the small universe of Stamps, Arkansas, in St. Louis, Missouri, and in San Francisco, California. We see Maya (nee Marguerite Johnson) and her brother Bailey shuttled to Grandmother Annie Henderson from the broken home of the mother Vivian Baxter, eventually back to Mother Vivian in St. Louis, then a return to Stamps with Grandmother Henderson, and a final return to California where Maya spends most of her time with her mother but also experiences a calamitous summer with her father, Bailey Johnson, in the southern part of the state. The book is rich in portraits of a wide assortment of blacks, descriptions of the rhythms of their lives and their confrontations with both elemental life and racial relations, and evocations of the patterns of the different environments. Their graphic depiction is always in relationship to the development of the child, but since all the experiences emerge from an imagination which has fully mastered them and, at will, turns them into symbols, they tend to operate on two levels: as mirrors of both the vigor and the unsteadiness of childhood innocence and imagination, and as near

From *African American Autobiography: A Collection of Critical Essays.* © 1993 by Prentice-Hall.

independent vibrations of the spirit of black life. The book ends with Maya's having become an unwed mother, a result of a confused move for sexual identity. Since the book ends with a dramatic episode which emphasizes Maya's beginning to face up to the terrors of motherhood, its resolution is somewhat tentative but complete enough to register the movement into a stance toward life beyond that of childhood.

Gather Together in My Name tells the story of the struggles of young womanhood to create an existence which provides security and love in a very unstable world; its time is the post–World War II period, and it involves settings in San Francisco, Los Angeles, Stamps, Arkansas, and then again various parts of California. On the one side of the tensions is Maya's combination of resourcefulness, imagination, and compulsive innocence; on the other, the intransigence of the world's obstacle courses which impel her into ill-advised love choices, an assortment of jobs ranging from that of short-order cook to setting up a house of prostitution staffed with two lesbians. Finally, in her quest for love and security, she is inveigled into prostitution by the forty-five year old pimp, L. D. Tolbrook, but forcibly argued out of it by her furious brother. Under the pressures of a loveless existence, she sees the decline of her brother into drug addiction and escapes the temptation herself by her new lover's demonstration of the unromantic degradation drugs have inflicted upon him. The book ends with Maya's statement, "I had no idea what I was going to make of my life, but I had given a promise and found my innocence. I swore I'd never lose it again." Technically, the resolution, again, has both tentativeness and a dramatic completeness. However, the feeling it gives is one of abruptness— the sensational character of it registers more fully than the definition of a new stance which it is supposed to impose.

Like *I Know Why*, *Gather Together* presents a wide assortment of personalities and conveys sharp and imaginative insights through them. It is a good book, well worth the doing. But it lacks the feeling of the fully mastered experience, the full measure and imaginative penetration, and the illusion of life vibrating as an entity in itself as well as in relationship to the heroine's own development.

It is thus *I Know Why* which I cite for creating a unique place in black autobiographical tradition. What is that tradition? Like American autobiography, in general, black autobiography has variety: the simple success story of John Mercer Langston's *From the Virginia Plantation to the National Capitol; or, the First and Only Negro Representative in Congress from the Old Dominion* (1894); the somewhat psychological analysis of Katherine Dunham's *A Touch of Innocence* (1959); the public memoir of John Roy

Lynch's *Reminiscences of an Active Life: The Autobiography of John Roy Lynch* (1970); and a varied assortment of autobiographical statements in connection with literary and public matters.

However, a main strand of black autobiographies takes us on a journey through chaos, a pattern established by the narratives of escaped slaves. The pattern takes shape in the first major black autobiography, Gustavus Vassa, *The Interesting Narrative of the Life of Olaudah Equiano, or Gustavus Vassa, the African* (1789). In relationship to later ex-slave statements, Vassa's account can be seen as emphasizing the instability of the black's relationship to all institutions devised to ward off chaos threatening human existence. And it is this instability of relationship to institutions which gives the particular tone and extremity described in much of black autobiography, those of the ex-slave and those born free. Vassa's and other ex-slave autobiographies required the achievement of tenuously held new identities: Vassa's "almost Englishman" and Christian man and usually, with the ex-slave, the combination of a definition implied by the ideals of the enlightenment and Christianity. Thus it is the temperature of urgencies which increases the root uncertainty of existence reflected by a large number of black autobiographies which eventually move from a reflection of the ambiguous dispensations of institutions of the slavery period to the ambiguous dispensations of post-slavery institutions. The autobiographies of Richard Wright (*Black Boy*, 1945), Anne Moody (*Coming of Age in Mississippi*, 1968), Malcolm X's *The Autobiography of Malcolm X* (1965), and others, will illustrate post-slavery journeys of the twentieth century and the persisting ambiguous relationship of blacks to American institutional dispensations.

Up through the early part of the twentieth century, black autobiographies had usually found grounds for a leap of faith and optimism in the complex of ideas known as The American Dream. Booker T. Washington's *Up From Slavery* (1901) is the classic example; it even fits well into the type of success story established by Benjamin Franklin's autobiography, with its emphasis upon common sense and optimism. James Weldon Johnson's *Along This Way: The Autobiography of James Weldon Johnson* (1933) focuses largely upon the public man and ends with a willed optimism: The Black must believe in the American Dream or destroy much that is of value within him. The optimism of such books can be seen as embracing the after-beat of rhythms picked up from those established by the abolitionist perspective in slave narratives. As weapons in the struggle, the narratives absorbed the tenets of Christianity, the ideals of the Enlightenment and of the American Constitution. Things were terrible, but the Great Day would come when the ideals were actualized.

Today the rhythms of the American Dream ideas run in a parallel pattern with a more serious questioning of the Dream itself. Thus Benjamin Mays's *Born to Rebel* (1971) recounts the encounter with nothingness during Mays's youth, but finds grounds for optimism in the fruits of public service. However, Richard Wright's *Black Boy* was the autobiography which began a questioning which shook the fabric of the American Dream, although the autobiography's ending leaves ground for hope of achieving the Dream in the Promised Land of the North. In the process of Wright's questioning, however, the cultural fabric of the black community is torn to shreds and tends to reflect a people teetering upon the brink of nothingness:

> After I had outlived the shocks of childhood, after the habit of reflection had been born in me, I used to mull over the strange absence of real kindness in Negroes, how unstable was our tenderness, how lacking in genuine passion we were, how void of great hope, how timid our joy, how bare our traditions, how hollow our memories, how lacking we were in those intangible sentiments that bind man to man, and how shallow was even our despair. After I had learned other ways of life I used to brood upon the unconscious irony of those who felt that Negroes led so passional an existence! I saw that what had been taken for our emotional strength was our negative confusions, our flights, our fears, our frenzy under pressure. (*Black Boy*, p. 33)

Wright was offended by the degree to which he found a black folk tradition oriented toward mere survival, base submission, and escapism, whereas, as he states in "Blueprint for Negro Writing" (*New Challenge*, Fall, 1937), he wished to mould the tradition into a martial stance. With the help of Marxism, he also wished to create the values by which the race was to live or die, to be not "only against exploiting whites, but against all of that within his own race that retards decisive action and obscures clarity of vision." He decried "a cowardly sentimentality [which had] deterred Negro writers from launching crusades against the evils which Negro ignorance and stupidity have spawned." Thus, from his autobiography and from several works of fiction, there emerges the hero as black rebel-outsider, embattled, particularly after *Uncle Tom's Children*, both with the pretensions of the American Dream and his own folk tradition.

Ralph Ellison's response to Wright's portrait of black life has been mixed. In his essay "Richard Wright's Blues" [*Shadow and Act*, 1964], he seems partly to condone and partly to reinterpret from his own perspective.

Among other things, he notes that the personal warmth of black communal life, in line with Wright's illustrations, "is accompanied by an ` equally personal coldness, kindliness by cruelty, regard by malice," that the opposite qualities are quickly set off "against the member who gestures toward individuality," and that "The member who breaks away is apt to be more impressed by its negative than by its positive character." He seems to defend the passage I quoted above from *Black Boy*: Wright was rejecting not only the white South in his autobiography but the South within himself—"As a rebel he formulated that rejection negatively, because it was the negative face of the Negro community upon which he looked most often as a child." Embattled himself with Irving Howe in his later essay "The World and the Jug" [*Shadow and Act*, 1964], Ellison at this time rejected the same quotation as having its source in Wright's attempts to see the forms of Negro humanity through the lens of Marxism and in Wright's paraphrase of Henry James's "catalogue of those items of a high civilization which were absent from American life during Hawthorne's day, and which seemed so necessary in order for the novelist to function." However, it must be said that Wright's intense rendering of negative images of black life in such works as *Black Boy* [1945], *Native Son* [1940], *Lawd Today* [1963], and *The Long Dream* [1958], without precluding assists from James and Marxism, would seem to require that we accept his negative remarks as an article of faith and belief. Ellison's earlier remarks, taking into consideration the stance of the rebel, and Wright's own aspiration to launch crusades against ignorance and stupidity seem to come closer to accounting for the degree of negativity in Wright's position. Certainly, another embattled rebel, Anne Moody in *Coming of Age in Mississippi*, seeing black communal life's frequent responses to the incursion of white power, gives off a similar tone of negativity and places beside the American Dream idea a large question mark. Such subsequent landmark autobiographies as Huey P. Newton's *Revolutionary Suicide* [1973] and the earlier *Autobiography of Malcolm X* [1965] seem to complete a rhythm of development away from a middle class consciousness or complex of ideas.

In the attempt to define a major strand of development in a black autobiographical tradition, then, I've outlined the theme of a journey through a highly heated chaos deriving from black life's ambiguous relationship to American institutions, an erosion of faith in the American Dream idea which earlier had provided grounds for optimism, and a controversially developing sense of negativity concerning the quality of black life in America.

I Know Why creates a unique place within black autobiographical tradition, not by being "better" than the formidable autobiographical landmarks described, but by its special stance toward the self, the community, and the universe, and by a form exploiting the full measure of imagination necessary to acknowledge both beauty and absurdity.

The emerging self, equipped with imagination, resourcefulness, and a sense of the tenuousness of childhood innocence, attempts to foster itself by crediting the adult world with its own estimate of its god-like status and managing retreats into the autonomy of the childhood world when conflicts develop. Given the black adult's necessity to compromise with prevailing institutions and to develop limited codes through which nobility, strength, and beauty can be registered, the areas where a child's requirements are absolute—love, security, and consistency—quickly reveal the protean character of adult support and a barely concealed, aggressive chaos.

We can divide the adults' resources, as they appear in the autobiography, into two areas of black life: the religious and blues traditions. Grandmother Henderson, of Stamps, Arkansas, represents the religious traditions; Mother Vivian Baxter, more of the blues-street tradition.

Grandmother's religion gives her power to order her being, that of the children, and usually the immediate space surrounding her. The spirit of the religion combined with simple, traditional maxims shapes the course of existence and the rituals of facing up to something called decency. For Maya and her brother Bailey, the first impact of the blues-street tradition is that of instability: at the ages of three and four, respectively, the children are suddenly shipped to Grandmother when the parents break up their "calamitous" marriage. A note "To Whom It May Concern" identifies the children traveling alone from "Long Beach, California, en route to Stamps, Arkansas, c/o Mrs. Annie Henderson." Angelou generalizes the children's situation as follows: "Years later I discovered that the United States had been crossed thousands of times by frightened Black children traveling alone to their newly affluent parents in Northern cities, or back to grandmothers in Southern towns when the urban North reneged on its economic promises."

Gradually, the children adjust to the new life, becoming an integral part of Grandmother Henderson's General Merchandise Store, Grandmother's church and religion, community school, and general community customs. In Chapters 1–8, we see the techniques by which the author is able to give a full registration of both the beauty and the root absurdity built into the traditions of the folk community. She carefully articulates the folk forms of responding to existence by the use of key symbols and patterns of those involved in religious and blues responses and the joining point between their ways of responding. For example, more than Grandmother Henderson is characterized through the following folk prayer, whose set phrases have accreted through a long tradition of bended knees in homes and small rural churches:

"Our Father, thank you for letting me see this New Day. Thank you that you didn't allow the bed I lay on last night to be my cooling board, nor my blanket my winding sheet. Guide my feet this day along the straight and narrow, and help me to put a bridle on my tongue. Bless this house, and everybody in it. Thank you, in the name of your Son, Jesus Christ, Amen."

The children are required to avoid impudence to adults, to respect religious piety, and to be obedient. Given the freshness of the childhood imagination, however, many meanings are turned into the absurdity often hovering near the fabric of human rituals. On the grim side, we see the poor giving thanks to the Lord for a life filled with the most meager essentials and a maximum amount of brute oppression. The church rituals create for the poor a temporary transcendence and an articulation of spirit, but their hardships are so graphically awaiting their re-confrontation with the trials of daily existence that the evoked spiritual beauty seems hard-pressed by the pathos of the grotesque. Still, it is from such religious rhythms that Grandmother Henderson possesses the strength to give much order to the children's lives, to set the family in initial order in California, and to provide them with the minimum resources to struggle for a world more attractive. The comic side is reflected through the autonomous imagination of the children: the incongruity between the piety of the shouters and the violence with which the religious gestures of one threatens the minister. Briefly, the author records the joining point between the blues and religious tradition: Miss Grace, the good-time woman, is also conducting rituals of transcendence through her barrelhouse blues for those whose uprush of spirit must have an earthly and fleshly source. The agony in religion and the blues is the connecting point: "A stranger to the music could not have made a distinction between the songs sung a few minutes before [in church] and those being danced to in the gay house."

Despite Grandmother Henderson's strength, the folk religious tradition leaves her with serious limitations. Her giant stature goes to zero, or almost, in any confrontation with the white Southern community, a startling and humiliating experience for the child worshipper of black adult omnipotence. In addition, there is what Ralph Ellison spoke of as a warmth in the folk communal life "accompanied by an equally personal coldness, kindliness by cruelty, regard by malice." It will be recalled that Ellison saw the negative qualities as being activated "against the member who gestures toward individuality." Maya Angelou dramatizes such an action in Chapter 15, a masterful section. Mrs. Bertha Flowers, the town's black intellectual, has ministered to Maya's ever-burgeoning hunger and quest for individuality by giving her a book of poetry, talking to her philosophically about life, and encouraging her to recite poems. Returning to Grandmother Henderson, she happens to say "by the way—." Grandmother gives her a severe beating for using the expression, much to the bewilderment of the child. Later, Grandmother explained that "Jesus was the Way, the Truth and the Light," that "by the way" is really saying "by Jesus," or "by God," and she had no intention of allowing the Lord's name to be taken in vain in her house. In *Gather Together* Grandmother Henderson gives her a severe, protective beating because Maya had endangered her life by responding to whites' abuse of her in the local clothing store by superlative abuse of her own. Thus, regarding folk religious tradition and other aspects of community confrontations with existence, the author imposes the illusion of striking a just balance between spiritual beauty and absurdity.

The confrontation of the self with blues-street tradition takes place while she is with her mother, Vivian Baxter, in St. Louis and California. The author manages the same just balance in portraying it. Because of the different levels of the tradition in which various members of the family are involved, because of the fluid movement some make between it and other traditions, and because of the originality with which the mother's portrait emerges, the exposure is fresh, vivid, lasting. Some of the strict man-woman codes reflected by folk ballads emerge from the character of the mother. Men are able to remain with her only so long as they honor the code, one having been cut and another shot for failure to show proper respect for the mother's prerogatives. In this fast-life area of black tradition, the children receive great kindness and considerable impact from built-in instabilities. Mother Vivian is kind in counseling Maya concerning her sexual confusions, in creating a celebrating atmosphere that children would love, in her matter-of-fact acceptance of Maya's unwed motherhood, and in the strong support she gives to the idea of self-reliance and excellence. She herself is the embodiment of bold aggressiveness and self-reliance. Her philosophy, too, has its brief maxims, involving the acceptance of the chaos swirling through and around "protective" institutions and meeting it with an on-topsmanship derived from the tough and alert self. Thus she believes in preparing for the worst, hoping for the best, and being unsurprised at anything which happens in between. At one point in the sequel autobiography, *Gather Together*, she tells Maya to be the best at anything she chooses to do—even should she choose to be a whore.

But in her fluid existence amidst threatening chaos, one drawback is the requirement of intense absorption in one's own life and in the alertness which makes on-topsmanship possible. Thus, the mother manages well her own relationship to one of her mates, a Mr. Freeman, but Maya finds herself raped by him at the tender age of eight, an act which involves her in ambiguous complicity—but also guilt and lingering shame and confusion. Her sense of innocence is stretched into dubious tenuousness by her instinctual and unconscious complicity. The fast-life tradition, unsatisfied with the actions of the court, provides for Mr. Freeman's murder—and Maya's increased sense of guilt. When she visits her hipsterish father, she suddenly is impelled into a battle with his girlfriend deriving from the girlfriend's jealousy and Maya's ambiguous emotions concerning her mother. In the process, Maya is cut.

Both children are in inner turmoil over their relationship to their beautiful, tough, and coping mother: Maya because of the paradox involved in being the ungainly and awkward daughter of the beautiful mother; Bailey, her brother, because the instability he is put through increases his oedipal ties to her. Chapter 17 is a poignant statement of Bailey's quest for his mother through a movie screen heroine who resembles her. In *Gather Together*, despite his consistent love and protectiveness of his sister Maya, he becomes involved in pimping, and after the loss of a young wife, he begins what seems to be a downward path through drugs. The problem is not that the mother did not love him, but that his earlier hunger was never resolved and her life style and codes helped to prevent his sense of security in relationship to her. Thus *Gather Together* reveals the tough and beautiful mother, who has held her poise in relationship to many men, now attempting to conceal the defeat she experiences in relationship to her son. The tough blues tradition, which is all for individuality, fails precisely where the religious tradition was strong: the provision of stable and predictable conditions.

Thus the author is able to give a just balance to the qualities of both traditions and to reveal the exact point where the universe becomes absurd. A good deal of the book's universality derives from black life's traditions seeming to mirror, with extraordinary intensity, the root uncertainty in the universe. The conflict with whites, of course, dramatizes uncertainty and absurdity with immediate headline graphicness. What intensifies the universalism still more is the conflict between the sensitive imagination and reality, and the imagination's ability sometimes to overcome. Maya and her brother have their reservoir of absurd miming and laughter, but sometimes the imagination is caught in pathos and chaos, although its values are frequently superior. When Grandmother Henderson's response to the insulting rejection by a white dentist to whom she has loaned money is humiliating, Maya finds consolation in the rituals she imagines the Grandmother using. The imaginative reproduction of the preacher's humiliating beating by an overbearing shouter is so productive of laughter that the beating the children receive becomes meaningless. Bailey, the brother, receives a very bitter experience when his imaginative simulation of sexual intercourse with girls while fully clothed suddenly leads to his encounter with a girl who demands reality, inveigles him into an exploitative love affair, and then runs away with a pullman porter.

The major function of the imagination, however, is to retain a vigorous dialectic between self and society, between the intransigent world and the aspiring self. Through the dialectic, the egos maintain themselves, even where tragic incident triumphs. In a sense, the triumph of circumstance for Maya becomes a temporary halt in a process which is constantly renewed, a fact evident in the poetic language and in the mellowness of the book's confessional form.

Finally, since *I Know Why* keeps its eyes upon the root existential quality of life, it makes its public and political statement largely through generalizing statements which broaden individual characters into types: Grandmother Henderson into the Southern mother; Maya into the young black woman, etc. And the after-rhythms of the American Dream can flow in occasionally without gaining the solemnity of a day in court.

The uniqueness of *I Know Why* arises then from a full imaginative occupation of the rhythms flowing from the primal self in conflict with things as they are, but balanced by the knowledge that the self must find its own order and create its own coherence.

MYRA K. McMURRY

Role-Playing as Art in Maya Angelou's "Caged Bird"

As a songwriter, journalist, playwright, poet, fiction and screen writer, Maya Angelou is often asked how she escaped her past. How does one grow up, Black and female, in the rural South of the thirties and forties without being crippled or hardened? Her immediate response, "How the hell do you know I did escape?" is subtly deceptive. The evidence of Angelou's creative accomplishments would indicate that she did escape; but a closer look reveals the human and artistic complexity of her awareness. For the first volume of her autobiography, *I Know Why the Caged Bird Sings*, is not an exorcism of or escape from the past, but a transmutation of that past. The almost novelistic clarity of *Caged Bird* results from the artistic tension between Angelou's recollected self and her authorial consciousness. Implicit in this dual awareness is the knowledge that events are significant not merely in themselves, but also because they have been transcended.

Angelou takes her title from Paul Laurence Dunbar's poem, "Sympathy." Dunbar's caged bird sings from the frustration of imprisonment; its song is a prayer. Angelou's caged bird sings also from frustration, but in doing so, discovers that the song transforms the cage from a prison that denies selfhood to a vehicle for self-realization. The cage is a metaphor for roles which, because they have become institutionalized and static, do not facilitate interrelationship, but impose patterns of behavior which deny true identity.

In *Caged Bird* Angelou describes her efforts to adapt to the role of a young Black girl, the painfully humorous failures, and the gradual realization of how to transcend the restrictions. At a very early age, the child Angelou,

From *South Atlantic Bulletin*, 41:2. © 1976 by South Atlantic Modern Language Association.

Marguerite Johnson, is an intensely self-conscious child; she feels that her true self is obscured. The autobiography opens with an episode in which Marguerite must recite a poem beginning, "What you looking at me for?" As she struggles for her lines in the Easter morning church service, she is conscious of her dual self, which is the constant subject of her fantasies. Beneath the ugly disguise—the lavender dress cut-down from a white woman's throwaway, the skinny legs, broad feet, nappy hair, and teeth with a space between—was the real Marguerite Johnson, a sweet little white girl with long blond hair, "everybody's dream of what was right with the world" (p. 1). She mixes elements of fairy tale and Easter story to imagine that a cruel fairy step-mother had changed her from her true self to her present condition. And she relishes the recognition scene in which people will say, "'Marguerite (sometimes it was "dear Marguerite"), forgive us, please, we didn't know who you were,' and [she] would answer generously, 'No, you couldn't have known. Of course I forgive you.'" This introductory episode is emblematic of the child's perspective. She is in a cage which conceals and denies her true nature, and she is aware of her displacement. Someone whispers the forgotten lines and she completes the poem, which suggests transcendence:

> What you looking at me for?
> I didn't come to stay.
> I just come to tell you its Easter Day.

But for Marguerite there is no transcendence. After painful confinement in the humiliating situation, the pressure of her true self to escape takes on a physical urgency. She signals request to go to the toilet and starts up the aisle. But one of the children trips her and her utmost control is then effective only as far as the front porch. In her view the choice was between wetting her pants or dying of a "busted head," for what was denied proper vent would surely back up to her head and cause an explosion and "the brains and spit and tongue and eyes would roll all over the place" (p. 3). The physical violence of the destruction imagined is the child's equivalent for the emotional violence of self-repression.

In Marguerite's world, rigid laws govern every aspect of a child's life: there are laws for addressing adults by proper title, laws for speaking and more for not speaking, laws about cleanliness and obedience, and about performance in school and behavior in church. Although she respects her brother Bailey for his ability to evade some laws, Marguerite is an obedient child. Her transgressions come, not of willful disobedience, but from loss of control in confrontations in which she is physically overpowered by a larger force.

Much of the story of growing up as Marguerite Johnson is the story of learning to control natural responses. Not to laugh at funny incidents in church, not to express impatience when the guest preacher says too long a blessing and ruins the dinner, not to show felt fear, are part of preparation for life in a repressive society.

Although much of Marguerite's repression is related to her being a child, the caged condition affects almost everyone in her world. The customers in her grandmother's store were trapped in the cotton fields; no amount of hope and work could get them out. Bailey, for all his clever manipulations, was "locked in the enigma . . . of inequality and hate" (p. 168). Her Uncle Willie's own body is his cage. Marguerite observes with the sensitivity of the adult Angelou looking back that he "must have tired of being crippled, as prisoners tire of penitentiary bars and the guilty tire of blame." When Marguerite catches Uncle Willie pretending not to be crippled before some out-of-town visitors, she finds the common condition of being caged and the desire to escape ground for sympathy. "I understood and felt closer to him in that moment then ever before or since" (p. 11).

Even the indomitable grandmother, Anne Henderson, rises each morning with the consciousness of a caged animal. She prays, "Guide my feet this day along the straight and narrow, and help me to put a bridle on my tongue" (p. 5). But it is from her that Marguerite begins to learn how to survive in the cage. Angelou recalls a particular incident that happened when she was about ten years old in which she began to realize her grandmother's triumph. Momma, as Marguerite calls her, has come onto the porch to admire a design that Marguerite had raked in the yard. At the approach of some troublesome "powhitetrash" children, Momma sends Marguerite inside where she cowers behind the screen door. Momma stands solidly on the porch humming a hymn. The impudent children tease, mimic, and insult the older, respectable woman who, by any measure that Marguerite can think of, is their superior. As Marguerite watches and suffers humiliation for her grandmother, she wants to scream at the girls and throw lye on them, but she realizes that she is "as clearly imprisoned behind the scene as the actors outside are confined to their roles" (p. 25). Throughout the performance, Momma stands humming so softly that Marguerite knows she is humming only because her apron strings vibrate. After the children leave, Momma comes inside and Marguerite sees that she is beautiful; her face is radiant. As Momma hums "Glory, glory, hallelujah when I lay my burden down," Marguerite realizes that whatever the contest had been, Momma had won. Marguerite goes back to her raking and makes a huge heart design with little hearts inside growing smaller toward the center, and draws an arrow piercing through all the hearts to the smallest one. Then she brings Momma to see. In essence she is using the design to organize feelings she could not otherwise order or express, just as Momma has used the song to organize her thoughts and feelings beyond the range of the children's taunts. She triumphs not only in spite of her restrictions, but because of them. It is because, as a Black woman, she must maintain the role of respect toward the white children that she discovers another vehicle for her true emotions. She has used her cage creatively to transcend it.

The same principle works for a group as well as for an individual. What Maya Angelou had understood intuitively or subconsciously as a ten-year-old comes to the level of conscious realization after her eighth-grade graduation. Marguerite's graduation ceremony begins in an aura of magic, but just after the national anthem and the pledge of allegiance, the point at which they normally would have sung the song they considered to be the Negro national anthem, the principal nervously signals the students to be seated. Then he introduces as commencement speaker a white politician who is on his way to another engagement and must speak out of order so that he can leave. His speech and the suppression of feeling his mere presence entails are humiliating reminders to the students of the restrictive white world in which they live. He talks of plans for an artist to teach at Central High, the white school, and of new microscopes and equipment for the Chemistry labs at Central. For Lafayette County Training School he promises the "only colored paved playing field in that part of Arkansas" and some equipment for the home economics building and the workshop. The implications of his talk are crushing to the graduates. For Marguerite the occasion is ruined; she remembers that

> Graduation, the hush-hush magic time of frills and gifts and congratulations and diplomas, was finished for me before my name was called. The accomplishment was nothing. The meticulous maps, drawn in three colors of ink, learning and spelling decasyllabic words, memorizing the whole of The Rape of Lucrece—it was for nothing. Donleavy had exposed us.
>
> We were maids and farmers, handymen and washerwomen, and anything higher that we aspired to was farcical and presumptuous. (p. 152)

The white politician rushes off to his next engagement, leaving a gloom over the ceremony. One student recites "Invictus"—"I am the master of my fate, I am the captain of my soul"—but now it is a farce. As Henry Reed, the valedictorian, gives his address, Marguerite wonders that he could go on. But at the end, Henry turns to the graduates and begins to sing the song omitted earlier, the Negro national anthem. The students, parents and visitors respond to the familiar song—their own song, and as they sing, "We have come over a way that with tears has been watered, / We have come, treading our path through the blood of the slaughtered," the separate, isolated individuals become a community with a common soul:

> We were on top again. As always again. We survived. The depths had been icy and dark, but now a bright sun spoke to our souls. I was no longer simply a member of the proud graduating class of 1940; I was a proud member of the wonderful, beautiful Negro race. (p. 156)

Maya Angelou abstracts from this incident that "we [the Negro race] survive in exact relationship to the dedication of our poets (include preachers, musicians and blues singers)" (p. 156). Art organizes consciousness; it brings people together with a sense of shared experience, and a sympathy of feeling. It provides a focal point that gives unified structure to emotional response. In this sense even a prize fighter becomes an artist, as when people gather at the store to listen to the radio broadcast of a Joe Louis fight. Joe Louis becomes symbolic of their repressed selves; his victory, limited and defined by the boxing ring, is nonetheless a spiritual victory for all Blacks. Like Marguerite's finally triumphant graduation, it is a victory, the significance of which largely depends on the sense of limitation overcome. Louis is simultaneously an oppressed man and "the strongest man in the world," and the full import of his achievement in winning the heavyweight championship lies in the context of the restrictions he overcame.

The same role that may be destructive to selfhood can, when played creatively, be transformed to a role that enhances self. The artist is able to do what the con men friends of Daddy Clidell do. They find a mark, someone who has obvious prejudices, and use these prejudices against him. Similarly the artist uses the bitter reality of his experience to produce a vehicle for essential human values. The artist achieves the same victory as the hero of the Black American ghettos, whom Maya Angelou describes as "that man who is offered only the crumbs from his country's table but by ingenuity and courage is able to take for himself a Lucullan feast" (p. 190). The artist also achieves a victory over reality; he too is able to take crumbs and "by ingenuity and courage" make a feast.

When Maya Angelou speaks of "survival with style" and attributes survival to the work of artists, she is talking about a function of art similar to that described by Ralph Ellison. Speaking of his own early discovery of the role of art, he calls it "a mode of humanizing reality and of evoking a feeling of being at home in the world. It is something which the artist shares with the group," and he describes how he and his friends yearned "to make any-and-everything of quality Negro-American; to appropriate it, possess it, re-create it in our own group and individual images. . . . [We] recognized and were proud of our group's own style wherever we discerned it—in jazzmen and prize fighters, ballplayers and tap dancers; in gesture, inflection, intona-tion, timbre and phrasing. Indeed, in all those nuances of expression and atti-tude which reveal a culture. We did not fully understand the cost of that style but we recognized within it an affirmation of life beyond all question of our difficulties as Negroes."

Such an affirmation of life, a humanizing of reality, is Maya Angelou's answer to the question of how a Black girl can grow up in a repressive system without being maimed by it. Art protects the human values of compassion, love, and innocence, and makes the freedom for the self-realization necessary for real survival. Her answer, like Ellison's, skirts the reformer's question: is "the cost of that style" too high? In this sense she and Ellison are religious writers rather than social ones, for their ultimate concern is self-transcen-dence. It is unlikely that either would deny the practical value of the past twenty years' progress toward attainment of Negroes' full citizenship in America. But ultimately, as artists, their concern is with the humanity which must survive, and even assimilate into its own creative potential, such restric-tions as these writers have encountered. For if this humanity cannot survive restriction, then it will itself become assimilated to the roles imposed upon it.

LILIANE K. ARENSBERG

Death as a Metaphor of Self in
I Know Why the Caged Bird Sings

When I think about myself,
I almost laugh myself to death,
My life has been one great big joke,
A dance that's walked
A song that's spoke
I laugh so hard I almost choke
When I think about myself.
                              —Maya Angelou

In 1970, at a time when most blacks and a growing number of liberal whites affirmed the ad-campaign motto that " Black is Beautiful," Maya Angelou's autobiography was published. An un-beautiful, awkward, rather morose, dreamy, and " too big Negro girl," young Maya Angelou seems an unlikely heroine. Neither the pretty and radiant prom queen of her all-black high school, like Anne Moody in *Coming of Age in Mississippi*, nor the acknowl- edged genius of her doting family like Nikki Giovanni in *Gemini*, the child Angelou writes of is unadmired, unenvied, uncoddled as she makes her precarious way (on "broad feet," she reminds us) into the world.

Spanning the first sixteen years of her life, *I Know Why the Caged Bird Sings* opens with Maya Angelou's arrival, at the green age of three, in dusty Stamps, Arkansas. Her parents' marriage dissolved, Maya and her older brother, Bailey, have been sent across country from their parents' home in

From *CLA Journal* 20:2. © 1976 by the College Language Association.

Long Beach, California, to Momma's, their paternal grandmother's in
Stamps. After five years of chores, books, fantasies and escapades with Bailey,
Maya rejoins her mother in teeming, gray St. Louis. There she is raped, at
eight, by her mother's lover, who in retaliation is murdered by her uncles. A
guilt-ridden, terrified and bewildered "woman," Maya is is sent to Stamps.
Upon her graduation from Lafayette County Training School, at fourteen
Maya rejoins her mother, now living in San Francisco. She spends part of one
summer at a trailer camp in Southern California with her father and his
lover, Dolores. When returning with him from a jaunt into Mexico, Maya is
stabbed in a quarrel with Dolores. Fearing another murderous reprisal, Maya
is unwilling to return to any of her homes. Instead, she seeks refuge in a car
junkyard. There "a collage of Negro, Mexican and white" youths initiate her
into a redeeming vision of universal brotherhood—one which Malcolm X
could only discover thousands of miles from the United States in Mecca. She
returns to San Francisco, a sobered and self-possessed young woman, challenges the racial bar to be hired as the town's first black female streetcar
conductor. At the end of the book Maya becomes mother to an illegitimate
son, the offspring of her " immaculate pregnancy."

This brief sketch, though excluding some very crucial personalities and
episodes in her youth, emphasizes the rootlessness of Maya Angelou's early
years. Angelou herself underscores this pattern of mobility in the opening
phrase of her introduction:

> "What are you looking at me for?
> I didn't come to stay. . . ."

Indeed, geographic movement and temporary residence become formative
aspects of her growing identity—equal in importance to experiences and
relationships more commonly regarded as instrumental in forming the adult
self. Appropriately, this poetic phrase becomes the young girl's motto or
"shield" (p. 58) as Angelou calls it; Maya's means of proclaiming her isolation while defending against its infringement.

Shuttled between temporary homes and transient allegiances, Maya
necessarily develops a stoic flexibility that becomes not only her "shield,"
but, more importantly, her characteristic means of dealing with the world.
This flexibility is both blessing and curse: it enables her to adapt to various
and changing environments, but it also keeps her forever threatened with
loss or breakdown of her identity, as will presently be shown.

Indeed, Angelou's descriptions of her younger self seem almost entirely
comprised of negatives: she is not wanted by her parents who hold over her

the unspoken, but everpresent, threat of banishment; she is not beautiful or articulate like her brother, Bailey; she is too introverted and passive to assert herself on her environment; and, finally, she is a child in a world of enigmatic adults, and a black girl in a world created by and for the benefit of white men.

Furthermore, Maya's geographic worlds are each separate and self-contained. There is the world of Momma and her Store in Stamps, a puritan world of racial pride, religious devotion and acquiescence to one's worldly lot. And there is her "wild and beautiful" mother's world of pool halls, card sharks, fast dancing, fast talking and fast loving. Combining and transcending both is the private and portable world of Maya's imagination.

If there is one stable element in Angelou's youth it is this dependence on books. Kipling, Poe, Austen and Thackeray, Dunbar, Johnson, Hughes and Du Bois, *The Lone Ranger, The Shadow* and *Captain Marvel* comics—all are equally precious to this lonely girl. Shakespeare, whose Sonnet 29 speaks to Maya's own social and emotional alienation, becomes her "first white love" (p. 11) . As it does for Mary Antin, Anaïs Nin, and other female auto-biographers, the public library becomes a quiet refuge from the chaos of her personal life. "I took out my first library card in St. Louis" (p. 64), she notes. And it is the public library she attempts to reach after her rape. Later, when running away from her father, she hides in a library. Indeed, when her life is in crisis, Maya characteristically escapes into the world of books.

As artifacts creating complete and meaningful universes, novels and their heroes become means by which Maya apprehends and judges her own bewildering world. Thus, Louise, her first girlfriend, reminds Maya of Jane Eyre; while Louise's mother, a domestic, Maya refers to as a governess. Mrs. Flowers, who introduces her to the magic of books, appeals to Maya because she was like "women in English novels who walked the moors . . . with their loyal dogs racing at a respectful distance. Like the women who sat in front of roaring fireplaces, drinking tea incessantly from silver trays full of scones and crumpets. Women who walked the 'heath' and read morocco-bound books and had two last names divided by a hyphen." Curiously, it is this imaginative association with a distant, extinct and colonial world that makes Mrs. Flowers one who "made me proud to be Negro, just by being herself " (p. 79).

But the plight of lovers, madmen and poets is also Maya's problem. "The little princesses who were mistaken for maids, and the long-lost children mistaken for waifs," writes Angelou, "became more real to me than our house, our mother, our school or Mr. Freeman" (p. 64). She is so consummately involved in the world of fantasy that even while being raped she "was sure any minute my mother or Bailey or the Green Hornet would burst in the door and save me" (p. 65).

As in this quotation, the style by which Angelou describes her youth seems in counterpoint to the meaning of her narrative. It is written with a humor and wry wit that belies the personal and racial tragedies recorded. Since style is such a revealing element in all autobiographies, hers, especially, seems a conscious defense against the pain felt at evoking unpleasant memories. Moreover, wit operates as a formidable tool of the outraged adult; by mocking her enemies, Angelou overcomes them. Thus the gluttonous Reverend Thomas gets his just desserts at church when "throwing out phrases like home-run balls" loses his dentures in a scuffle with an over-zealous parishioner; the self-serving condescension of "fluttering" Mrs. Cullinan is ridiculed in a "tragic ballad" on "being white, fat, old and without children"; so, too, with the vanity and carelessness of her mother's "lipstick kisses" and her father's pompous "*ers* and *errers*" as he struts among Stamps' curious "down-home folk." The adult writer's irony retaliates for the tongue-tied child's helpless pain.

The primary object, however, for Angelou's wit is herself. At times maudlin, always highly romantic and withdrawn, the young Maya is a person the older writer continually finds comic. Her idolatrous attachment to Bailey, her projections of fantasy upon reality, her reverence of her mother's stunning beauty, her strained attempts at sympathy for her self-enamoured father, her ingenuous attitude towards sexuality—these are but a few of the many and recurring aspects of her younger self the adult mocks.

The basic motive for writing one's autobiography, some believe, is to be understood, accepted, and loved. Angelou's willingness to ridicule former self-deceptions—more precisely, her former self—indicates the adult's fear-lessness of the reader's judgments and her own critical stance towards herself. If Angelou's voice in re-creating her past is, therefore, ironic, it is however supremely controlled.

Nevertheless, despite the frankness of her narrative, Angelou avoids charting a direct path to her present self. Unlike *Gemini*, or *Coming of Age in Mississippi*, or *The Autobiography of Malcolm X*, or Richard Wright's *Black Boy* —books in the same genre—Angelou's autobiography barely mentions the emergent woman within the girlish actor. Although Roy Pascal believes that "the autobiographer must refer us continually outwards and onwards, to the author himself and to the outcome of all the experiences," Maya Angelou proves an exception to the rule.

Because Angelou's apprehension of experience and, indeed, herself, is essentially protean and existential, it is difficult to find one overriding identity of the adult self controlling her narrative. For what connects the adult and the child is less a linear development towards one distinct version of the self through career or philosophy, than an everchanging multiplicity of possibilities. It is, in fact, her mutability, born of and affirmed through repeated movement, reorientation and assimilation, that becomes Angelou's unique identity, her "identity theme," to use Heinz Lichtenstein's more precise term. And if "work, in man, serves the maintenance of the individual's identity theme," as Lichtenstein asserts, then the numerous careers of the adult Angelou—as dancer, prostitute, S. C. L. C. organizer, actor, poet, journalist and director—document restlessness and resilience.

The unsettled life Angelou writes of in *I Know Why the Caged Bird Sings* suggests a sense of self as perpetually in the process of becoming, of dying and being reborn, in all its ramifications. Thus death (and to some extent its companion concept, rebirth) is the term by which her "identity theme" operates. It is the metaphor of self which most directly and comprehensively communicates Angelou's identity. Moreover, the compulsion to repeat—a necessary instrument for the maintenance of any "identity theme"—adds credence to the power of this major motif in Angelou's narrative. For, while the book's tone is predominantly witty, even light, resonating just below the surface of almost every page of Angelou's autobiography is the hidden, but everpresent, theme of death.

Angelou introduces *I Know Why the Caged Bird Sings* with an anecdote. It is Easter Sunday at the Colored Methodist Episcopal Church in Stamps. In celebration of the event, Momma has prepared a lavender taffeta dress for Maya. Believing it to be the most beautiful dress she has ever seen, Maya attributes to it magical properties: when worn, the dress will change Maya into the lovely, blond and blue-eyed "sweet little white girl" she actually believes herself to be.

But on Easter morning the dress reveals its depressing actuality: it is "a plain, ugly cut-down from a white woman's once-was-purple throwaway." No Cinderella metamorphosis for Maya; instead she lives in a "black dream" from which there is no respite. Unlike Christ, whose resurrection from death the church is celebrating, Maya cannot be reborn into life. Overcome with the impossibility of her white fantasy, she escapes the church "peeing and crying" her way home. Maya must, indeed, lose control of her body and feelings. "It would probably run right back up to my head," she believes, "and my poor head would burst like a dropped watermelon, and all the brains and spit and tongue and eyes would roll all over the place" (p. 3). By letting go of her fantasy—physically manifested by letting go of her bladder—Maya will not "die from a busted head."

But, to " let go," as Erik Erikson observes in *Childhood and Society*, "can turn into an inimical letting loose of destructive forces." For, on this Easter

Sunday Maya Angelou comprehends the futility of her wish to become "one of the sweet little white girls who were everybody's dream of what was right with the world." "If growing up is painful for the Southern Black girl," the adult writer concludes, "being aware of her displacement is the rust on the razor that threatens the throat." Although she acknowledges the "unnecessary insult" of her own white fantasy, Angelou nevertheless puts the rust on the razor by her awareness of its insidious and ubiquitous presence.

The form an autobiography takes is as revealing as its style and content. By placing this anecdote before the body of her narrative, Angelou asserts the paradigmatic importance of this particular event on her life. The atemporality of this experience (Maya's age remains unmentioned) coupled with the symbolic setting of Easter Sunday, suggests a personal myth deeply imbedded in Angelou's unconscious. One could, indeed, speculate that this event, introducing Maya Angelou's autobiography, is the "epiphanic moment" of her youth. For this short narrative presents the two dynamic operatives that circumscribe Angelou's self: her blackness and her outcast position.

Immediately striking in the anecdote is Maya's fantastic belief that "I was really white," that "a cruel fairy stepmother, who was understandably jealous of my beauty" (p. 2) had tricked Maya of her Caucasian birthright. The fairy tale imagery employed to depict her creation is characteristic of the imaginative and impressionable girl, but the meaning of her tale cannot be overlooked. For, according to her schema, Maya's identity hinges on the whims of this fairy stepmother. If benevolent, she will transform Maya back into a pretty white girl; if she remains cruel, her spell over Maya will rest unbroken. When her dress does not produce the longed-for results, Maya is forced to contend with her blackness. But if she acknowledges this blackness, Maya must also acknowledge the existence of an arbitrary and malevolent force beyond her control which dictates her personal and racial identity.

As if mourning the death of the lovely white body beyond her possession, Maya describes her dress as sounding "like crepe paper on the back of hearses" (p. 1). Maya's body indeed becomes a symbolic hearse, containing not only her dead dream but also a life whose very existence is threatened by the whims of a murderous white culture.

Angelou's highly personal confession of racial self-hatred is, unfortunately, not unique in Afro-American experience. Many works of contemporary black novelists and autobiographers—from Ralph Ellison and Imamu Baraka / LeRoi Jones to Richard Wright and Malcolm X—assert that invisibility, violence, alienation and death are part and parcel of growing up black in a white America. Likewise, psychological and sociological studies affirm that the first lesson in living taught the black child is how to ensure his / her survival. "The child must know," write Grier and Cobbs, "that the white world is dangerous and that if he does not understand its rules it may kill him." It is, then, pitifully understandable for Maya to wish herself white, since blackness forebodes annihilation.

Of equal significance in this introductory anecdote is Maya's belief that a stepmother has put her under this spell and then abandoned her. Her image of herself, for at least the first five years of life, is that of an orphan. Even later, when forced to recognize the existence of both her parents, she still clings to this orphan identity. Although acknowledging that Bailey, by dint of beauty and personality, is his parents' true son, she describes herself as "an orphan that they had picked up to provide Bailey with company" (p. 45).

While her father is as culpable as her mother in Maya's abandonment, it is nevertheless her mother whom Maya most yearns for and consequently blames. No real mother would "laugh and eat oranges in the sunshine without her children" (p. 42), Maya reflects bitterly when first confronted with her mother's existence. No proper mother should let her child so profoundly mourn her passing as Maya has done.

> I could cry anytime I wanted by picturing my mother (I didn't
> know what she looked like) lying in her coffin. Her hair, which
> was black, was spread out on a tiny little pillow and her body was
> covered with a sheet. The face was brown, like a big O, and since
> I couldn't fill in the features I printed M O T H E R across the
> O, and tears would fall down my cheeks like warm milk (p. 43).

Maya's image of her dead mother is deeply comforting to the child. The protective and nurturing maternal love Maya yearns for is symbolically created through her own tears: they "would fall down my cheeks like warm milk." Consider then, the shock, the affront to her tottering self-image as well as to the image of her dead mother, when Maya receives her mother's first Christmas presents. Not only is her mother alive, but Maya herself must have been as good as dead during those early years of separation.

Adding insult to injury are the "awful presents" themselves: "a tea set —a teapot, four cups and saucers and tiny spoons—and a doll with blue eyes and rosy cheeks and yellow hair painted on her head" (p. 43). Symbols of a white world beyond Maya's reach or everyday experience, these toys not only evidence her mother's exotic and alien life, but also intimate questions of guilt and banishment no five-year-old can answer. The doll, especially, whose description so closely parallels Maya's own wished-for physical appearance, is an intolerable presence. It serves as an effigy of her mother by virtue of being female and her gift, as well as of Maya's impossible fantasy; Maya and Bailey "tore the stuffing out of the doll the day after Christmas" (p. 44).

Abandonment by a dead mother is forgivable, but abandonment by a living one evokes a rage so threatening that it must undergo massive repression. Thus, Maya becomes passive, inhibiting her deep anger and hostility. The fear of abandonment, even when living with her mother in St. Louis, never abates. "If we got on her nerves or if we were disobedient, she could always send us back to Stamps. The weight of appreciation and the threat, which was never spoken, of a return to Momma were burdens that clogged my childish wits into impassivity. I was called Old Lady and chided for moving and talking like winter's molasses" (p. 57). Maya's fears come true; after her rape she is again banished to Stamps.

Nevertheless, Maya repeatedly protests fondness for her mother. Beautiful, honest, gay and tough, Vivian Baxter leaves her daughter awestruck. "I could never put my finger on her realness," Angelou writes, "She was so pretty and so quick that . . . I thought she looked like the Virgin Mary" (p. 57). So much is Vivian Baxter idealized that Angelou capitalizes "Mother" in her narrative, while "father" remains in lowercase. But Vivian Baxter is diametrically opposite to the brown-faced nurturing mother Maya had mourned and yearned for in Stamps. Her beauty and animation keep Maya suspicious of their consanguinity.

Maya's ambivalence about her mother—her fear and love, her rage and need for her, her isolation and her desire for closeness—is never fully resolved. Although she insists verbally on this love, her affect reveals sullenness, resignation, depression and overwhelming passivity. Maya's aggression against her mother is well-defended, and thus specific suggestions of hostility towards her are rare. But the proliferating references to death in Angelou's autobiography provide another route for releasing Maya's (and Angelou's) repressed violent aggression.

This aspect of death's overdetermined significance is important but by no means the only level of reference; at least five sub-themes, each bearing on the major theme of death, emerge in *I Know Why the Caged Bird Sings*. The first is the most obvious: the realistic fear of whites which Momma and the Southern black community have drummed into Maya. Momma, Angelou writes, "didn't cotton to the idea that whitefolks could be talked to at all without risking one's life" (p. 39). The white lynchers whom Uncle Willie hides from in the vegetable bin, the taunting "powhitetrash" girls, the bloated dead man fished out of the river—all are daily proof of a predatory white world. This fact leads Angelou to a bitter conclusion: "the Black woman in the South who raises sons, grandsons and nephews had her heartstrings tied to a hanging noose" (p. 95).

The daily fear of murder at the hands of whites leads the Southern black community into the haven of religion and the belief of a blessed reward in "the far off bye and bye." Thus, Southern black religion celebrates death, since life itself is too precarious to pin one's hopes on. Even at the revival meeting attended by members from a variety of Southern churches, death continually asserts its presence: the cardboard fans flourished by the worshippers advertise Texarkana's largest Negro funeral parlor. "People whose history and future were threatened each day by extinction," comments Angelou, "considered that it was only by divine intervention that they were able to live at all" (p. 101) .

Balancing this image of a white world threatening her own and her people's lives, is Maya's revenge fantasy of murdering the offending whites. When Dentist Lincoln refuses to treat her toothache, Maya creates an elaborate revery wherein a Herculean Momma has the cowering dentist pleading for his life: "Yes, ma'am. Thank you for not killing me. Thank you, Mrs. Henderson" (p. 162) .

Far and away the most dramatic instance of this revenge theme occurs the day of Maya's graduation from Lafayette County Training School. Unable to stand the invited white speaker's "dead words" which systematically destroy the dreams and aspirations of the black children and their elders Maya wills them all dead.

> Then I wished that Gabriel Prosser and Nat Turner had killed all whitefolks in their beds and that Abraham Lincoln had been assassinated before the signing of the Emancipation Proclamation, and that Harriet Tubman had been killed by that blow on her head and Christopher Columbus had drowned in the *Santa Maria*.
>
> It was awful to be Negro and have no control over my life. It was brutal to be young and already trained to sit quietly and listen to charges brought against my color with no chance of defense. We should all be. I thought I should like to see us all dead, one on top of the other. A pyramid of flesh with the whitefolks on the bottom, as the broad base, then the Indians with their silly tomahawks and teepees and wigwams and treaties, the Negroes with their mops and recipes and cotton sacks and spirituals sticking out of their mouths. The Dutch children should all stumble in their wooden shoes and break their necks. The French should choke to death on the Louisiana

Purchase (1803) while silkworms ate all the Chinese with their stupid pigtails. As a species, we were an abomination. All of us (pp. 152–53).

Operating on a more personal level is the violence Maya witnesses within the members of her own family. Angelou introduces her Uncle Willie by describing his method of pushing her and Bailey onto the Store's red heater if they neglect their lessons. Momma, too, does not spare the rod when she believes her grandchildren remiss in hygiene, schooling, manners or piety. But this corporal punishment—executed more in love than in rage —is small matter, indeed, when compared to the fundamental brutality of Maya's maternal relations in St. Louis. Her maternal grandfather and uncles revel in their own "meanness": "They beat up whites and Blacks with the same abandon" (p. 56). Even her mother is not immune from her family's violent streak. Once, in retaliation for being cursed, Vivian Baxter, with the aid of her brothers, "crashed the man's head with a policemen's billy enough to leave him just this side of death" (p. 55). Later Vivian Baxter, again in response to an insult, shoots the partner of her gambling casino.

As the climax of this familial violence, Mr. Freeman's rape is performed under the threat of death: "If you scream, I'm gonna kill you. And if you tell, I'm gonna kill Bailey" (p. 65). But her family's response to Maya's subsequent withdrawal into silent passivity is itself another form of violence. "For a while I was punished for being so uppity that I wouldn't speak; and then came the thrashings, given by any relative who felt himself offended" (p. 73) . The rape itself is the most flagrant example of her maternal family's characteristic combination of aggression and neglect. Not only is Mr. Freeman her mother's lover, but mother and children all live under his roof. Ruthless in her quest for material comfort, Vivian Baxter is not above taking full advantage of Freeman's obvious adoration. Already at eight a sagacious observer, Maya responds with mixed emotions to her mother's relationship with Freeman. "I felt sorry for Mr. Freeman. I felt as sorry for him as I had felt for a litter of helpless pigs born in our backyard sty in Arkansas. We fattened the pigs all year long for the slaughter on the first good frost, and even as I suffered for the cute little wiggly things, I knew how much I was going to enjoy the fresh sausage and hog's headcheese they could give me only with their deaths" (p. 60).

Of course, Maya's sympathy for Freeman has another cause: she feels as neglected by Vivian Baxter as he does. And while Freeman's motives in the earlier masturbatory episodes and even the rape itself probably stem as much from revenge against the mother as easy access to the daughter, Maya's own need for attention and physical closeness cannot be overlooked. After the first of these episodes, Angelou writes, "came the nice part. He held me so softly that I wished he wouldn't ever let me go. I felt at home. From the way he was holding me I knew he'd never let me go or let anything bad ever happen to me. This was probably my real father and we had found each other at last" (p. 61). Pitifully unable to distinguish lust from paternal love (never having experienced the latter), Maya projects onto Freeman this physical warmth missing from all her relationships with adults. "I began to feel lonely for Mr. Freeman and the encasement of his big arms," Angelou recalls. "Before, my world had been Bailey, food, Momma, the Store, reading books and Uncle Willie. Now, for the first time, it included physical contact" (p. 62).

Freeman's subsequent murder (he was kicked to death by her uncles) evokes overwhelming guilt in Maya. At Freeman's trial Maya gives false testimony about their encounters, and now "a man was dead because I lied" (p. 72). Associating her spoken word with death, Maya stops talking.

Maya as bearer of death is the fourth dimension of death and violence in Angelou's narrative. In disgrace with God because "I had sold myself to the Devil and there could be no escape," Maya conceives herself to be the cursed instrument of violent death. This conviction is part of the pattern of self-rejection and inferiority well-established within Maya's psyche; it lies but one small step beyond a personal sense of inherent gross repulsiveness. Introjecting this repulsiveness—which she believes everyone except Bailey feels towards her—Maya generalizes on her role in Freeman's death and perceives herself as death's tool. "The only thing I could do," she reasons, "was to stop talking to people other than Bailey. Instinctively, or somehow, I knew that because I loved him so much I'd never hurt him, but if I talked to anyone else that person might die too. Just my breath, carrying my words out, might poison people and they'd curl up and die like the black fat slugs that only pretended" (p. 73) .

In this psychic state Maya conceives of her own body mythically as a Pandora's Box containing a degeneracy so virulent that, if left uncontrolled, will contaminate the universe. So profound is her hatred and rage, she recalls, that "I could feel the evilness flowing through my body and waiting, pent up, to rush off my tongue if I tried to open my mouth. I clamped my teeth shut, I'd hold it in. If it escaped, wouldn't it flood the world and all the innocent people" (p. 72). As a vessel containing a death-inducing fluid, Maya must control the physical force within her with all the strength and will she can muster. Thus, her resolve not to speak, and her consequent impassivity become outward manifestations of an inner struggle no less cosmic than Jacob and the Angel's. This same struggle is the one which opens Angelou's autobiography.

Upon her return to Stamps, Maya projects her own deathlike inertness on the whole town. It is described as "exactly what I wanted, without will or consciousness. . . . Entering Stamps, I had the feeling that I was stepping over the border lines of the map and would fall, without fear, right off the end of the world. Nothing more could happen, for in Stamps nothing happened" (p. 74).

An outcast in a community of outcasts, Maya avoids emotional ties with others. In fact, for six years, until Louise befriends her, Maya is without an intimate friend her own age. It is not surprising, then, that when Mrs. Bertha Flowers takes an active interest in her, Maya describes her as "the lady who threw me my first life line" (p. 77). Nor is it surprising that Maya turns to the safety of books for the exciting relationships shunned in real life.

Yet, this pathological paralysis which inhibits Maya's ability to express her resentment and anger also opens the door to a gratification of her desire for a union with her mother. For Maya's passivity and obsession with death serve more than one unconscious need. While keeping her emotionally isolated from, and invulnerable to, others, they also gratify her regressive strivings for her mother.

Indeed, Maya's decision to lie at Freeman's trial was motivated not simply by mortal terror of her maternal clan and by fear of revealing her own complicity in the sexual episodes, but more importantly by her desire for her mother's warmth and approving love.

> I couldn't say yes and tell them how he had loved me once for a few minutes and how he had held me close before he thought I had peed in my bed. My uncles would kill me and Grandmother Baxter would stop speaking, as she often did when she was angry. And all those people in the court would stone me as they had stoned the harlot in the Bible. And Mother, who thought I was such a good girl, would be so disappointed. . . .
>
> . . . I looked at his heavy face trying to look as if he would have liked me to say No. I said No.
>
> The lie lumped in my throat and I couldn't get air. . . . Our lawyer brought me off the stand and to my mother's arms. The fact that I had arrived at my desired destination by lies made it less appealing to me (p. 70–71).

When Maya's attempts at physical closeness with her mother— pathetically by way of Mr. Freeman's arms and her lie—prove unsuccessful, she reverts to the most primitive of all longings: to die. If death is "the condition in which identification with mother can be achieved," as Barchelon and Kovel postulate about *Huckleberry Finn*, then its "ultimate expression is passivity, of doing nothing." Thus, "in the unconscious, death can be represented as that dissolution of self necessary for reunion with the source of life, as a recapitulation of that self-less time in the womb." Consequently, for a major portion of her autobiography, Maya Angelou evokes the notion of her willful dissolution—still another dimension in her book of the death-motif.

Thanatos, or the unconscious drive toward dissolution and death, exists in Angelou's narrative before the crucial episode of her rape and courtroom lie. Indeed, it first emerges when Maya is confronted with recognizing the existence of her parents. Deeply attached to the image of her dead mother, her indecision about joining the living one in St. Louis evokes the thought of suicide. "Should I go with father? Should I throw myself into the pond, and not being able to swim, join the body of L. C., the boy who had drowned last summer?" (pp. 46–47). Even her choice of method—death by water—calls up her yearning for a return to the source of all life, the mother.

Although her second residence in Stamps includes episodes wherein Maya considers her own death, these are generally handled more with humor than pathos. At any rate, the very abundance of references to her own extinction, regardless of Angelou's tone, is evidence of this theme's powerful hold over both the actor's and the author's unconscious. Three examples out of many will suffice. When cautioned by Mrs. Flowers to handle her books well, Maya can only imagine the most extreme punishment if she proves negligent: "Death would be too kind and brief" (p. 82) . Later, having survived to see the day of her graduation, Angelou relates that "somewhere in my fatalism I had expected to die, accidentally, and never have the chance to walk up the stairs in the auditorium and gracefully receive my hard-earned diploma. Out of God's merciful bosom I had won reprieve" (p. 147). Again, referring to the overwhelming sway books had over hers and Bailey's imaginations, Angelou writes that "ever since we read *The Fall of the House of Usher*, we had made a pact that neither of us would allow the other to be buried without making 'absolutely, positively sure' (his favorite phrase) that the person was dead" (p. 166).

Included in this part of her experience is Angelou's first conscious cognizance of her own mortality. So crucial an aspect of her identity is this awareness, that Angelou devotes an entire chapter to it. Beneath the mock-Gothic melodrama of Mrs. Taylor's funeral and her posthumous nocturnal returns to visit her husband (neither of whom are mentioned again in the book), exists Maya's real and growing apprehension of her own mortal state:

"I had never considered before that dying, death, dead, passed away, were words and phrases that might be even faintly connected with me" (p. 135).

This deathward drift is arrested and altered when Maya moves to California. Just as Stamps reflects Maya's impassivity, so does San Francisco evoke her resiliency; while Stamps projects the worst side of Maya, so San Francisco affirms the best: "The city became for me the ideal of what I wanted to be as a grownup. Friendly but never gushing, cool but not frigid or distant, distinguished without the awful stiffness" (p. 180). In San Francisco Maya's own identity happily merges with her environs. "In San Francisco, for the first time, I perceived myself as part of something," writes Angelou. "I identified . . . with the times and the city. . . . The undertone of fear that San Francisco would be bombed which was abetted by weekly air raid warnings, and civil defense drills in school, heightened my sense of belonging. Hadn't I, always, but ever and ever, thought that life was just one great risk for the living?" (p. 179).

Death in its many manifestations is, indeed, pivotal to Maya Angelou's sense of self. But the life instinct, Eros, coexists with Thanatos in her autobiography, as it does in life. In fact, the tension between Maya's quest for a positive, life-affirming identity and her obsession with annihilation provide the unconscious dynamism affecting all aspects of her narrative, and endowing it with power and conviction. Thus, the ultimate challenge to death is Maya's own active assertion of self and her willingness to face annihilation and overcome it. The remainder of Angelou's autobiography addresses itself to this end.

It is not until she visits Mexico with her father that Maya tenaciously struggles for her life. Leaving Maya to her own wits in a Mexican *cantina*, Bailey Johnson, Sr., takes off with his Mexican lover. When he finally returns, intoxicated beyond help, Maya must drive them both home. Although she has never driven, Maya defies and masters the bucking Hudson.

> The Hudson went crazy on the hill. It was rebelling and would have leaped over the side of the mountain, to all our destruction, in its attempt to unseat me had I relaxed control for a single second. The challenge was exhilarating. It was me, Marguerite, against the elemental opposition. As I twisted the steering wheel and forced the accelerator to the floor I was controlling Mexico, and might and aloneness and inexperienced youth and Bailey Johnson, Sr., and death and insecurity, and even gravity (pp. 202–03).

But, as in the incident of Freeman's rape, the fatal pattern of reversal again appears. Maya's temporary safety is followed by Dolores's stabbing. When, in order to save face, Johnson hides Maya at a friend's home rather than bring her to a hospital, Maya is again confronted with the specter of her own death. She survives the night, however, sleeping "as if my death wish had come true" (p. 212). But morning presents the inevitable questions: "What would I do? Did I have the nerve to commit suicide? If I jumped in the ocean wouldn't I come up all bloated like the man Bailey saw in Stamps?" (212). Although she has evoked her childish alternative of death by water and its unconscious wish for a return to mother, this time Maya resolves to make it on her own.

The decision not to retreat to her mother's home becomes the turning-point in Maya Angelou's autobiography. " I could never succeed in shielding the gash in my side from her," she argues. "And if I failed to hide the wound we were certain to experience another scene of violence. I thought of poor Mr. Freeman, and the guilt which lined my heart, even after all those years, was a nagging passenger in my mind" (p. 213). With this gesture, Maya not only triumphs over her regressive longing for death and mother, but also, by sparing her father and Dolores, overcomes her sense of herself as death's tool.

Employing the same simile she had earlier used to describe her mother—"She was like a pretty kite that floated just above my head" (p. 54)—Maya now describes herself as "a loose kite in a gentle wind floating with only my will for anchor" (p. 214). Put more plainly, Maya rises in her own estimation, incorporates the best of her mother and becomes her own guardian. It is only then that Maya is ready to return to the human fold.

The outcast children of the dead-car junkyard where she seeks refuge eliminate Maya's "familiar insecurity," especially in relation to her mother. She learns "to drive . . . to curse and to dance" (p. 215), with the best of them. But of signal importance is that these children disprove the racial prejudice —and its concurrent death fantasies—of her earlier experiences.

> After hunting down unbroken bottles and selling them with a white girl from Missouri, a Mexican girl from Los Angeles and a Black girl from Oklahoma, I was never again to sense myself so solidly outside the pale of the human race. The lack of criticism evidenced by our ad hoc community influenced me, and set a tone of tolerance for my life (p. 216).

That Angelou concludes her autobiography with the birth of her son is final evidence of the substantive power of death as metaphor of self in *I Know*

Why the Caged Bird Sings. Her body, which she had earlier described as not only ugly and awkward but also contaminated with a death-inducing power, brings forth a living child. But the vestiges of her former self-image are not so easily excised. When her mother brings to Maya's bed her three-week-old baby, Maya is terror-stricken: "I was sure to roll over and crush out his life or break those fragile bones" (p. 245). But later, when her mother wakens her, the apprehensive Maya discovers her son safe: Under the tent of blanket, which was poled by my elbow and forearm, the baby slept touching my side" (p. 246).

This final picture of Vivian Baxter as a confident and compassionate mother lovingly bent over her daughter's bed, evokes the brown, nurturing figure of Maya's childhood fantasy. By asserting her faith in Maya's instinctive, preserving motherhood, Vivian Baxter not only qualifies the book's implicit image of her as cruel stepmother, but also consummates Maya's growing sense of herself as an adult, life-giving woman.

When writing one's autobiography one's primary concern is the illumination of personal and historical identity while giving shape and meaning to the experiences out of which that identity has developed. Through the abyss of social and emotional death, Angelou emerges as a tenacious and vital individual. Indeed, in keeping with her death-and-rebirth fantasy, Maya Angelou is reborn: once, into a life-affirming identity recorded within the pages of her narrative, and again, when she re-creates that life as author of her autobiography. If one must enter a dark night of the soul in order to emerge radiant, then Maya Angelou's "terrible beauty" shines clear to the sky.

CHRISTINE FROULA

The Daughter's Seduction: Sexual Violence and Literary History

A still, small voice has warned me again to postpone the
description of hysteria.
[FREUD to Fliess, January 1, 1896]

I felt sorry for mama. Trying to believe his story kilt her.
[ALICE WALKER'S Celie]

In her speech before the London/National Society for Women's Service
on January 21, 1931, Virginia Woolf figured the woman novelist as a fisherwoman who lets the hook of her imagination down into the depths "of
the world that lies submerged in our unconscious being. "Feeling a violent
jerk, she pulls the line up short, and the "imagination comes to the top in
a state of fury":

> Good heavens she cries—how dare you interfere with me. . . .
> And I—that is the reason—have to reply, "My dear you were
> going altogether too far. Men would be shocked." Calm yourself.
> . . . In fifty years I shall be able to use all this very queer knowl-
> edge that you are ready to bring me. But not now. You see I go
> on, trying to calm her, I cannot make use of what you tell me—
> about women's bodies for instance—their passions—and so on,

From *Signs* 11:4. © 1986 by The University of Chicago Press.

because the conventions are still very strong. If I were to overcome the conventions I should need the courage of a hero, and I
am not a hero. . . .

Very well says the imagination, dressing herself up again in
her petticoat and skirts. . . . We will wait another fifty years. But
it seems to me a pity.

Woman's freedom to tell her stories—and indeed, as this fable shows, to
know them fully herself—would come, Woolf went on to predict, once she
is no longer the dependent daughter, wife, and servant. Given that condition,
Woolf envisioned "a step upon the stair": "You will hear somebody coming.
You will open the door. And then—this at least is my guess—there will take
place between you and some one else the most interesting, exciting, and
important conversation that has ever been heard" (*Pargiters*, xliv).

But that was to be in "fifty years." In 1931, Woolf still felt a silence
even within all the writing by women that she knew—even, indeed, within
her own. Woolf's fable of silences that go unheard within women's writing
points to a violence that is all the more powerful for being nearly invisible.
and it interprets women's silence in literary history as an effect of repression,
not of absence. In this essay, I will explore the literary history implied by
Woolf's fisherwoman image, reading it backward, through Homer and
Freud, to elucidate the "conventions" that bound her imagination; and
forward, to contemporary works by women that fulfill Woolf's "guess" that
women would soon break a very significant silence. Drawing upon feminist
analyses of Freud's discovery and rejection of the seduction theory of
hysteria, I will argue that the relations of literary daughters and fathers
resemble in some important ways the model developed by Judith Herman
and Lisa Hirschman to describe the family situations of incest victims: a
dominating, authoritarian father; an absent, ill, or complicitous mother; and
a daughter who, prohibited by her father from speaking about the abuse, is
unable to sort out her contradictory feelings of love for her father and terror
of him, of desire to end the abuse and fear that if she speaks she will destroy
the family structure that is her only security. By aligning a paradigmatic
father-daughter dialogue in Homer's *Iliad* with Freud's dialogue with the
hysterics, we can grasp the outline of what I shall call the hysterical cultural
script: the cultural text that dictates to males and females alike the necessity
of silencing woman's speech when it threatens the father's power. This
silencing insures that the cultural daughter remains a daughter, her power
suppressed and muted; while the father, his power protected, makes culture
and history in his own image. Yet, as the hysterics' speech cured their symp-

toms, so women, telling stories formerly repressed, have begun to realize the prediction of Woolf's fisherwoman. Maya Angelou's *I Know Why the Caged Bird Sings* (1969) and Alice Walker's *The Color Purple* (1982) exemplify the breaking of women's forbidden stories into literary history—an event that reverberates far beyond their heroes' individual histories to reshape our sense of our cultural past anti its possible future directions.

Cultural Fathers and Daughters: Some Interesting Conversations

What is the fisherwoman's story, the one that got away? The answer I wish to pursue begins with the earliest conversation between man and woman in our literary tradition, that between Helen and Priam in the *Iliad*, book 3. Although readers tend to remember the Helen of the *Iliad* as silent—beauty of body her only speech—the text reveals not Helen's silence but her silenc*ing*. As they stand upon the city wall gazing down at the battlefield, the Trojan king and patriarch Priam asks Helen to point out to him the Greek heroes whose famous names he knows. Her answer exceeds Priam's request:

> "Revere you as I do,
> I dread you, too, dear father. Painful death
> would have been sweeter for me, on that day
> I joined your son, and left my bridal chamber,
> my brothers, my grown child, my childhood friends!
> But no death came, though I have pined and wept.
> Your question, now: yes, I can answer it:
> that man is Agamemnon, son of Atreus,
> lord of the plains of Argos, ever both
> a good king and a formidable soldier—
> brother to the husband of a wanton . . .
>   or was that life a dream?"

Helen first invokes her own fear of and reverence for Priam. But this daughterly homage to her cultural father only frames her expression of her longing for her former life and companions. Helen, however, is powerless to escape the male war economy that requires her presence to give meaning to its conflicts, and so she translates her desire for her old life into a death wish that expresses at once culturally induced masochism and the intensity of her resistance to her own entanglement in the warriors' plot. Priam appears to reply only to the words that answer his query:

The old man gazed and mused and softly cried
"O fortunate son of Atreus! Child of destiny,
O happy soul! How many sons of Akhaia
serve under you! In the old days once I went
into the vineyard country of Phrygia
and saw the Phrygian host on nimble ponies,

. . . .

And they allotted me as their ally
my place among them when the Amazons
came down, those women who were fighting men;
but that host never equaled this,
the army of the keen-eyed men of Akhaia.'

[*Iliad*, 74]

Priam seems not to notice Helen's misery as he turns to imaginary competi-
tion with the admired and envied Agamemnon. What links his speech to
Helen's, however, is the extraordinary fact that the occasion he invokes as his
most memorable experience of troops arrayed for battle is a battle against the
Amazons. That Amazons come to his mind suggests that, on some level, he
has heard Helen's desires. Priam's speech recapitulates his conflict with
Helen, and hers with Greek culture, as an archetypal conflict between male
and female powers. Significantly, Priam does not say which of these forces
triumphed. But in leaving the action suspended, he connects past with
present, the Amazons' challenge with this moment's conflict between his
desires and Helen's who, merely in having desires that would interfere with
her role as battle prize, becomes for Priam the Amazon.

What does it mean that Helen should become the Amazon in Priam's
imagination? Page duBois and William Blake Tyrrell analyze the Amazon
myth as a representation of female power that has escaped the bounds
within which Greek culture, specifically the marriage structure, strives to
contain it. The Amazon myth, Tyrrell writes, is about daughters, warriors,
and marriage. It projects male fear that women will challenge their subor-
dinate status in marriage and with it the rule of the father. In Varro's
account of the mythology of Athens's origins, the female citizens of Athens
were, under Cecrops, dispossessed of their social and political authority
after they banded together to vote for Athena as their city's presiding deity
and brought down Poseidon's jealous wrath: "'They could no longer cast a
vote, no new-born child would take the mother's name,' . . [and] they are no
longer called Athenians but daughters of Athenians." From the Greek
woman's lifelong role of daughter, her deprivation of political, economic, and

social power, the Amazon myth emerges as "the specter of daughters who refuse their destiny and fail to make the accepted transition through marriage to wife and motherhood" (*Amazons*, 65). Such unruly daughters threatened to be "rivals of men," "opposed or antithetical to the male as father (*Amazons*, 83). Becoming a rival in the male imagination, the daughter also becomes a warrior—as Helen does to Priam, as Clytemnestra does to Apollo when, in the *Eumenides*, he laments that Agamemnon was not cut down by an Amazon instead of by her, as Dido does to Aeneas in his premon- itory conflation of her with Penthesilea in *Aeneid*. These allusions suggest that the Amazon figure, a figment of the male imagination, expresses male desire to contain the threat of a female uprising within the arena of the battlefield; that is, to transform the invisible threat of female revolt into a clear and present danger that males might then band together to combat in the regulated violence of war. In linking Helen with the Amazons, Priam dramatizes the threat that female desire poses to the male war culture pred- icated on its subjugation. Their conversation replicates the larger design of Homer's epic, which, being 'his" story, not hers, turns the tale of a woman's abduction and silencing into the story of a ten-year war between two male cultures. Priam's battle with the Amazons remains suspended in his speech because that battle has not ended. But in this conversation, it is Priam, the cultural father, who triumphs, while Helen's story, by his refusal to hear it, becomes the repressed but discernible shadow of Priam's own.

Helen's exchange with Priam is one skirmish in her culture's war against the Amazons, and a subsequent conversation between Helen and Aphrodite depicts another battle in the form of a cultural daughter's seduc- tion. Here, Helen opposes Aphrodite's demand that she join Paris in bed while the battle rages outside: "'O immortal madness, / why do you have this craving to seduce me? / . . . Go take your place beside Alexandros! / . . . Be / unhappy for him, shield him, till at last / he marries you—or, as he will, / enslaves you. / I shall not join him there!'" (*Iliad*, 81–82). Helen passionately and eloquently resists her cultural fate, but Homer's Olympian magic conquers her. Aphrodite silences Helen and enforces her role as object, not agent, of desire by threatening her: "Better not be so difficult. / . . . I can make hatred for you grow / amid both Trojans and Danaäns, / and if I do, you'll come to a bad end" (*Iliad*, 82). The male-authored goddess, embodying the sublimated social authority of Greek culture, forces Helen to relinquish control over her sexuality to the "higher" power of male culture and, like a complicitous mother, presses her to conform to its rule. Helen easily resists being "seduced," angrily thrusting back upon Aphrodite the role of compliant wife/slave that the goddess recommends to her. But this scene makes no distinction between seduction and rape—between being "led astray" and being sexually violated—for Helen can resist sexual complicity only on pain of being cast out altogether from the social world, which is constructed upon marriage. She can be a faithful wife or a "wanton," a "nightmare," a "whore"; she can be a dutiful daughter or an unruly one. But she cannot act out her own desire as Menelaus and Paris, Agamemnon and Akhilleus, Khryses and Hektor, can theirs. Indeed, if wanton in Troy and wife in the bridal chamber are the only choices her culture allows her, she cannot choose even from these. Whereas Paris can propose to settle the dispute by single combat with Menelaus, or the Trojan elders, seeing Helen on the wall, can murmur "let her go [back to Greece] in the ships / and take her scourge from us" (*Iliad*, 73), there is never a question of Helen's deciding the conflict by choosing between the two men.

Although not literally silenced by Aphrodite's metaphysical violence, Helen, surrendering her sexuality, is simultaneously subdued to her culture's dominant text of male desire. "Brother dear," she tells Hektor,

> dear to a whore, a nightmare of a woman!
> That day my mother gave me to the world
> I wish a hurricane blast had torn me away
> to wild mountains, or into tumbling sea
> to be washed under by a breaking wave,
> before these evil days could come! . . .
>
> [*Iliad*, 152]

Helen's will to escape the warriors' marriage plot here turns against the only object her culture permits: herself. She names herself from its lexicon for wayward daughters and passionately imagines death as her only possible freedom. Using the names her culture provides her, weighted with its judgments, Helen loses power even to name herself, her speech confined between the narrow bounds of patriarchal culture and death. That she imagines her death as an entering into the wild turbulence of nature allegorizes the radical opposition of male culture to female nature which the Greek marriage plot enforces: Helen, the Greeks' most exalted image of woman, is also a powerfully expressive subject who must, because of her power, be violently driven back into nature.

Death failing, Helen fulfills her prescribed role by participating in her culture's metaphysical violence against herself: "You [Hektor] are the one afflicted most / by harlotry in me and by his madness, / our portion, all of misery, given by Zeus / that we might live in song for men to come" (*Iliad*,

153). She sacrifices herself upon the altar of patriarchal art, a willing victim who not only suffers but justifies her culture's violence. (Men too suffer the violence of the Greek marriage plot—Helen's "we" includes Hektor—but whereas Hektor resists Andromakhe's pleas and follows his desire for honor into battle, Helen's and Andromakhe's desires are entirely ineffectual.) If the poem, like the war, seems to glorify Helen, in fact she and all the female characters serve primarily to structure the dynamics of male desire in a culture that makes women the pawns of men's bonds *with each other* and the scapegoats for their broken allegiances. The poem's opening scene portrays woman's role in Greek culture as the silent object of male desire, not the speaker of her own. While Agamemnon and Akhilleus rage eloquently over their battle prizes Khryseis and Briseis, the women themselves do not speak at all. They are as interchangeable as their names make them sound, mere circulating tokens of male power and pride—as Akhilleus's apology to Agamemnon upon rejoining the battle confirms: "Agamemnon, was it better for us / in any way, when we were sore at heart, / to waste ourselves in strife over a girl? / If only Artemis had shot her down / among the ships on the day I made her mine, / after I took Lyrnessos!" (*Iliad*, 459).

The *Iliad* suggests that women's silence in culture is neither a natural nor an accidental phenomenon but a cultural achievement, indeed, a constitutive accomplishment of male culture. In Helen's conversations, Homer writes the silencing of woman into epic history as deliberate, strategic, and necessary—a crucial aspect of the complex struggle that is the epic enterprise. In Helen the *Iliad* represents the subjugation of female desire to male rule by means of a continuum of violence, from physical abduction to the metaphysical violence that Greek culture exerts against woman's words and wishes. To a greater extent than we have yet realized, Homer's epic is about marriage, daughters, and warriors. It is about the Amazon.

The *Iliad* is an ancient text, and we have moved very far from the world that produced it—a fact often invoked to distance readers from the violence against women in which the poem participates. But if we set Helen's conversations next to a powerful analogue of our century, Sigmund Freud's dialogues with hysterics and with the phenomenon of hysteria, the paradigmatic force of her "abduction" into the cultural father's script becomes apparent. As the *Iliad* tells the story of a woman's abduction as a male war story, so Freud turned the hysterics' stories of sexual abuse into a tale to soothe a father's ear. And just as Priam's repressed fears seep into his speech in his allusion to the Amazons, so Freud's repression of the daughter's story generates symptomatic moments that "chatter through the fingertips of his psychoanalytic theory.

Freud's conversations with hysterical patients began in the 1880s. At first, Freud, unlike Priam, was able to hear his patients' stories, and he· found that in every case, analysis elicited an account of sexual abuse suffered in childhood at the hands of a member of the patient's own family—almost always the father, as he belatedly reported. On this evidence, Freud developed his "seduction theory"—the theory that hysterical symptoms have their origin in sexual abuse suffered in childhood which is repressed and eventually assimilated to later sexual experience. Freud first formulated the seduction theory in a letter to his colleague and confidant Wilhelm Fliess in October 1895, and he presented it to the Vienna psychiatric establishment on April 21, 1896, in a paper titled "The Aetiology of Hysteria." The paper, Freud wrote to Fliess, "met with an icy reception," summed up in Krafft-Ebing's dismissal of it as "a scientific fairytale" (*Origins*, 167n.). For a time Freud pursued the research by which he hoped to prove the seduction theory, writing to Fliess in December 1896: "My psychology of hysteria will be preceded by the proud words: "*Introite et hic dii sunt* [Enter, for here too are gods]" (*Origins*, 172). His pride in his discovery was shortlived, however, for within a year, he would write again to confide "the great secret which has been slowly dawning on me in recent months. I no longer believe in my *neurotica*" (*Origins*, 215). From this point, Freud went on to found psychoanalytic theory upon the oedipal complex.

Historians of psychoanalysis consider Freud's turn from the seduction theory to the oedipal complex crucial to the development of psychoanalysis. Anna Freud wrote that "keeping up the seduction theory would mean to abandon the Oedipus complex, and with it the whole importance of phantasy life. . . . In fact, I think there would have been no psychoanalysis afterwards." But a more critical reading of Freud's abandonment of his seduction theory has emerged from feminist scholarship over the last decade. Several critics have argued—Luce Irigaray from feminist theory, Alice Miller as well as Herman and Hirschman from clinical evidence, Marie Balmary from a psychoanalytic reading of the "text" of Freud's life and work, Florence Rush and Jeffrey Moussaieff Masson from historical evidence, among others—that Freud turned away from the seduction theory not because it lacked explanatory power but because he was unable to come to terms with what he was the first to discover: the crucial role played in neurosis by the abuse of paternal power.

For purposes of the present argument, the issue is best put in terms of credit or authority: the hysterics, Breuer's and his own, confronted Freud with the problem of whose story to believe, the father's or the daughter's. From the first, Freud identified with the hysterics strongly enough that he could hear what they told him. Yet, although he could trace the etiology of hysteria to sexual abuse suffered in childhood, Freud could not bring himself to draw the conclusion that his evidence presented to him that the abuser was most often the father. The cases of Anna O., Lucy R., Katharina, Elizabeth von R., and Rosalia H. described in *Studies on Hysteria* all connect symptoms more or less closely with fathers or, in Lucy's case, with a father substitute. In two cases, however, Freud represented the father as an uncle, a misrepresentation that he corrected only in 1924; and his reluctance to implicate the father appears strikingly in a supplemental narrative of an unnamed patient whose physician-father accompanied her during her hypnotic sessions with Freud. When Freud challenged her to acknowledge that "something else had happened which she had not mentioned," she "gave way to the extent of letting fall a single significant phrase; but she had hardly said a word before she stopped, and her old father, who was sitting behind her, began to sob bitterly." Freud concludes: "Naturally I pressed my investigation no further; but I never saw the patient again." Here Freud's sympathies divide: had the father not intruded, Freud undoubtedly would have heard her out as he had Katharina; but, made aware of the father's anguish, he "naturally" cooperated with it even to the extent of repressing from his text the "single significant phrase" that may have held the key to her neurosis.

In larger terms, too, Freud's work on hysteria posed the dilemma of whether to elicit and credit the daughter's story, with which rested, as other cases had shown, his hope of curing her limping walk; or to honor the father's sob, which corroborated even as it silenced the girl's significant word. The list of reasons Freud gave Fliess for abandoning the seduction theory is, as Balmary points out, not very compelling; indeed, it contradicts the evidence of *Studies on Hysteria*. Freud complains that he cannot terminate the analyses, even though several cases (notably Anna O./Bertha Pappenheim, who was Breuer's patient) are there described as terminating in a lasting cure. He complains of not being able to distinguish between truth and "emotionally charged fiction" in his patients, even though he had linked the vanishing of symptoms with the recovery of traumatic experience through memory—whether narrated with apparent fidelity to literal fact, as in Katharina's case, or in dream imagery, as by Anna O., whom Breuer wrote that he always found "entirely truthful and trustworthy" (*Studies on Hysteria*, 43). And Freud claims to have been frustrated in his attempt to recover the buried trauma, despite his success in some instances. Only one item on the list is upheld by the earlier cases: "the astonishing thing that in every case *my own not excluded*, blame was laid on perverse acts by the father, and realization of the unexpected frequency of hysteria, in every case of which the same thing applied, though it was hardly credible that perverted acts against children were so general."

The problem was precisely that sexual abuse of children by fathers appeared "so general." In the years between conceiving and abandoning the seduction theory, Freud was engaged in his own self-analysis, in which he discovered, through dreams, his own incestuous wishes toward his daughter Mathilde and, through symptoms exhibited by his siblings, the possibility that his father Jakob had abused his children. Jakob himself died on October 23, 1896, initiating in Freud a complex process of mourning that ultimately strengthened his idealization of his father. Freud's dream of Irma's injection, which concerned a patient who shared his daughter Mathilde's name, superimposed a destructive father-daughter relationship upon one between physician and patient. Nor could the father's fault be contained within the bounds of the hysterics' individual histories. Recent research, for example Herman's, has traced many continuities between the problem of father-daughter incest and the dominance of male/paternal authority in society as a whole; Freud too faced implications that would have changed the focus of his work from individual therapy to social criticism. The "icy reception" with which the professional community of fin de siècle Vienna greeted his 1896 lecture, which did not explicitly implicate fathers in hysteria, was indication enough that Freud, if he credited the daughters, would risk sharing their fate of being silenced and ignored. The stakes for Freud were very high, for the fathers who paid him his (at that time meager) living also represented, as had Jakob, the privileged place that Freud, as a male, could himself hope to attain in the culture. Acceding, upon Jakob's death, to the place of the father, he acceded also to the father's text, which gave him small choice but to judge the daughters stories "hardly credible."

Yet Freud could not easily call in the credit that he had already invested in the daughters' stories. As Jane Gallop notes, he continued to speak of "actual seduction" long after he had supposedly repudiated it, with the difference that he now deflected guilt from the father to, variously, the nurse, the mother, and, by way of the oedipal complex, the child herself. Balmary argues persuasively that Freud's own hysterical symptoms grew more pronounced as he undertook to deny what he was the first to discover, that "the secret of hysteria is the father's hidden fault"; and that the texts documenting his turn to the oedipal complex betray that turn as a symptomatic effort to conceal the father's fault. Seduced by the father's sob story, Freud took upon himself the burden his patients bore of concealing the father's fault in mute symptomology. Hysterics, Freud wrote, suffer from reminiscence. As Priam in his reply to Helen does not forget her words, so Freud in his later writings does not forget the daughter's story but rewrites it as the story of "femininity," attributing to mothers, nurses, and a female "Nature" the damage to female subjectivity and desire wrought by specific historical events. Yet when Freud concludes in "Femininity" that woman has an inferior sense of justice and suggests that the "one technique" she has contributred to culture, the invention of plaiting and weaving, is designed to conceal the shame of her genital lack, it is he who, like Priam, is weaving a cultural text whose obscured but still legible design is to protect the *father* (conceived broadly as general and cultural, that is, as male authority) from suspicion of an insufficiently developed sense of justice. Like Priam, Freud makes subtle war on woman's desire and on the credibility of her language in order to avert its perceived threat to the father's cultural preeminence. If, in doing so, he produces a theory that Krafft-Ebing could have approved, he also composes a genuine "scientific fairytale."

It appears, then, that Freud undertook not to believe the hysterics not because the weight of scientific evidence was on the father's side but because so much was at stake in maintaining the father's credit: the innocence not only of particular fathers—Freud's, Freud himself, the hysterics'—but also of the cultural structure that credits male authority at the expense of female authority, reproducing a social and political hierarchy of metaphorical fathers and daughters. The history of the seduction theory shows Freud's genius, but it also shows his seduction by the hysterical cultural script that protects the father's credit, and Freud's consequent inability, not unlike Helen's, the hysterics', or Woolf's fisherwoman's, to bring the story of sexual abuse and silencing to light. When Helen sublimely paints herself and Hektor as willing victims upon the altar of an art that serves the divine plan of Zeus, "father of gods and men," she speaks this cultural script; as Priam does in reminiscing about Amazons, as the hysterics with their bodily reminiscences and Freud with his theory of femininity did; and as Woolf's fisherwoman does, with her imagination gagged and petticoated in deference to the "conventions."

Women's literary history has important continuities with the actual and imaginative histories told by Homer, Freud, and Herman. Woman's cultural seduction is not merely analogous to the physical abuses that Freud's patients claimed to have suffered but *continuous* with them. Herman shows that the abusive or seductive father does serious harm to the daughter's mind as well as to her body, damaging her sense of her own identity and depriving her voice of authority and strength. For the literary daughter—the woman reader/writer as daughter of her culture—the metaphysical violence against women inscribed in the literary tradition, although more subtle and no less difficult to acknowledge and understand, has serious consequences. Metaphysically, the woman reader of a literary tradition that inscribes violence against women is an abused daughter. Like physical abuse, literary violence against women works to privilege the cultural father's voice and story over those of women, the cultural dauther's and indeed to silence women's voices. If Freud had difficulty telling the difference between his patients' histories and their fantasies, the power of such cultural fantasies as Homer's and Freud's to shape their audiences' sense of the world is self-evident.

But the Freud of 1892 understood the power of language to cure. Woolf, we remember, predicted a moment when women would break through the constraints of the cultural text. If the literary family history resembles the histories Freud elicited from his patients, we could expect the cultural daughter's telling of her story to work not only a "cure" of her silence in culture but, eventually, a more radical cure of the hysterical cultural text that entangles both women and men. To explore these possibilities, I will turn to a daughter's text that breaks even as it represents the daughter's hysterical silence, in doing so, crossing images of literal and literary sexual abuse: Maya Angelou's autobiographical *I Know Why the Caged Bird Sings.*

The Daughter's Story and the Father's Law

Early in her memoir, Angelou presents a brief but rich *biographia literaria* in the form of a childhood romance: "During these years in Stamps, I met and fell in love with William Shakespeare. He was my first white love. Although I enjoyed and respected Kipling, Poe, Butler, Thackeray and Henley, I saved my young and loyal passion for Paul Lawrence Dunbar, Langston Hughes, James Weldon Johnson and W. E. B. DuBois' 'Litany at Atlanta.' But it was Shakespeare who said, 'When in disgrace with fortune and men's eyes.' It was a state with which I felt myself most familiar. I pacified myself about his whiteness by saying that after all he had been dead so long that it couldn't matter to anyone any more." Maya and her brother Bailey reluctantly abandon their plan to memorize a scene from Shakespeare—"we realized that Momma would question us about the author and that we'd have to tell her that Shakespeare was white, and it wouldn't matter to her whether he was dead or not" (*I Know Why*, 11)—and choose Johnson's "The Creation" instead. This passage, depicting the trials attending those interracial affairs of the mind that Maya must keep hidden from her vigilant grandmother, raises the question of what it means for a female reader and fledgling writer to carry on a love affair with Shakespeare or with male authors in general. While the text overtly confronts and disarms the issue of race, the seduction issue is only glancingly acknowledged. But this literary father-daughter romance resonates quietly alongside Angelou's more disturbing account of the quasi-incestuous rape of the eight-year-old Maya by her mother's lover, Mr. Freeman—particularly by virtue of the line she finds so sympathetic in Shakespeare, "When in disgrace with fortune and men's eyes." Mr. Freeman's abuse of Maya occurs in two episodes. In the first, her mother rescues her from a nightmare by taking her into her own bed, and Maya then wakes to find her mother gone to work and Mr. Freeman grasping her tightly. The child feels, first, bewilderment and terror: "His right hand was moving so fast and his heart was beating so hard that I was afraid that he would die." When Mr. Freeman subsides, however, so does Maya's fright: "Finally he was quiet, and then came the nice part. He held me so softly that I wished he wouldn't ever let me go. . . . This was probably my real father and we had found each other at last" (*I Know Why*, 61). After the abuse comes the silencing: Mr. Freeman enlists the child's complicity by an act of metaphysical violence, informing her that he will kill her beloved brother Bailey if she tells anyone what "they" have done. For the child, this prohibition prevents not so much telling as asking, for confused as she is by her conflicting feelings, she has no idea what has happened. One day, however, Mr. Freeman stops her as she is setting out for the library, and it is then that he commits the actual rape on the terrified child, "a breaking and entering when even the senses are torn apart" (*I Know Why*, 65). Again threatened with violence if she tells, Maya retreats to her bed in a silent delirium, but the story emerges when her mother discovers her stained drawers, and Mr. Freeman is duly arrested and brought to trial.

At the trial, the defense lawyer as usual attempts to blame the victim for her own rape. When she cannot remember what Mr. Freeman was wearing, "he snickered as though I had raped Mr. Freeman" (*I Know Why*, 70). His next question, as to whether Mr. Freeman had ever touched her prior to that Saturday, reduces her to confusion because her memory of her own pleasure in being held by him seems to her to implicate her in his crime: "I couldn't say yes and tell them how he had loved me once for a few minutes and how he had held me close. . . . My uncles would kill me and Grandmother Baxter would stop speaking. . . . And all those people in the court would stone me as they had stoned the harlot in the Bible. And mother, who thought I was such a good girl, would be so disappointed" (*I Know Why*, 70–71). An adult can see that the daughter's need for a father's affection does not cancel his culpability for sexually abusing her. But the child cannot resolve the conflict between her desire to tell the truth, which means acknowledging the pleasure she felt when Mr. Freeman gently held her, and her awareness of the social condemnation that would greet this revelation. She knows the cultural script and its hermeneutic traditions, which hold all female pleasure guilty, all too well, and so she betrays her actual experience with a lie: "Everyone in the court knew that the answer had to be No. Everyone except Mr. Freeman and me. . . . I said No (*I Know Why*, 71). But she chokes on the lie and has to be taken down from the stand. Mr. Freeman is sentenced to a year and a day, but somehow manages to be released that very afternoon; and not long thereafter, he is killed by her Baxter uncles. Hearing of Mr. Freeman's death, Maya is overwhelmed with terror and remorse: "A man was dead because I lied" (*I Know Why*, 72). Taking his death as proof that her words have power to kill she descends into a silence that lasts for a year. Like Helen's sacrificial speech, Maya's silence speaks the hysterical cultural script: it expresses guilt and anguish at her own aggression against the father and voluntarily sacrifices the cure of truthful words.

Maya's self-silencing recalls the the link between sexual violation and silence in the archetypal rape myth of Philomela. Ovid's retelling of the Greek myth entwines rape with incest as Tereus, watching Philomela cajole her father into allowing her to visit her sister Procne, puts himself in her father's place: "He would like to be / Her father at that moment, and if he were / He would be as wicked a father as he is a husband." After the rape, in Ovid's story as in Angelou's, the victim's power of speech becomes a threat to the rapist and another victim of his violence: "Tereus did not kill her. He seized her tongue / With pincers, though it cried against the outrage, / Babbled and made a sound like *Father*, / Till the sword cut it off." The tongue's ambiguous cry connects rape/incest with the sanctioned ownership of daughters by fathers in the marriage structure and interprets Procne's symmetrical violation of killing her son Itys: she becomes a bad mother to her son as Tereus has been a bad father to the daughter entrusted to him. In the suspension wrought by metamorphosis, Tereus becomes a war bird and Procne and Philomela become nightingales whose unintelligible song resembles the hysterics' speech. In silencing herself, Maya—who knows why the caged bird sings—plays all the parts in this cultural drama. She suffers as victim, speaks the father's death, and cuts out her own tongue for fear of its crying "Father."

Maya breaks her silence when a woman befriends her by taking her home and reading aloud to her, then sending her off with a book of poems, one of which she is to recite on her next visit. We are not told which poem it was, but later we find that the pinnacle of her literary achievement at age twelve was to have learned by heart the whole of Shakespeare's *Rape of Lucrece*—nearly two thousand lines. Maya, it appears, emerges from her literal silence into a literary one. Fitting her voice to Shakespeare's words, she writes safe limits around the exclamations of her wounded tongue and in this way is able to reenter the cultural text that her words had formerly disrupted. But if Shakespeare's poem redeems Maya from her hysterical silence, it is also a lover that she embraces at her peril. In Angelou's text Shakespeare's Lucrece represents that violation of the spirit which Shakespeare's and all stories of sleeping beauties commit upon the female reader. Maya's feat of memory signals a double seduction: by the white culture that her grandmother wished her black child not to love and by the male culture which imposes upon the rape victim, epitomized in Lucrece, the double silence of a beauty that serves male fantasy and a death that serves male honor. The black child's identification with an exquisite rape fantasy of white male culture violates her reality. Wouldn't everyone be surprised, she muses, "when one day I woke out of my black ugly dream and my real hair, which was long and blond, would take the place of the kinky mass that Momma wouldn't let me straighten? My light-blue eyes were going to hypnotize them. . . . Because I was really white and because a cruel fairy stepmother, who was understandably jealous of my beauty, had turned me into a too-big Negro girl, with nappy black hair, broad feet, and a space between her teeth that would hold a number two pencil" (*I Know Why*, 2). Maya's fantasy bespeaks her cultural seduction but Angelou's powerful memoir, recovering the history that frames it, rescues the child's voice from this seduction by telling the prohibited story.

Re-creating the Universe

If Angelou presents one woman's emergence from the hysterical cultural text, Alice Walker's *The Color Purple* deepens and elaborates its themes to work a more powerful cure. Published in 1982 (right on schedule with respect to Woolf's prediction), Walker's novel not only portrays a cure of one daughter's hysterical silence but rewrites from the ground up the cultural text that sanctions her violation and dictates her silence. Whereas the memoir form holds Angelou's story within the limits of history, Walker stages her cure in the imaginary spaces of fiction. Yet Walker conceived *The Color*

Purple as a historical novel, and her transformation of the daughter's story into a fiction that lays claim to historical truth challenges the foundation of the "conventions," social and cultural, that enforce women's silence. Walker retells the founding story of Western culture from a woman's point of view, and in an important sense, her historical novel—already celebrated as a landmark in the traditions of Black women's, Black, and women's writing—also stands in the tradition inaugurated by Homer and Genesis. Her hero Celie is a woman reborn to desire and language; and Walker, while not one with Celie as Angelou is with Maya, is a woman writer whom Woolf might well have considered a hero.

The Color Purple tells the story of a fourteen-year-old daughter's rape by her "Pa." It begins in its own prohibition: its first words, inscribed like an epigraph over Celie's letters, are her "Pa"'s warning, "*You better not never tell nobody but God. It'd kill your mammy*" (*Color*, 11). Thus is Celie robbed, in the name of her mother, of her story and her voice. Later, her pa further discredits her when he hands Celie over to Mr. _____ (ironically reduced to generic cultural father), a widower in need of a wife-housekeeper-caretaker of his children, with the warning: "She tell lies" (*Color*, 18). Isolated, ignorant, and confused, Celie follows her pa's prohibition literally, obediently silencing her speech but writing stumblingly of her bewilderment in letters to God: "Dear God, I am fourteen years old. ~~I am~~ I have always been a good girl. Maybe you can give me a sign letting me know what is happening to me" (*Color*, 11). Celie's rape leaves her with guilt that blocks her words. But through her letter writing she is able at once to follow the letter of the father's law and to tell her story, first to that imaginary listener, the God of her father's command, and later, to the friend who saves her from silence, Shug Avery.

These ends are all the more powerful in that they emerge from Celie's seemingly hopeless beginnings. With the first of Celie's two pregnancies by her pa, he forces her to leave school: "He never care that I love it (*Color*, 19). Celie keeps studying under her younger sister Nettie's tutelage, but the world recedes from her grasp. "Look like nothing she say can git in my brain and stay," Celie writes God. "She try to tell me something bout the ground not being flat. I just say, Yeah, like I know it. I never tell her how flat it look to me" (*Color*, 20). While this passage conveys the pathos of Celie's isolation, it also reveals what will eventually prove the source of her strength, for Celie's eventual emergence from silence, ignorance, and misery depends upon her fidelity to the way things look to her. One important instance is her feeling for her mother, who is too weak and ill to intervene in the incest and who dies soon after Celie's second child is born. "Maybe cause my mama cuss me you think I kept mad at her," Celie tells God. "But I ain't. I felt sorry for mama. Trying to believe his story kilt her" (*Color*, 15).

As Celie never loses her identification with her mother, so she is saved from her isolation by three other women who become her companions and examples and whose voices foil Celie's submissive silence. Sofia, who marries Mr. _____'s son Harpo, is at first a problem for Celie, who tells God: "I like Sofia, but she don't act like me at all. If she talking when Harpo and Mr. _____ come in the room, she keep right on. If they ast her where something at, she say she don't know. Keep talking" (*Color*, 42). When Harpo consults her about how to make Sofia mind, Celie advises: "Beat her (*Color*, 43)— propounding the cultural script of violent male rule in marriage, the only one she knows. But when Sofia angrily confronts Celie, friendship forms, and Celie begins to abandon her numb allegiance to the father's law. Shug Avery, a brilliant blues singer and Mr. _____'s longtime lover, enters Celie's life when Mr. _____ brings her home ill for Celie to nurse. Like Sofia, Shug talks: "she say whatever come to mind, forgit about polite (*Color*, 73). Mary Agnes, Harpo's girl friend after Sofia's departure, begins, like Celie, as a relatively weak and silent woman. Yet when she is elected to go ask help from the white warden for Sofia in prison, she returns from her mission battered and bruised, and only after some urging—"Yeah, say Shug, if you can't tell us, who you gon tell, God?" (*Color*, 95)—is she able to tell the others that the warden has raped her. Telling the story, she becomes her own authority, symbolized in her self-naming: when Harpo says, "I love you, Squeak," she replies, "My name Mary Agnes" (*Color*, 95).

Mary Agnes's example is important for Celie, who, until now, has buried her story in her letters. One night soon afterward, when their husbands are away, Shug comes into bed with Celie for warmth and company, and Celie tells her everything: "I cry and cry and cry. Seem like it all come back to me, laying there in Shug arms. . . . Nobody ever love me, I say. She say, I love you, Miss Celie. And then she haul off and kiss me on the mouth. *Um*, she say, like she surprise. . . . Then I feels something real soft and wet on my breast, feel like one of my little lost babies mouth. Way after while, I act like a little lost baby too" (*Color*, 108–9). To know all alone, Balmary writes, is to know as if one did not know. To know with another is conscious knowledge, social knowledge, *con-science*. Celie's telling of her story is an act of knowing-with that breaks the father's law, his prohibition of conscience. Knowing her story with Shug begins to heal Celie's long-hidden wounds of body and voice.

The radical conscience of Walker's novel goes beyond restoring Celie's voice to break down the patriarchal marriage plot that sanctions violence against women. This dismantling begins with another wound when Shug and Celie find the letters from Nettie that Mr. _____ has spitefully hidden since the sisters' separation. From them, Celie learns her lost history: that their father had been lynched when they were babies for having a store that did too well; that their mother, then a wealthy widow had lost her reason and married a stranger, the man Celie knew as her " Pa"; that he had given Celie's two children to Samuel and Corrine, the missionaries to whom Nettie had also fled; and that, Corrine having died, Samuel, Nettie, and Celie's children are returning to the United States from their African mission. Celie's first response when she finds the intercepted letters is a murderous fury toward fathers both physical and metaphysical. Shug has to disarm her of the razor she is about to use to kill Mr. _____, and the scales fall from her eyes with respect to the God to whom she has been writing: "Dear God, . . . My daddy lynch. My mama crazy. All my little half-brothers and sisters no kin to me. My children not my sister and brother. Pa not pa. You must be sleep" (*Color*, 163).

With Shug's help, Celie is able to translate her murderous rage into powerful speech and to meet Mr. _____ on the battlefield of language. Patriarchal family rule and patriarchal metaphysics break down simultaneously as Shug and Celie leave Mr. _____'s house for Shug's Memphis estate. Celie's self-assertion is met with scorn by Mr. _____: "Shug got talent, he say. She can sing. She got spunk, he say. She can talk to anybody Shug got looks, he say. She can stand up and be notice. But what you got? You ugly. You skinny. You shape funny. You too scared to open your mouth to people" (*Color*, 186). But Celie's voice gains strength as she comes into possession of her history, and for the first time, she finds words to resist Mr. _____:

> I curse you, I say.
> What that mean? he say.
> I say, Until you do right by me, everything you touch will crumble.
> He laugh. Who you think you is? he say. . . .
> A dust devil flew up on the porch between us, fill my mouth with dirt. The dirt say, Anything you do to me, already done to you.
> Then I feel Shug shake me. Celie, she say. And I come to myself.
> I'm pore, I'm black, I may be ugly and can't cook, a voice say to everything listening. But I'm here.
> Amen, say Shug. Amen, amen. [*Color*, 187]

Celie's curse, which Walker enhances with epic machinery, is powerful. But unlike the razor which Shug takes out of her hand, it does not return Mr. _____'s violence in kind. Instead, the decline of the father's law in Walker's novel creates temporary separate spheres for women and men in which gender hierarchy breaks down in the absence of the "other," enabling women and men eventually to share the world again. Celie's authority is consolidated as she comes into economic independence Earlier, Shug had distracted Celie from her murderous rage toward Mr. _____ by suggesting that the two of them sew her a pair of pants. "What I need pants for?" Celie objects. "I ain't no man" (*Color*, 136). In Memphis, while trying to think what she wants to do for a living, Celie sits "making pants after pants" (*Color*, 190) and soon finds her vocation founding "Folkpants, Unlimited." In this comic reversal, the garment that Celie at first associates strictly with men becomes the means, symbolic and material, of her economic independence and her self-possession.

The magical ease with which Celie emerges from poverty and silence classes Walker's "historical novel" with epic and romance rather than with realist or socialist realist fiction. Walker's Shug has a power that is historically rare indeed, and Celie's and Nettie's inheritance of their father's house, in particular, indulges in narrative magic that well exceeds the requirements of the plot. But Celie's utopian history allegorizes not only women's need to be economically independent of men but the daughter's need to inherit the symbolic estate of culture and language that has always belonged to the father, a "place" in culture and language from which she, like Archimedes, can move her world. When Celie comes into the power of language, work, and love, her curse temporarily comes true. As the daughter learns to speak, Mr. _____ falls into a hysterical depression. Mr. _____'s crisis signals the death of the cultural father whom he had earlier embodied: "Harpo ast his daddy why he beat me. Mr. _____ say, Cause she my wife. Plus, she stubborn. All women good for—he don't finish. He just tuck his chin over the paper like he do. Remind me of Pa" (*Color*, 30). As cultural father, Mr. _____'s law was unspoken, his ways immutable, and his words so close to the patriarchal script that he didn't have to finish his sentences. By the end of the novel, however, Mr. _____ has abandoned that role to become Albert and to "enter into the Creation" (*Color*, 181). By the novel's last scenes, Albert's life is scarcely differentiable from Celie's, and he tells her, "Celie, I'm satisfied this the first time I ever lived on Earth as a natural man" (*Color*, 230).

An important effect of Albert's transition from patriarch to natural man is the abandonment of that strictly literal stake in paternity that the marriage structure serves. As a "natural man," Albert, like everyone else, spends a lot of time concocting devious recipes to hide the taste of yams from Henrietta—who, Celie explains, has to eat yams to control her chronic blood disease but "Just our luck she hate yams and she not too polite to let us know" (*Color*, 222). Henrietta, Sofia's youngest child. Whose "little face always look like stormy weather" (*Color*, 196), is a crucial figure in the novel. Though Harpo tries to claim her as his sixth child, she is nobody's baby; only Sofia (if anyone) knows who her father is. Nonetheless Harpo, Albert, and everyone else feel a special affection for "ole evil Henrietta" (*Color*, 247), and, as they knock themselves out making yam peanut butter and yam tuna casserole, it becomes apparent that, in Walker's recreated universe, the care of children by men and women without respect to proprietary biological parenthood is an important means of undoing the exploitative hierarchy of gender roles. If Celie's discovery that "Pa not pa" liberates her from the law of the father that makes women and children its spiritual and sexual subjects, Albert, in learning to "wonder" and to "ast" (*Color*, 247) and to care for Henrietta, escapes the confines of the patriarchal role. As the functions of father and mother merge, the formerly rigid boundaries of the family become fluid: Celie, Shug, and Albert feel "right" sitting on the porch together; love partners change with desire; and, most important, children circulate among many parents: Samuel, Corrine, and Nettie raise Celie's; Celie raises Mr. _____'s and Annie Julia's; Sofia, Odessa, and Mary Agnes exchange theirs and the whole community, including the white Eleanor Jane, becomes involved with yams and Henrietta. Whereas, in the patriarchal societies analyzed by Lévi-Strauss, the exchange of women forges bonds between men that support male culture, in Walker's creation story children are the miracle and mystery that bond all her characters to the world, each other, and the future.

Undoing the gender hierarchy necessitates a rewriting of the Creation myth and a dismantling of the hierarchical concepts of God and authority that underwrite them in Western tradition. The God to whom Celie writes her early letters loses credibility once she learns, through Nettie's letters, that nothing is as the law of the father proclaimed it. When Shug hears her venting her wrath, she is shocked: "Miss Celie, You better hush. God might hear you." "Let 'im hear me, I say. If he ever listened to poor colored women the world would be a different place, I can tell you." Shug deconstructs Celie's theology: "You have to git man off your eyeball, before you can see anything a 'tall," she explains. "He on your box of grits, in your head, and all over the radio. He try to make you think he everywhere. Soon as you think he everywhere, you think he God. But he ain't"; "God ain't a he or a she, but a It. . . . It ain't something you can look at apart from everything else, including yourself. I believe God is everything . . . that is or ever was or ever will be. And when you can feel that, and be happy to feel that, you've found It" (*Color*, 175–79). In Walker's cosmos, the monotheistic Western myth of origins gives way to one of multiple, indeed infinite, beginnings that the new myth of Celie's fall and self-redemption celebrates. Hers is not a Creation finished in the first seven days of the world but one in which all creators are celebrated, if at times reluctantly. When Sofia, with what Harpo calls her "amazon sisters," insists on bearing her mother's casket, Harpo asks,

> Why you like this, huh? Why you always think you have to do things your own way? I ast your mama bout it one time, while you was in jail.
> What she say? ast Sofia.
> She say you think your way as good as anybody else's. Plus, it yours. [*Color*, 196]

Walker echoes this moment in her epigraph, which translates Harpo's "here come the amazons" (*Color*, 198) into: "Show me how to do like you. Show me how to do it" (*Color*, i). She fills her historical novel with creators, authorities, beginnings, "others." Like all authors of epic, she collapses transcendence and history; but her history differs from that of earlier epics. Originating in a violation of the patriarchal law, it undoes the patriarchal cultural order and builds upon new ground. "Womanlike," Walker writes, "my 'history' starts not with the taking of lands, or the births, battles, and deaths of Great Men, but with one woman asking another for her underwear." The violation of "conventions" that this exchange of underwear stages breaks through the patriarchal sexual and spiritual economy, writing into history a story long suppressed and revising history by doing so. Celie's last letter—addressed to "Dear God. Dear stars, dear trees, dear sky, dear peoples. Dear Everything. Dear God"—records a conversation about history:

> Why us always have family reunion on July 4th, say Henrietta, mouth poke out, full of complaint. It so hot.
> White people busy celebrating they independence from England July 4th, say I Harpo, so most black folks don't have to work. Us can spend the day celebrating each other.
> Ah, Harpo, say Mary Agnes, sipping some lemonade. I didn't know you knowed history. [*Color*, 249–50]

Harpo's decentering history is a microcosm of Walker's, which ends with a beginning: "I feel a little peculiar round the children," Celie writes. "And I see they think [us] real old and don't know much what going on. But I don't think us feel old at all. . . . Matter of fact, I think this the youngest us ever felt" (*Color,* 251). As Celie's beginning could have been a silent end, so her ending continues the proliferating beginnings that the novel captures in its epistolary form, its characters' histories, and the daily revelations that Shug names "God."

Walker's telling of the daughter's long-repressed story marks an important beginning for literary history. In her hands, the forbidden story recreates the world by reclaiming female subjectivity. "What I love best about Shug," Celie tells Albert, "is what she been through. When you look at Shug's eyes, you know she been where she been, seen what she seen, and what she did. And now she know. . . . And if you don't git out the way, she'll tell you about it" (*Color,* 236). Walker's woman as hero, whose history is her identity and who recreates the universe by telling her story to the world, is not new in real life. But she is only now making her presence felt in the literary tradition, opening a powerfully transformative dialogue between herself and the world, between her story and his, and between ourselves and our cultural past. As she does so, we can look forward to that "most interesting, exciting, and important conversation" that Woolf predicted would begin once woman recovered her voice.

KENETH KINNAMON

Call and Response: Intertextuality in Two Autobiographical Works by Richard Wright and Maya Angelou

In his provocative account of Afro-American literary criticism from the 1940s to the present, Houston A. Baker, Jr., traces three stages of development: integrationism, the "Black Aesthetic," and the "Reconstruction of Instruction." As his major representative of the first stage, "the dominant critical perspective on Afro-American literature during the late 1950s and early 1960s," Baker makes a strange choice—Richard Wright, in the 1957 version of "The Literature of the Negro in the United States." According to Baker, Wright, sanguine because of the Supreme Court school desegregation decision of 1954, believed that the leveling of racial barriers in American society would lead to a homogenous American literature in which minority writers would be absorbed into the mainstream of cultural expression. Even the verbal and musical folk forms of the black masses would eventually disappear with the inevitable triumph of democratic pluralism in the social order. Actually, Wright's essay is not basically an optimistic statement of integrationist poetics. It is, rather, a document in the proletarian-protest stage of Afro-American literature and literary criticism that dominated the Thirties and Forties, constituting the stage immediately preceding Baker's first stage. The proletarian-protest stage anticipates elements of all three of Baker's stages. Like the integrationist stage it postulates a fundamental unity of human experience transcending racial and national (but not economic)

From *Studies in Black American Literature, Vol. II: Beliefs vs. Theory in Black American Literary Criticism*. © 1986 by The Penkevill Publishing Co.

boundaries. Its commitment to an engaged literature is as fierce as that of the Black Aestheticians. And in "Blueprint for Negro Writing," at least, it advocates a sophisticated modern literary sensibility, as does the Stepto-Gates school. What it does not do is examine the special perspective of black women writers, a failing shared by the following three stages. This deficiency seems particularly conspicuous now that good women writers are so abundant and female critics are beginning to assess their achievement in relation to the total Afro-American literary tradition.

Despite its unfortunate effort at social disengagement, to my mind the most illuminating effort to provide a theoretical framework for the interpretation of Afro-American literature is Robert B. Stepto's *From Behind the Veil: A Study of Afro-American Narrative* (Urbana: University of Illinois Press, 1979). In this seminal work Stepto argues that the central myth of black culture in America is "the quest for freedom and literacy." Shaped by the historical circumstances of slavery and enforced illiteracy, this myth exists in the culture prior to any literary expression of it. Once this "pregeneric myth" is consciously articulated, it begins to take generic shape, especially as autobiography or fiction. The resulting narrative texts interact with each other in complex ways that constitute a specifically Afro-American literary tradition and history. In his book Stepto explores this intertextual tradition, dividing it into what he designates "The Call" and "The Response." In "The Call," he treats four slave narratives (by Bibb, Northup, Douglass, and Brown), *Up From Slavery*, and *The Souls of Black Folk*. To this call he discusses the twentieth century response of *The Autobiography of an Ex-Coloured Man*, *Black Boy*, and *Invisible Man*. All would agree that, of these nine works, those by Douglass, Washington, Du Bois, Johnson, Wright, and Ellison are classics of Afro-American literature, but notice that all of these authors are not only men, but race men, spokesmen, political activists. By way of complementing Stepto's somewhat narrow if sharp focus, I propose here to examine some intertextual elements in *Black Boy* and *I Know Why the Caged Bird Sings* to ascertain how gender may affect genre in these two autobiographical quests for freedom and literacy and, in Angelou's case, community as well.

In many ways these two accounts of mainly Southern childhoods are strikingly similar. Both narratives cover a period of fourteen years from earliest childhood memories to late adolescence: 1913 to 1927 (age four to eighteen) in Wright's case, 1931 to 1945 (age three to seventeen) in Angelou's case. Both Wright and Marguerite Johnson (Angelou's given name) are products of broken homes, children passed back and forth among parents and other relatives. Both have unpleasant confrontations with their fathers' mistresses. Both spend part of their childhoods in urban ghettoes (Memphis and St. Louis) as well as Southern small towns. Both suffer physical mistreatment by relatives. Both are humiliated by white employers. Lethal white violence comes close to both while they are living in Arkansas. Each child is subjected by a domineering grandmother to rigorous religious indoctrination, but each maintains a skeptical independence of spirit. From the trauma or tedium of their surroundings, both turn to reading as an escape. Both excel in school, Wright graduating as valedictorian from the eighth grade of Smith-Robinson School in Jackson, Mississippi, and Johnson as salutatorian of Lafayette County Training School in Stamps, Arkansas, fifteen years later.

In addition to these general similarities, some highly specific resemblances suggest more than mere coincidence or common cultural background. In *Black Boy Wright* recalls an incident in Memphis involving a preacher invited to Sunday dinner, the main course being "a huge platter of golden-brown fried chicken." Before the boy can finish his soup the preacher is picking out "choice pieces": "My growing hate of the preacher finally became more important than God or religion and I could no longer contain myself. I leaped up from the table, knowing that I should be ashamed of what I was doing, but unable to stop, and screamed, running blindly from the room. 'That preacher's going to eat all the chicken!' I bawled." The gluttonous preacher's counterpart in *I Know Why the Caged Bird Sings* is Reverend Howard Thomas, whose "crime that tipped the scale and made our hate not only just but imperative was his actions at the dinner table. He ate the biggest, brownest and best parts of the chicken at every Sunday meal." Wright's literary imagination was first kindled by the story of Bluebeard. As a child Angelou also learned of Bluebeard. A later common literary interest was Horatio Alger, who nurtured Wright's dreams of opportunities denied in the South. To Marguerite Johnson, however, Alger was a reminder that one of her dreams would be permanently deferred: "I read more than ever, and wished my soul that I had been born a boy. Horatio Alger was the greatest writer in the world. His heroes were always good, always won, and were always boys. I could have developed the first two virtues, but becoming a boy was sure to be difficult, if not impossible" (p. 74). One is tempted to think that Angelou had Wright specifically in mind in this passage, but even if she did not, her text provides an instructive gloss on Wright's, pointing out that sexism as well as racism circumscribes opportunity.

Other parallel passages provide additional intertextual clues to a basic difference in perspective on childhood experiences. One of the numerous relatives with whom young Richard could not get along was Aunt Addie, his teacher in a Seventh-Day Adventist school in Jackson. After a bitter confrontation in which the twelve-year-old boy threatens his aunt with a knife, she finds occasion for revenge:

> I continued at the church school, despite Aunt Addie's never calling upon me to recite or go to the blackboard. Consequently I stopped studying. I spent my time playing with the boys and found that the only games they knew were brutal ones. Baseball, marbles, boxing, running were tabooed recreations, the Devil's work: instead they played a wildcat game called popping-the-whip, a seemingly innocent diversion whose excitement came only in spurts, but spurts that could hurl one to the edge of death itself. Whenever we were discovered standing idle on the school grounds, Aunt Addie would suggest that we pop-the-whip. It would have been safer for our bodies and saner for our souls had she urged us to shoot craps.
>
> One day at noon Aunt Addie ordered us to pop-the-whip. I had never played the game before and I fell in with good faith. We formed a long line, each boy taking hold of another boy's hand until we were stretched out like a long string of human beads. Although I did not know it, I was on the tip end of the human whip. The leading boy, the handle of the whip, started off at a trot, weaving to the left and to the right, increasing speed until the whip of flesh was curving at breakneck gallop. I clutched the hand of the boy next to me with all the strength I had, sensing that if I did not hold on I would be tossed off. The whip grew taut as human flesh and bone could bear and I felt that my arm was being torn from its socket. Suddenly my breath left me. I was swung in a small, sharp arc. The whip was now being popped and I could hold on no more; the momentum of the whip flung me off my feet into the air, like a bit of leather being flicked off a horsewhip, and I hurtled headlong through space and landed in a ditch. I rolled over, stunned, head bruised and bleeding. Aunt Addie was laughing, the first and only time I ever saw her laugh on God's holy ground. (pp. 96–97)

In Stamps pop-the-whip was considerably less dangerous: "And when he [Maya's brother Bailey] was on the tail of the pop the whip, he would twirl off the end like a top, spinning, falling, laughing, finally stopping just before my heart beat its last, and then he was back in the game, still laughing" (p.

23). Now pop-the-whip is not among the gentlest of childhood activities, but surely it is less potentially deadly than Wright makes it out, surely it is closer to Angelou's exciting but essentially joyous pastime. With his unremittingly bleak view of black community in the South, Wright presents the game as sadistic punishment inflicted by a hateful aunt. In Angelou's corrective it becomes a ritual of ebullient youthful bravado by her "pretty Black brother" who was also her "unshakable God" and her "Kingdom Come" (p. 23).

Another pair of passages shows the same difference. Both Wright's Grandmother Wilson and Johnson's Grandmother Henderson ranked cleanliness close to godliness. On one occasion Wright remembers his grandmother bathing him:

> I went to her, walking sheepishly and nakedly across the floor. She snatched the towel from my hand and began to scrub my ears, my face, my neck.
>
> "Bend over," she ordered.
>
> I stooped and she scrubbed my anus. My mind was in a sort of daze, midway between daydreaming and thinking. Then, before I knew it, words—words whose meaning I did not fully know—had slipped out of my mouth.
>
> "When you get through, kiss back there," I said, the words rolling softly but unpremeditatedly. (p. 36)

Naturally the response to this call is a severe beating. Angelou treats a similar situation with humor:

> "Thou shall not be dirty" and "Thou shall not be impudent" were the two commandments of Grandmother Henderson upon which hung our total salvation.
>
> Each night in the bitterest winter we were forced to wash faces, arms, necks, legs and feet before going to bed. She used to add, with a smirk that unprofane people can't control when venturing into profanity, "and wash as far as possible, then wash possible." (p. 26)

No children like to scrub or be scrubbed, but Wright uses the occasion to dramatize hostility between himself and his family, while Angelou's purpose is to portray cleanliness as a bonding ritual in black culture: "Everyone I knew respected these customary laws, except for the powhitetrash children" (p. 27).

In *Black Boy* the autobiographical persona defines himself *against* his environment, as much against his family and the surrounding black culture as against the overt hostility of white racism. Like the fictional persona Bigger Thomas, the protagonist of *Black Boy* is all archetypal rebel who rejects all social norms. In the opening scene he sets his family's house on fire, eliciting a traumatically severe whipping from his mother. His father "was always a stranger to me, always alien and remote" (p. 9). Young Richard subverts his paternal authority by a disingenuous literalism in the cat-killing episode. At the end of the first chapter he recalls his last meeting with his father in 1940, providing an exaggerated geriatric description complete with toothless mouth, white hair, bent body, glazed eyes, gnarled hands. His father was a brutalized "black peasant," "a creature of the earth" without loyalty, sentiment, tradition, joy, or despair—all in contrast to his son, who lives "on a vastly different plane of reality," who speaks a different language, and who has traveled to "undreamed-of shores of knowing" (pp. 30, 31). Wright's symbolic effort to bury his father corresponds to a persistent attempt to come into his own by opposing or ignoring all members of his family, who consistently try to stifle his articulation of his individuality, to inhibit his quest for freedom. Shouting joyously at the sight of a free-flying bird outside his window, Richard is rebuked in the opening scene by his younger brother with the words "'You better hush.'" His mother immediately steps in to reinforce the message: "'You stop that yelling, you hear?'" (p. 3). These are the first words spoken to Richard in *Black Boy*, but they reverberate in other mouths throughout the work. His brother plays an exceedingly minor role before being sent to Detroit to live with an aunt. His mother is presented more sympathetically than are other members of the family, but even she functions as a harsh disciplinarian striving to suppress her son's dangerous individualism. His grandmother and other relatives join this effort leading often to violent arguments in which Richard threatens them with knife or razor blade.

Outside the family the boy's relations to other black children are marked by fights on the street and in the schoolyard described with the same hyperbolic violence employed in the pop-the-whip episode. In the classroom he has to struggle against a paralyzing shyness that renders him almost mute and unable to write his own name: "I sat with my ears and neck burning, hearing the pupils whisper about me, hating myself, hating them: I sat still as stone and a storm of emotion surged through me" (p. 67). In describing his contacts with the general black community Wright emphasizes brutalization and degradation, as in his account of saloons in Memphis or in this paragraph on life in West Helena:

We rented one half of a double corner house in front of which ran a stagnant ditch carrying sewage. The neighborhood swarmed with rats, cats, dogs, fortunetellers, cripples, blind men, whores, salesmen, rent collectors, and children. In front of our flat was a huge roundhouse where locomotives were cleaned and repaired. There was an eternal hissing of steam, the deep grunting of steel engines, and the tolling of bells. Smoke obscured the vision and cinders drifted into the house, into our beds, into our kitchen, into our food; and a tarlike smell was always in the air. (p. 52)

Richard learns about sex voyeuristically by peeping at the whores at work in the other half of the duplex in the Arkansas town, as he had earlier watched the exposed rears of privies in Memphis. When he does manage to establish some degree of rapport with other boys, "the touchstone of fraternity was my feeling toward white people, how much hostility I held toward them, what degrees of value and honor I assigned to race" (p. 68). But as the reader of "Big Boy Leaves Home," *The Long Dream*, or biographies of Wright knows, in *Black Boy* the author minimizes the important role his friendship with peers actually played in his adolescent life. Religion is also rejected, whether the peripteral Seventh-Day Adventism of his grandmother or the mainstream black Methodism of his mother. So estranged and isolated from the nurturing matrices of black culture, an estrangement as much willed from within as imposed from without, Wright was able to utter this famous indictment:

(After I had outlived the shocks of childhood, after the habit of reflection had been born in me, I used to mull over the strange absence of real kindness in Negroes, how unstable was our tenderness, how lacking in genuine passion we were, how void of great hope, how timid our joy, how bare our traditions, how hollow our memories, how lacking we were in those intangible sentiments that bind man to man, and how shallow was even our despair. After I had learned other ways of life I used to brood upon the unconscious irony of those who felt that Negroes led so passional an existence! I saw that what had been taken for our emotional strength was our negative confusions, our flights, our fears, our frenzy under pressure.

(Whenever I thought of the essential bleakness of black life in America, I knew that Negroes had never been allowed to catch the full spirit of Western civilization, that they lived somehow in it but not of it. And when I brooded upon the cultural barrenness of black life, I wondered if clean, positive tenderness, love, honor, loyalty, and the capacity to remember were native with man. I asked myself if these human qualities were not fostered, won, struggled and suffered for, preserved in ritual form from one generation to another.) (p. 33)

In part this passage attempts to shame whites by showing them what their racism has wrought, but in a more crucial way it defines Wright's individual-istic alienation from all sense of community, that permanent spiritual malaise that is both the key biographical fact and the ideological center of his art.

With Maya Angelou the case is quite otherwise. If she never experi-enced the physical hunger that characterized much of Wright's childhood, he was not raped at the age of eight. Yet here youthful reponse to rejection and outrage is to embrace community, not to seek alienation. *I Know Why the Caged Bird Sings* is a celebration of black culture, by no means uncritical, but essentially a celebration. Toward her family, young Marguerite is depicted as loving, whether or not her love is merited. She idolizes her slightly older brother Bailey. Her Grandmother Henderson is presented not only as the matrifocal center of her family but as the leader of the black community in Stamps, strong, competent, religious, skilled in her ability to coexist with Jim Crow while maintaining her personal dignity. She is a repository of racial values, and her store is the secular center of her community. Crippled Uncle Willie could have been presented as a Sherwood Anderson grotesque, but Angelou recalls feeling close to him even if he was, like Grandmother Henderson, a stern disciplinarian. Angelou would seem to have every reason to share Wright's bitterness about parental neglect, but she does not. When her father shows up in Stamps she is impressed by his appearance, his proper speech, and his city ways. Her mother beggars description: "To describe my mother would be to write about a hurricane in its perfect power. Or the climbing, falling colors of a rainbow. . . . My mother's beauty literally assailed me" (p. 58). Absorbed in their own separate lives, her parents neglect or reject her repeatedly, but she is more awed by their persons and their person-alities than she is resentful. Her maternal family in St. Louis is also impres-sive in its worldly way, so different in its emphasis on pleasure and politics from the religious rectitude of the paternal family in Stamps. Even Mr. Freeman, her mother's live-in boyfriend who first abuses and then rapes the child, is presented with more compassion than rancor.

Afflicted with guilt after Freeman is killed by her uncles, Marguerite lapses into an almost catatonic silence, providing an excuse to her mother to send her back to Stamps. Southern passivity provides a good therapeutic environment for the child, especially when she is taken under the wing of an elegant, intelligent black woman named Mrs. Bertha Flowers, who treats her to cookies, Dickens, and good advice. Better dressed and better read than anyone else in the community, she nevertheless maintains good relations with all and urges Marguerite not to neglect the wisdom of the folk as she pursues literary interests: "She said that I must always be intolerant of ignorance but understanding of illiteracy. That some people, unable to go to school, were more educated and even more intelligent than college professors. She encouraged me to listen carefully to what country people called mother wit. That in those homely sayings was couched the collective wisdom of generations" (p. 97). In contrast to Wright's grandmother, who banished from her house the schoolteacher Ella for telling the story of Bluebeard to Richard, Grandmother Henderson is quite friendly with "Sister" Flowers, both women secure in their sense of self and their mutual respect.

Angelou also recalls favorably the larger rituals of black community. Religious exercises, whether in a church or in a tent revival meeting, provide a festive atmosphere for Marguerite and Bailey. Racial euphoria pervades the black quarter of Stamps after a Joe Louis victory in a prizefight broadcast on Uncle Willie's radio to a crowd crammed into the store. A summer fish fry, the delicious feeling of terror while listening to ghost stories, the excitement of pregraduation activities—these are some of the pleasures of growing up black so amply present in *I Know Why the Caged Bird Sings* and so conspicuously absent in *Black Boy*.

A comparison of the graduation exercises in the two works is particularly instructive. Marguerite is showered with affectionate attention and gifts, and not only from her family and immediate circle of friends: "Uncle Willie and Momma [her Grandmother Henderson] had sent away for a Mickey Mouse watch like Bailey's. Louise gave me four embroidered handkerchiefs. (I gave her three crocheted doilies.) Mrs. Sneed, the minister's wife, made me an undershirt to wear for graduation, and nearly every customer gave me a nickel or maybe even a dime with the instruction 'Keep on moving to higher ground,' or some such encouragement" (p. 169). Richard feels more and more isolated as graduation nears: "My loneliness became organic. I felt walled in and I grew irritable. I associated less and less with my classmates" (p. 152). Refusing to use a speech prepared for him by the school principal, he resists peer and family pressure as well as the implicit promise of a teaching job, in order to maintain his sense of individual integrity. Giving his own speech, he rejects utterly the communal ceremony implicit in the occasion:

On the night of graduation I was nervous and tense: I rose and faced the audience and my speech rolled out. When my voice stopped there was some applause. I did not care if they liked it or not: I was through. Immediately, even before I left the platform, I tried to shunt all memory of the event from me. A few of my classmates managed to shake my hand as I pushed toward the door, seeking the street. Somebody invited me to a party and I did not accept. I did not want to see any of them again. I walked home, saying to myself: The hell with it! With almost seventeen years of baffled living behind me, I faced the world in 1925. (p. 156)

The valedictorian of Marguerite's class accepts the help of a teacher in writing his speech, but before he mounts the podium a white politician delivers the Washingtonian message that "we were maids and farmers, handymen and washerwomen, and anything higher that we aspired to was farcical and presumptuous" (pp. 175–176). But this ritual of racial humiliation is immediately followed by a ritual of racial survival and solidarity. After giving his speech, the valedictorian improvises by singing "Lift Ev'ry Voice and Sing" with renewed meaning, joined by all present, the white man having left. From shame the collective emotion is transformed by the song of a black poet to pride: "We were on top again. As always, again. We survived. The depths had been icy and dark, but now a bright sun spoke to our souls. I was no longer simply a member of the proud graduating class of 1940; I was a proud member of the wonderful, beautiful Negro race" (p. 179). Unlike Wright, Angelou stresses the intimate relation of the black creator to the black audience. Gathering his material from the stuff of the black experience, with its suffering and its survival, James Weldon Johnson transmutes the experience into art, giving it back to the people to aid them to travel the stony road, to fortify their spirit by reminding them of their capacity to endure. The episode is a paradigm of Angelou's own artistic endeavor in *I Know Why the Caged Birds Sings.*

It is important to recognize that Angelou's Southern environment is as grievously afflicted by white racism as Wright's. Just as young Richard is tormented by whites, so is Marguerite by her employer Mrs. Cullinan who calls her out of her name, or by Dentist Lincoln, who owes Grandmother Henderson money but will not treat the child's toothache because ". . . my policy is I'd rather stick my hand in a dog's mouth than in a nigger's'" (p. 184). White violence comes dangerously close to both Uncle Willie and Bailey. Indeed, the town is quintessentially Southern in its racial attitudes, comparable to Wright's Elaine or West Helena or Jackson: "Stamps,

Arkansas, was Chitlin' Switch, Georgia: Hang 'Em High, Alabama; Don't Let the Sun Set on You Here, Nigger, Mississippi; or any other name just as descriptive. People in Stamps used to say that the whites in our town were so prejudiced that a Negro couldn't buy vanilla ice cream. Except on July Fourth. Other days he had to be satisfied with chocolate" (p. 47). It is not that Angelou de-emphasizes the racist assault on Black personality and community; it is just that she shows with respect if not always agreement the defensive and compensatory cultural patterns developed to survive in such an environment. This is Maya Angelou's response in *I Know Why the Caged Bird Sings* to the call of *Black Boy*.

One hesitates to generalize on the basis of a single book by one woman writer, but a quick recall of such writers as Linda Brent, Zora Neale Hurston, Gwendolyn Brooks, Margaret Walker, Paule Marshall, Sonia Sanchez, Toni Morrison, Sherley Anne Williams, Nikki Giovanni, Carolyn M. Rodgers, Ntozake Shange, Alice Walker, Gayl Jones, and numerous others suggests that, more than male writers, women are concerned with such themes as community, sexism (especially sexual exploitation), and relations with family and friends. They seem correspondingly less interested in individual rebellion, alienation, and success against the odds. A theory which can encompass both visions, adding community to the myth of freedom and literacy, accommodating *I Know Why the Caged Bird Sings* as easily as *Black Boy*, may follow the stages delineated by Houston Baker and become the primary contribution of the present decade to Afro-American literary criticism.

SUSAN GILBERT

Maya Angelou's I Know Why the Caged Bird Sings: *Paths to Escape*

Maya Angelou's first autobiographical book, *I Know Why the Caged Bird Sings* (1970), opens in church on Easter Sunday with the child dressed up in a lavender taffeta dress lovingly tucked by "Momma," her grandmother. She hopes to wake from her "black ugly dream" (p. 4) to "look like one of the sweet little white girls who were everybody's dream of what was right with the world" (p. 4). The book closes with the heroine a sixteen-year-old mother, unmarried, who has gazed on her beautiful baby afraid to handle him until one night her mother puts the baby in bed beside her. Though she fears she will roll over and crush him, Maya wakes to find him sleeping safely by her side under the tent of covers she has made with her arm. Her mother whispers comfortingly, "See, you don't have to think about doing the right thing, if you're for the right thing, then you do it without thinking" (p. 281).

The writer neither wishes to be white nor fears for her black son. From the conflicts of black and white worlds and from the conflicts of styles at her rural religious Grandmother, "Momma," and her streetwise urban mother, she has found the strengths that will lead her beyond them both. But she has not done it "without thinking." Between the years when she was the sixteen-year-old mother, in 1944, and when as a woman of forty-two, in 1970, she published her book, she did a great deal of thinking about "doing the right thing" and did her thinking through a very varied career and wide experience of the world. The reader of the book must deal throughout with the dual perspective of the child, growing to consciousness of herself and the limits of her world, and the author, experienced, confident, and didactic.

From *Mount Olive Review* 1:1. © 1987 by Mount Olive College.

It is a story of hurt, and loneliness, and anger, and love. The first memory is of separation; when she was three and her brother Bailey four, they were sent alone by train from California, where their parents had broken up their marriage, to Stamps, Arkansas, to live with their paternal grandmother. Fixed forever in the woman's consciousness are her love for her beautiful, clever brother, their grief, and their dreams of the mother who has sent them away. Intertwined with these memories is the enormous presence of the grandmother, "Momma," a shopkeeper, a devout Christian who prays morning and evening. By her faith she endures this world, for whose injustice she has no explanation to give the children, and hopes for her reward and retribution in the next world. The child sees and the author remembers the crushing poverty of those farm workers who trudge through Momma's store, hopeful and singing in the morning, bone weary and no richer at evening.

The whites of Stamps live across town and appear in the earliest memories only in scattered terrible vignettes: of nights when the Klan rides and all the black men hide, some in the chicken droppings under their homes, her Uncle Willie in the bottom of a barrel of potatoes; of days when "po-white-trash" girls call the dignified grandmother "Annie" and mock her in word and obscene gesture; of a grammar school graduation day robbed of its luster by the careless hurt of a white speaker, a politician, who promises new laboratories for the white high school and a paved sports field for the black.

At eight she goes with her brother to live with their mother in St. Louis. Here she is introduced to the ways of street-wise urban blacks with laws independent of the white dominant culture. It is a worldly rich environment. Their gay and beautiful mother charms her children with her singing and dancing as she charms the patrons of the bars. And she turns the other cheek to no one. Her gang of fierce brothers hold a covenant of loyalty as strong as that of the church brethren of Arkansas, but utterly different in its rules of reciprocity. The children at this stage belong to neither world but live in awe of their mother, never secure that she will be really there forever. And Maya, at age eight, is first fondled then raped by her mother's boyfriend. In the court of white justice he is found guilty, given a year's sentence, allowed to go free the same night of the trial. In the other court of the black streets the retribution is more terrible. He is kicked to death.

Maya and Bailey return to Stamps. She suffers guilt for having caused the man's death and the separation of her brother from the mother he adores. For a year she retreats to silence, one of the most terrible of the "Silences" that women writers have described.

That she emerged from this silence, Angelou attributes to the strength of Momma, who finds her a sympathetic adult friend and who later, bravely takes the children to California to their mother's guardianship, and, far beyond Momma, to her mother, Vivian Baxter, a force not daunted by sexual or racial prejudice: "To describe my mother would be to write about a hurricane in its perfect power" (p. 58). It is strength imparted with little tenderness; it is strength to endure hurts, not a strength which can protect her from them. The strengths and weaknesses of the family and the relationship of the girl to her family are the most important topics of discussion about the book, to which we will return.

The last year the book recounts is tumultuous. Maya spends a summer with her father and his new girl friend and feels close to neither. On a day trip to Mexico with her father she sees him relax in a Mexican bar, a great man, tall, handsome, funny, admired by an easy crowd, and imagines the man he might have been in another culture. She drives him back dead drunk, she who had never driven a car, in a feat of success born of desperation and courage. Then after a fight with the father's girl friend, she is dumped at someone else's house, and wanders off to sleep in a junk yard of abandoned cars and to awake to find herself in a community of homeless, run-away children. It is an odd setting for Eden but an idyll of the Golden Age nonetheless. Under the benign rule of a tall boy, "Bootsie," there was "no stealing"; "everyone worked at something," collecting bottles, mowing lawns, odd jobs. "All money was held by Bootsie and used communally" (p. 246).

The experience has a crucial place in the work. Angelou writes:

> After a month my thinking processes had so changed that I was hardly recognizable to myself. The unquestioning acceptance by my peers had dislodged the familiar insecurity. Odd that the homeless children, the silt of war frenzy, could initiate me into the brotherhood of man. After hunting down unbroken bottles and selling them with a white girl from Missouri, a Mexican girl from Los Angeles and a Black girl from Oklahoma, I was never again to sense myself so solidly outside the pale of the human race. The lack of criticism evidenced by our ad hoc community influenced me, and set a tone of tolerance for my life (p. 247).

The brotherhood of man is a distant fellowship. With the sense of tolerance comes no closeness or love. When she returns to her mother's house, the good-by's are simple and the welcome casual. Her oldest intimacy, with her brother Bailey, in ruptured first by his growing identification with "a group of slick street boys" (p. 249) then by his leaving the house to live with a white prostitute.

Maya lives in lonely uncertainty over approaching womanhood and dismay over her looks. However universal the experience, it does not make any young person feel close to others. In a desperate attempt to affirm her sexuality, she accosts a neighbor boy. After one sexual encounter—without feeling, without a word being spoken—she is pregnant. It is a last mark of the isolation in which she has lived that no one notices her pregnancy until she tells her parents of it, in her eighth month.

If they have not protected her, they do not desert her, but give her care and encouragement. Maya Angelou will be a loving mother without having known tender love as a child. The book is dedicated to: "My son, Guy Johnson and all the strong black birds of promise who defy the odds and gods and sing their songs."

It is our task now to see where this book fits into several literary traditions, especially a tradition of Southern literature. For background and locale, it's hard to be more Southern than Stamps, Arkansas; St. Louis is debatable; California is OUT. Although Maya Angelou has returned to the South to become Reynolds Professor at Wake Forest, it is by a very circuitous route.

Her career, since the close of *I Know Why the Caged Bird Sings*, has made her a citizen of the world. Her works have been among all strata of humanity. The last of her teenage years she spent on the streets of California, where she was waitress, barmaid, dishwasher, nightclub entertainer, prostitute, and madam, and where she barely escaped a life of drug addiction. From this life she became a part of a world tour of *Porgy and Bess*. She has since been actress, dancer, and producer of shows for Broadway and TV. She has been journalist and editor, poet and author of her autobiographical books. She has lived and worked in Africa. She has served as a coordinator for the Southern Christian Leadership Conference. She has been university administrator and professor in Ghana, in California, in Kansas, and at Wake Forest. She holds honorary degrees from a dozen institutions.

The South that she lived in, Stamps, Arkansas, and that her kinsmen close and distant fled, makes part of her past. But she has been eager to put as much distance between herself and its white bourgeoisie traditions in literature as in life. The only black she speaks of with real scorn in this book is the father's priggish girl friend who apes the ways of middle class white women. She is a "small tight woman from the South" who "kept the house clean with the orderliness of a coffin;" who "was on close terms with her washing machine and ironing board;" who "had all the poses of the Black bourgeoisie without the material bases to support the postures" (p. 221). With more pity but no closer identification, she recounts that the poor black girls of Stamps were marked by the trivial traditions of Southern white women: "Ridiculous and even ludicrous. But Negro girls in small Southern towns, whether poverty-stricken or just munching along on a few of life's necessities, were given as extensive and irrelevant preparations for adulthood as rich white girls shown in magazines," the irrelevancies of "mid-Victorian values" (p. 101). With money earned picking cotton and with fingers too coarse for the work, they yet bought tatting or embroidery thread, and Maya herself has "a lifetime's supply of dainty doilies that would never be used in sacheted dresser drawers" (p. 101).

Although in ceasing to be Marguerite Johnson of Stamps, Arkansas, and in becoming Maya Angelou the writer, she denies the traditions—for blacks or for women—of the white South, the same themes most often called Southern fill her work. None, of course, is exclusively or originally Southern, and looking at the other traditions her work pertains to makes this very clear.

Speaking of her years in Africa and her marriage to an African, Angelou said that Ghana taught her to see the survival of distinctly African ways among the Afro-Americans. These affect her portrayal of character, individually and collectively. In *I Know Why the Caged Bird Sings* she describes Momma's reluctance to be questioned or to tell all she knows as her "African-bush secretiveness and suspiciousness" which has been only "compounded by slavery and confirmed by centuries of promises made and promises broken" (p. 189). She relates the habits of address, calling neighbors "Uncle," "Sister," "Cousin" to a heritage of tribal belonging.

As a writer she says she works from her ear, from listening to her people's cadences and habits of speech. Here she is like other Southern writers, Faulkner, Welty, O'Connor, Lee Smith whose works capture the language as spoken in particular places by particular people; she differs from them in her insistence on the uniqueness of black American speech. Here and throughout her work Angelou regards language as the means of black survival and of triumph: "It may be enough, however, to have it said that we survive in exact relationship to the dedication of our poets (include preachers, musicians and blues singers)" (p. 180). But she nowhere limits herself to the tongues of black Arkansas or ghetto streets. One critic has praised her "avoidance of a monolithic Black language" and the fact that she "does not overburden black communicants with clumsy versions of home-spun black speech" (p. 35). In the white high school she attended in San Francisco, Angelou became conscious that she would use two languages: "We learned to slide out of one language and into another without being conscious of the effort. At school, in a given situation, we might respond with 'That's not unusual.' But in the street, meeting the same situation, we easily

said, 'It be's like that sometimes'" (p. 219). I have said that the point of view
of the book goes back and forth between that of the inexperienced girl and
the experienced writer. The language also moves between a strong, colloquial simplicity and a sometimes over-blown literary mannerism. Though
she does not over-use black folk speech, she never errs when she uses it as she
does in such literary passages as this one, describing her self-pride on graduation day: "Youth and social approval allied themselves with me and we
trammeled memories of slights and insults. The wind of our swift passage
remodeled my features. Lost tears were pounded to mud and then to dust.
Years of withdrawal were brushed aside and left behind, as hanging ropes of
parasitic moss" (p. 167). (Whether this is more embarrassing to Southern
literature than the false inflections of Southern accents offered us by
Hollywood or TV—it's for you to judge!).

The literary traditions not often allied to Southern literature which
undergird this work are those of a long Western tradition of the
Bildungeroman—a novel, often autobiographical, of a young person's
growing up and finding his way among the traditions and values of the
family and culture in which he or she is reared—and a long tradition in this
country of Afro-American autobiography. In a sense both come together in
this book; some critics have referred to it inter-changeably as "novel" and
autobiography. But the traditions are diametrically opposite in the ways the
hero or heroine is portrayed.

In the *Bildungeroman* the loneliness of the hero is expected. Youth is
self-conscious; the hero feels that the values of his family and culture are
oppressive to him; he must make his escape. It is an international genre
including Goethe's *Wilhelm Meister* and James Joyce's *A Portrait of the
Artist as a Young Man*, with outstanding examples in Southern literature,
Thomas Wolfe's *Look Homeward, Angel* and Richard Wright's *Native Son*.
It influences women's works like Kate Chopin's *The Awakening*, and with
the publication of this first of Angelou's works in 1970 and a host of other
important books that appeared in the same decade, it affects a vital new
tradition in black women's writings.

Before the publication in 1940 of Wright's *Native Son*, fiction by
American black writers constituted a smaller and less important body of
work than the long tradition of Afro-American autobiographies arising
from the narratives of escaped or redeemed slaves. In these autobiographies, the primary mode of black American prose, the role of the hero is
altogether different, not a lonely misfit, not a rejector of this people but
their exemplum. One critic, Selwyn R. Cudjoe, says that the authority of
these writings derives from the impersonality of the hero-narrator:

. . . the Afro-American autobiographical statement as a form tends to be bereft of any excessive subjectivism and mindless egotism. Instead, it presents the Afro-American as reflecting a much more *im-personal* condition, the autobiographical subject emerging as an almost random member of the group, selected to tell his/her tale. As a consequence, the Afro-American autobiographical statement emerges as a public rather than a private gesture, *me-ism* gives way to *our-ism* and superficial concerns about *individual subject* usually give way to the collective subjection of the group. The autobiography, therefore, is objective and realistic in its approach and is presumed generally to be of service to the group.

This critic, Cudjoe, lumps together autobiography and fiction: "Autobiography and fiction, then, are simply different means of arriving at or (re)cognizing the same truth: the reality of American life and the position of the Afro-American subject in that life. Neither genre should be given a privileged position in our literary history and each should be judged on its ability to speak honestly and perceptively about Black experience in this land" (p. 8).

Asked this question, "Do you consider your quartet to be autobiographical novels or autobiographies?" Angelou replied, "They are autobiographies," and she went on to define her intent there as reporting on a collective, not a lone individual's story. "When I wrote *I Know Why the Caged Bird Sings*, I wasn't thinking so much about my own life or identity. I was thinking about a particular time in which I lived and the influences of that time on a number of people. I kept thinking, what about that time? What were the people around young Maya doing? I used the central figure—myself—as a focus to show how one person can make it through those times."

Whether we call the work "fiction or "autobiography" *does* really matter more than just giving English teachers something to argue about. Different traditions affect the stance of the writer to her work and the responses of the reader. Especially on the most important questions of debate about this work, the nature of the family or group she portrays and the nature of the relationship of the central character to that group, the two traditions we have looked at pose different solutions. In a *Bildungeroman*— or apprenticeship novel—we expect detachment from or rejection of the group mores. In the tradition of black autobiography here described we expect total or unconscious absorption in the group. The role of the black woman in this tradition has been called that of "an all-pervading absence" (Cudjoe, p. 7). Few of many thousand such autobiographies written were by or about women.

In those written by men they play a distinctly subservient role: "they never really seemed to have lived worthy of emulation. They invariably seemed to live for others, for Black men or White; for children, or for parents; bereft, always it appeared, of an autonomous self" (Cudjoe, p. 11).

Two important breaks in tradition have come in the twentieth century. In 1945 Richard Wright published his autobiography, *Black Boy*, and touched off a debate that has not ended about the nature of the black experience in America. His hero is not a random member of a group who are victims of white oppression. The white oppressors are there, but the boy suffers as much from his black family who have become, under the heritage of slavery, sub-human in their hunger, fear, ignorance, superstition, brutality, and despair. By the miracle of books he is awakened to a life none of his family could comprehend. Years later, as a grown man, he saw the father who laughed at his hunger, saw him as a peasant of the soil and as an animal: "how chained were his actions and emotions to the direct, animalistic impulses of his withering body." The mature Wright pitied and forgave his father, but he left the lesson that he had to distance himself from his family or perish. Black writers especially have argued against his assertions:

> After I had outlived the shocks of childhood, after the habit of reflection had been born in me, I used to mull over the strange absence of real kindness in Negroes, how unstable was our tenderness, how lacking in genuine passion we were, how void of great hope, how timid our joy, how bare our traditions, how hollow our memories, how lacking we were in those intangible sentiments that bind man to man, and how shallow was even our despair (*Black Boy*, p. 45).

Much in *I Know Why the Caged Bird Sings* and in what Angelou has said about her writing shows her in opposition to Wright's dogma. Though the girl is lonely and hurt, she finds her way to survival in terms of the traditions of her family, her mother and her grandmother, not in opposition to them. She does remark that she knew few expressions of tenderness. The grandmother was embarrassed to discuss any emotions not associated with her religious faith; the mother imparted power but not tenderness. She describes her:

> . . . Vivian Baxter had no mercy. There was a saying in Oakland at the time which, if she didn't say it herself, explained her attitude. The saying was, 'Sympathy is next to shit in the dictionary,

and I can't even read . . . She had the impartiality of nature, with
the same lack of indulgence or clemency. (pp. 201–202)

In stressing her discovery of continuance of African ways among American
blacks she argues with Wright's judgment that black traditions were "bare."
In her description of her use of the mode autobiography, she says she was
writing of one who typifies, not one who opposes or escapes the group.

I Know Why the Caged Bird Sings appeared in 1970. In the same year
appeared Toni Morrison's *The Bluest Eye*, Alice Walker's *The Third Life of
Grange Copeland*, Louise Meriwether's *Daddy Was a Numbers Runner*, Michele
Wallace's *Black Macho and the Myth of Superwoman*, and Nikki Giovanni's *Black
Feeling, Black Talk/Black Judgement*. In these and other notable works of the
1970's—Ntozake Shange's *For Colored Girls Who Have Considered Suicide/When
the Rainbow is Enuf*—black woman writers have debated the effects of black
sexism, and many have asserted that they must find their identity not merely in
opposition to an oppressive white culture but in opposition to the traditions for
the woman that the black culture imposes.

Angelou has put herself apart consistently from the movement of white
women's liberation. Black women, she says, have never been as subservient
within their community as white women in theirs: "White men, who are in
effect their fathers, husbands, brothers, their sons, nephews and uncles, say
to white women, or imply in any case: 'I don't really need you to run my
institutions. I need you in certain places and in those places you must be kept
—in the bedroom, in the kitchen, in the nursery, and on the pedestal.' Black
women have never been told this." Though they have not occupied the
pulpits, black women have been leaders in their communities, according to
Angelou. She is pleased with the dialogue that these black women's works
have begun. Though she has been criticized for including the rape in *I Know
Why the Caged Bird Sings*, she says the whole truth must be told, and she says
there is much truth still to be told of the male point of view of such works as
For Colored Girls Who Have Considered Suicide.

Angelou's works and words point to her conviction that the black
tradition is adequate and good, that black women emerge from it
triumphant and strong. Critics have noted that absence of significant men
in her autobiographies, and she certainly has been, since her years of teenage motherhood, a woman who had to survive on her own strengths. In
the midst of the debate of the 70's over the place of women in black
culture, she affirmed that, subservient to no one, she was willing and
honored to "serve." As one who had to work to survive, she says she has
always been "liberated":

I am so "liberated" that except on rare occasions my husband does not walk into the house without seeing his dinner prepared. He does not have to concern himself about a dirty house, I do that, for myself but also for my husband. I think it is important to make that very clear.

I think there is something gracious and graceful about serving. Now, unfortunately, or rather the truth is, our history in this country has been the history of the servers and because we were forced to serve and because dignity was absolutely drained from the servant, for anyone who serves in this country, black or white, is looked upon with such revilement, they are held in such contempt while that is not true in other parts of the world. In Africa it is a great honor to serve. . . ."

I Know Why the Caged Bird Sings is sixteen years old now, the experience it recounts more than forty years old. Yet nothing, it seems, could be more timely.

It is an admirable story; and it is not typical. Typically the black girl who has no permanent father in her home, who is shuffled between mother and grandmother, city and country, who is raped at eight, a mother at sixteen, who supports her child without help from its father or from her own mother, with odd jobs, waitress, barmaid, prostitute—typically such girls do not become *Ladies Home Journal's* Woman of the Year for Communications or Reynolds Professor at Wake Forest or recipients of a dozen honorary degrees. For all Angelou's heroic assertion that the black woman emerges victorious from oppression and abuse, most of them do not. They are not equipped to succeed by any of the traditions here laid out, not that of the dominant white bourgeoisie which taught a generation of Southern women, black and white, to sew and crochet and be debutantes; not that of the pious black churchwomen who look for reward and vindication in the next life; not that of the black streets where one of her mother's boy friends was kicked to death, another one shot, where Angelou once herself took a pistol to the home of a boy who had threatened her son. Few black women have had work so well for them the swift vengeance outside the law; they have been victims of lawlessness as cruel as the law which first held them oppressed and then neglected their victimization.

Angelou knows it is a heroic, not typical model. The dedication, you remember, is to her son and to "all the strong Black birds of promise who defy the odds and gods."

One last note. Bearing the emphasis on family with tradition we have seen common to Southern literature, this book bears no mark of the provincialism of which not only Southern literature but much American literature of recent decades, especially the literature of American women, has been accused.

You have probably been reading, as I have, of the recent writers' congress, PEN, in New York. The complaints of non-American writers, Salmon Rushdie, Nadine Gordimer, were loud that ours has become a literature of the misunderstood individual. It abounds in complaints and self-centered pre-occupations—will the heroine, like Gail Godwin's Odd Woman, achieve orgasm; it finds little room for the hunger of the children of the world or for the brutalities of police states.

Artistically Maya Angelou may err on the side of didacticism but she is free of exaggerated self-concern. The voice in the story shifts, from the girl of limited experience and perspective to that of the writer who speaks with the authority of truths gleaned from the traditions as diverse as Shakespeare and Ghanian folk tale. By her work she has not only contributed to but expanded the American literary tradition and the perspective from which this literature views—and serves—the world.

JOANNE M. BRAXTON

A Song of Transcendence: Maya Angelou

Maya Angelou's *I Know Why the Caged Bird Sings* (1970) and Ann Moody's *Coming of Age in Mississippi* (1968) appeared at the end of the civil rights movement of the 1960s, and they carry with them the bitter and hard-won fruit of this era. Angelou and Moody know the harsh realities of life in the Deep South in the mid-twentieth century—in Arkansas and Mississippi, respectively. As the critic Roger Rosenblatt has asserted, "No black American author has ever felt the need to invent a nightmare to make [her] point." As Maya Angelou writes of her childhood: "High spots in Stamps were usually negative: droughts, floods, lynchings and deaths." Touched by the powerful effects of these destructive forces, Maya Angelou and Ann Moody hold themselves together with dignity and self-respect. They move forward toward a goal of self-sufficiency, combining a consciousness of self, an awareness of the political realities of black life in the South, and an appreciation of the responsibility that such an awareness implies. For this chapter, I have selected *I Know Why the Caged Bird Sings* as representative of autobiographies written by black women in the post-civil rights era.

In the Arkansas South of Maya Angelou's childhood, recognized patterns of etiquette between the races asserted white superiority and black inferiority. This etiquette served as a form of social control that pervaded the daily experiences of blacks, who negotiated narrow paths of safety:

> Momma intended to teach Bailey and me to use the paths of life
> that she and her generation and all the Negroes gone before had

From *Black Women Writing Autobiography: A Tradition Within a Tradition.* © 1989 by Temple University.

found, and found to be safe ones. She didn't cotton to the idea
that white folks could be talked to at all without risking one's life.
And certainly they couldn't be spoken to insolently. In fact, even
in their absence they could not be spoken of too harshly unless
we used the sobriquet "They." If she had been asked to answer
the question of whether she was cowardly or not, she would have
said that she was realist. (*Caged Bird*, 39)

Throughout the course of *Caged Bird*, Maya Angelou moves toward this
same realism, which is not only a practical political philosophy but also one
of the dominant modes of the autobiography. *I Know Why the Caged Bird
Sings* distills the essence of the autobiographical impulse into lyric imagery
touched by poignant realism. Angelou once said, "I speak to the black experience, but I am always talking about the human condition—about what we
can endure, dream, fail at, and still survive." In this spirit, she faithfully
depicts her home ground as a version of the universal human experience.

This chapter undertakes the task of defining the characteristics that identify the text in terms of a tradition of black women's writing. George Kent has
argued that *I Know Why the Caged Bird Sings* "creates a unique place within
black autobiographical tradition . . . by its special stance toward the self, the
community, and the universe, and by a form exploiting the full measure of
imagination necessary both to beauty and absurdity." In *Caged Bird*, we witness
the full outward extension of the outraged mother. Although, in some sense,
this text seems yet too close to be explicated adequately, the availability of criticism outweighs the problem of dealing with a recent text, for as James Olney
has noted, "Here we have an autobiography by a black woman, published in
the last decade (1970), that already has its own critical literature." Not only
does the preponderance of criticism herald "full literary enfranchisement" for
"black writers, women writers, and autobiography itself," but it indicates the
importance of the text to black autobiographical tradition.

Although I have selected *Caged Bird* because of the availability of criticism and because it covers a wider span of time than Angelou's subsequent
autobiographies, one of the added advantages in considering this particular
volume is that it can be read in relation to Angelou's other autobiographical
works. In 1974, *Gather Together in My Name* followed *Caged Bird*, and *Singin'
and Swingin' and Gettin' Merry Like Christmas* appeared in 1976, followed by
The *Heart of a Woman in* 1981 and *All God's Children Need Traveling Shoes* in
1986. Additionally, Angelou has published several collections of poetry;
almost all this poetry has some autobiographical content, and through much
of it, Angelou celebrates her dark womanhood, as in "Woman Me":

Your smile, delicate
rumor of peace.
Deafening revolutions nestle in the
cleavage of
your breasts
Beggar-Kings and red-ringed Priests
seek glory at the meeting
of your thighs
A grasp of Lions, a Lap of Lambs.

Thus Angelou's autobiographical impulse manifests itself in lyrical forms as well as the prose narrative.

In *Black Autobiography*, Stephen Butterfield compares the dramatic structure, setting, and content of *I Know Why the Caged Bird Sings* with that of Richard Wright's *Black Boy* and concludes that "Maya Angelou's complex sense of humor and compassion for other people's defects . . . endow her work with a different quality of radiance." Elements of humor and compassion contribute greatly to the effect, but this "different quality of radiance" actually derives from *Caged Bird*'s special relationship to a tradition of black women writing autobiography. When Butterfield writes, "Ida Wells created the identity of mother and protectress: Maya Angelou in *I Know Why the Caged Bird Sings* inspires the urge to protect," he both demonstrates his respect for and betrays his ignorance of the black female autobiographical tradition. The identity of the mother and protectress is already firmly established in Harriet Brent Jacobs's *Incidents in the Life of a Slave Girl* of 1861. Angelou extends and enlarges that identity.

I Know Why the Caged Bird Sings treats themes that are traditional in autobiography by black American women. These include the importance of the family and the nurturing and rearing of one's children, as well as the quest for self-sufficiency, self-reliance, personal dignity, and self-definition. Like Ida B. Wells, Maya Angelou celebrates black motherhood and speaks out against racial injustice; but unlike Wells, she does so from a unified point of view and in a more coherent form. This derives, in part, from Wells's identity as a public figure and Angelou's identity as an artist. As a creative autobiographer, Angelou may focus entirely on the inner spaces of her emotional and personal life. In *I Know Why the Caged Bird Sings*, the mature woman looks back on her bittersweet childhood, and her authorial voice retains the power of the child's vision. The child's point of view governs Angelou's principle of selection. When the mature narrator steps in, her tone is purely personal, so it does not seem unusual that Angelou feels compelled to explore aspects of her coming of age that Ida B. Wells (and Zora Neale Hurston) chose to omit.

Here emerges the fully developed black female autobiographical form that began to mature in the 1940s and 1950s. Like Zora Neale Hurston and Era Bell Thompson, Maya Angelou employs rhythmic language, lyrically suspended moments of consciousness, and detailed portraiture. Her use of folklore and humor help to augment the effect she creates as tale-teller *par excellence*. Maya Angelou takes the genre of autobiography to the heights that Zora Neale Hurston took the novel in *Their Eyes Were Watching God*. If *I Know Why the Caged Bird Sings* reads like a novel, it carries the ring of truth. Speaking in terms of its literary merits, it is perhaps the most aesthetically satisfying autobiography written by a black woman in this period.

Necessarily, analysis begins with the title *I Know Why the Caged Bird Sings*, which originally appeared in the poem "Sympathy" by the great black poet, Paul Laurence Dunbar:

I know why the caged bird beats his wings
Till its blood is red on the cruel bars
For he must fly back to his perch and cling
When he would fain be on the bough aswing
And a pain still throbs in the old, old scars
And they pulse again with a keener sting—
I know why he beats his wings!

I know why the caged bird sings, ah me.
When his wing is bruised and his bosom sore,—
When he beats his bars and would be free
It is not a carol of joy or glee,
But a prayer that he sends from his heart's deep core,
But a plea, that upward to Heaven he flings—
I know why the caged bird sings!

The sentiment of this poem, one of Dunbar's best lyrics, presages the tone of Angelou's autobiography, and some of the feeling of her struggle to transcend the restrictions of a hostile environment. Clearly, Angelou is in "sympathy" with the "real" Dunbar, the bleeding bird behind the mask. And it seems likely that Dunbar would have been in "sympathy" with Angelou as well. For like the Dunbar poem and the spirituals sung by southern blacks, *I Know Why the Caged Bird Sings* displays a tremendous "lift" and an impulse toward transcendence. And like the song of the caged bird, the autobiography represents a prayer sent from the "heart's deep core," sent from the depth of emotion and feeling. The autobiographer prays that the bird be released from the cage of its oppression to fly free from the definitions and limitations imposed by a hostile world.

Development occurs on multiple levels in *I Know Why the Caged Bird Sings*. As in the autobiographies considered in the previous chapter, a maturation of consciousness parallels geographical movement (South to North and East to West). Sidonie Ann Smith argues that Angelou's narrative strategy in *Caged Bird* "itself is a function of the autobiographer's self-image at the moment of writing, for the nature of that self-image determines the pattern of self-actualization [she] discovers while attempting to shape [her] past experiences. Such a pattern must culminate in some sense of an ending, and it is this sense of an ending that informs certain earlier moments with significance and determines the choice of what [she] recreates, what she discards. . . . Ultimately, then, the opening material assumes the end, the end the opening movement."

In *Caged Bird*, Maya Angelou does not progress only from a state of semi-orphanhood to one of motherhood; she develops through various stages of self-awareness. At the beginning of the narrative, Angelou depicts her arrival in Stamps, Arkansas, as a "tagged orphan."

> When I was three and Bailey four, we had arrived in a musty little town, wearing tags on our wrists which instructed—"To Whom It May Concern"—that we were Marguerite and Bailey Johnson, Jr., from Long Beach, California, en route to Stamps, Arkansas, c/o Mrs. Annie Henderson. (*Caged Bird*, 3–4)

The autobiographer, receptive rather than active in her early childhood, absorbs the "hometraining" and humble teachings of her grandmother, Annie Henderson, a self-sufficient woman who provides for her two grandchildren and her crippled son, Marguerite's Uncle Willie. "Momma" owns a store that seems to cater to and survive on the support of poor blacks; Mrs. Henderson also owns some of the land rented by the "poor white trash." She is the only colored woman in Stamps whom the whites refer to as "Mrs."—a clear mark of respect. Throughout the autobiography, her mother and grandmother play an important role, both as protective and nurturing figures, and as models for Marguerite, who, at the end of the narrative, has become a mother herself and assumed a positive, if still somewhat problematic, identity.

For critic Myra K. McMurry, *Caged Bird* is "an affirmation . . . Maya

Angelou's answer to the question of how a Black girl can grow up in a repressive system without being maimed by it." As in the autobiographies of Era Bell Thompson, Zora Neale Hurston, and Laura Adams, *I Know Why the Caged Bird Sings* reveals the autobiographer's sense of geographic, cultural, and social displacement. "If growing up is painful for the Southern black girl," Angelou writes, "being aware of her displacement is the rust on the razor that threatens the throat. It is an unnecessary insult" (*Caged Bird*, 3). Once again, the quest is not only for survival but also for an authentic, self-defining black female identity, one that evinces care and concern for others. Angelou's treatment of the theme of limitation and restriction resembles Dunbar's treatment in the poem "Sympathy." Like the caged bird, the young Marguerite Johnson feels removed from the larger world. Marguerite is "big, elbowy and grating"; her playmates describe her as being "shit color." Her hair, she thinks, is like "black steel wool" (*Caged Bird*, 17). Still, Angelou finds "hope and a hope of wholeness" in the love and support received from Momma, Bailey, and Uncle Willie. Never considered attractive by the standards of her community, Marguerite develops her intellect:

> During these years in Stamps, I met and fell in love with William Shakespeare. He was my first white love. Although I enjoyed and respected Kipling, Poe, Butler, Thackeray and Henley, I saved my young and loyal passion for Paul Laurence Dunbar, Langston Hughes, James Weldon Johnson and W. E. B. Du Bois' "Litany in Atlanta." But it was Shakespeare who said, "When in disgrace with fortune and men's eyes." It was a state with which I found myself most familiar. (*Caged Bird*, 11)

Later she will become acquainted with Gorky, Dostoyevsky, Turgenev, and other writers who influence her choice of form and style, but during her childhood, Shakespeare and Dunbar speak directly to her dilemma—the problem of developing a positive self-image in a culture whose standards of beauty are uniformly white, and the problem of finding a place for herself in that culture.

The strongest portraits, the strongest images in *Caged Bird*, are the respected figures of Marguerite's mother and grandmother. She celebrates her grandmother's feminine heroism, wisdom, and unselfishness in much the same way that Harriet Brent Jacobs celebrates similar qualities in her own dear grandmother. George Kent argues that "Grandmother's religion gives her the power to order her being, that of the children, and usually the immediate space surrounding her. The spirit of the religion combined with simple, traditional maxims shapes the course of existence and rituals of facing up to something called decency." Mrs. Henderson nurtures Marguerite through her Stamps childhood and beyond, doing what she can to protect her son's young children from frequent intrusions of "white reality." Such painful confrontations can occur at any time, and can be instigated by whites from any age group or social class. Mrs. Henderson is even insulted by the poor white trash children whose parents rent land from her. The autobiographer writes of this as "the most painful experience I ever had with my grandmother":

> For an awful second I thought they were going to throw a rock at Momma, who seemed (except for the apron strings) to have turned into stone herself. But the big girl turned her back, bent down and put her hands flat on the ground she didn't pick up anything. She simply shifted her weight and did a hand stand.
>
> Her dirty bare feet and long legs went straight for the sky. Her dress fell down around her shoulders, and she had on no drawers. The slick pubic hair made a brown triangle where her legs came together. She hung in the vacuum of that lifeless morning for only a few seconds, then wavered and tumbled. The other girls clapped her on the back and slapped their hands.
>
> Momma changed her song to "Bread of Heaven, feed me till I want no more."
>
> I found that I was praying too. (*Caged Bird*, 25–26)

Through this depiction of her experience, Maya Angelou praises her grandmother's courage. It is from her grandmother and from people who raise and nurture her that Maya learns to use and develop this courage, which she views as the most important virtue of all. "Without courage," she had said, "you cannot practice any other virtue with consistency" (*ODU*).

There were ample opportunities for the development of courage in Maya Angelou's young life, and the fine edge of this virtue was honed in facing the commonplace dangers of life in Stamps, such as lynching. Lynching constituted a real danger and hence a legitimate fear in the minds of Arkansas blacks. The terror of lynching persists as a theme throughout the sections of the autobiography set in Arkansas. Early in the narrative, we are told how Mrs. Henderson hid a would-be lynch victim and provided him with supplies for a journey, even though she jeopardized her own security to do so. On another occasion, it is necessary to conceal Uncle Willie one night after an unknown black man is accused of "messing with" a white woman.

Angelou forcefully conveys the emotional and psychological impact of the threat of lynching as she experienced it:

> Even after the slow drag of years, I remember the sense of fear which filled my mouth with hot, dry air, and made my body light. . . . We were told to take the potatoes and onions out of their bins and knock out the dividing walls that kept them apart. Then with a tedious and fearful slowness Uncle Willie gave me his rubber-tipped cane and bent down to get into the now enlarged empty bin. It took forever before he lay down flat, and then we covered him with potatoes and onions, layer upon layer, like a casserole. Grandmother knelt praying in the darkened store. (*Caged Bird*, 14–15)

Like Aunt Marthy in *Incidents in the Life of a Slave Girl*, Mrs. Henderson, "Momma," fulfills the archetypal role of the outraged mother by concealing her innocent child. Angelou succeeds in communicating a sense of the frustration and humiliation her family feels in these encounters. Without polemics, she shows the absurdity of lynching: Why should a crippled old man be forced to spend the night in a bin full of potatoes and onions in fear of his life because some unnamed black man has been accused of an unnamed crime?

Unlike Ida B. Wells, Maya Angelou speaks about lynching from a personal point of view, articulating her experience and her pain. On one occasion, Momma, Marguerite, and Uncle Willie wait for Bailey, who is late returning from the theater in town. Momma's apprehension, Angelou writes, "was evident in the hurried movements around the kitchen and in her lonely fearing eyes" (*Caged Bird*, 95). Later in the narrative (after the return from St. Louis and just before the permanent move to California), Bailey sees the body of a lynch victim whose "things had been cut off and put in his pocket and had been shot in the head, all because whitefolks said he 'did it' to a white woman" (*Caged Bird*, 30). These are harsh experiences for young children to endure, but Bailey and Marguerite survive, due in no small measure to the protection and sense of security they receive from their grandmother. Through Momma, Marguerite absorbs values and concepts that make it possible to maintain and replenish a sense of self-worth. Through Momma, Marguerite learns to pray.

An important theme throughout the autobiography, religion represents a sustaining force in the life of Mrs. Henderson, who derives spiritual sustenance and fortitude from the "Bread of Heaven." When threatened, Momma turns to her faith, which is clearly a source of her personal power. The early religious experiences of Maya Angelou resemble those of Zora Neale Hurston more nearly than those of any other autobiographer studied here; like Era Bell Thompson and Laura Adams, Maya Angelou displays the old "church of emotion," but unlike them, she is no stranger to it. Mrs. Henderson, a respected church elder, requires that Bailey and Marguerite participate fully in church activities and in the religious life of the community. Angelou's regard for black spirituality and black religion does not exempt the church from criticism. Like Wright, she finds comedy in the Sunday performances of "sisters" possessed by the spirit, and she ridicules the greedy minister when he eats more than his fair share of the fried chicken at Sunday dinner. But unlike Wright, she evokes this ridicule and paints this portrait without condescension—still recognizing the solvency of the basic spiritual trust.

Respecting her grandmother's homespun teaching, Maya became a part of the fabric of her culture, absorbing both literary and folk influences through observation, study, and loving imitation. Of the sermons and the spirituals, Angelou has said, "they run through my veins like blood." From her point of view, literature includes written as well as oral tradition, and she sees the spirituals as American classics; "to deny it [the spirituals as unwritten literature] is to spit upon your grandfather's grave. Like all art, it belongs to everyone who appreciates it" (*ODU*). *Caged Bird* shows the influence of myriad folk forms, including the sermon, the ghost story, the preacher tale, the tale of exaggeration, a children's rhyme, and secular and religious songs. The use of these oral forms, together with folk language, contributes to the unique tone, texture, and style of the autobiography. Their presence also helps identify the autobiographer in a relationship with her community and culture.

In *Caged Bird*, as in *American Daughter* and *Dust Tracks*, closeness to the land and continual involvement with nature are essential to the mood and imagery of the autobiography. Marguerite notes the passage of time by watching "the field across from the Store turn caterpillar green, then gradually frosty white. She knew exactly how long it would be before the big wagons would pull into the front yard and load on the cotton pickers at daybreak to carry them to the remains of slavery's plantations" (*Caged Bird*, 5). This mood is enhanced by the use of portraiture, rhythmic language, and the careful depiction of lyrically suspended moments of consciousness.

In the dying sunlight the people dragged rather than their empty sacks. . . . The sounds of the new morning had been replaced

with grumbles about cheating houses, weighted scales and dusty
rows. . . . In cotton-picking time, the late afternoons revealed the
harshness of Black Southern life, which in the early morning had
been softened by nature's blessing of grogginess, forgetfulness
and the soft lamplight. (*Caged Bird*, 7)

The entire "black community of Stamps," Sidonie Smith argues, is itself
caged in the "social reality of racial subordination and impotence."
Marguerite's "personal displacement is counterpointed by the ambiance of
displacement within the larger black community."

Because she works in her grandmother's store, Marguerite has no
direct experience of the intense labor of picking cotton, but she observes the
workers as they go out into the fields and return. She has "seen the fingers
cut by the mean little cotton bolls" and "witnessed the backs and arms and
legs resisting any further demands" (*Caged Bird*, 7).

The use of portraiture and the feeling of being close to nature and the
land contribute to the lyric sensibility of *Caged Bird*, but unlike the earlier
autobiographies by Thompson and Hurston, *Caged Bird* admits harsh and
painful aspects of the southern black experience before the civil rights era—
the economic oppression and racial violence that Thompson and Hurston
either knew little about or chose to ignore. This awareness lends Angelou's
lyric imagery the knife-sharp edge of realism, something contributed to
black female autobiographical tradition through the Richard Wright school
of the 1940s and 1950s. Thematic and structural similarities between the
autobiographies of Wright and Angelou result from their common descent
from the slave narrative and from the influence of Russian writers, which
both read. Another common denominator between Wright and Angelou
concerns their view of the "Great Migration," of which both were a part.
They depict themselves as participants in a vast historical drama—the movement of rural blacks from the Deep South to the urban centers of the North,
hoping to improve their economic and social horizons by escaping the racism
and exploitation of the South. Although Wright's tone seems more political
than Angelou's, they respond to the same historic moment.

Afro-Americans who participated in the Great Migration can be
compared with Europeans who emigrated to America only to find "identity
problems in their mental baggage." As Erik Erikson has observed of the
European-American group, "Emigration can be a hard and heartless matter,
in terms of what is abandoned in the old country and what is usurped in the
new one. Migration means cruel survival in identity terms, too, for the very
cataclysms in which millions perish open up new forms of identity to the

survivors." From her autobiography and her life work, Angelou has emerged as a survivor, a "whole" person, with her identity, her sense of humor, her dignity, and her style intact.

One of the important early turning points in the autobiography centers on Marguerite's move to St. Louis. Initially more of a change in geographic location than the beginning of a change of consciousness, the move precipitates profound problems of identity. After four years of living happily with Momma and Uncle Willie in Stamps, Marguerite and Bailey become aware of the impending move during Christmas. Having received presents from their mother and father, they conclude that their parents are about to come and get them. This occurrence raises strong emotions in the two young children, who have come to regard Stamps as their home:

> The gifts opened the door to questions neither of us wanted to ask. Why did they send us away? And what did we do so wrong? So Wrong? Why, at three and four, would we have tags put on our arms to be sent alone from Long Beach, California, to Stamps, Arkansas, with only the porter to look after us? (Besides, he got off in Arizona.) (*Caged Bird*, 43)

A year later, Bailey, Sr., arrives in Stamps without warning. And in a relatively short time the children are on their way west, headed for California or so they think. En route, their father tells them that they are actually going to St. Louis to visit their mother. In Pig Latin, Marguerite asks Bailey, Jr., "Ooday ooyay inkthay isthay is our atherfay, or ooday ooyay inkthay atthay eeway eeingbay idkay appednay?" Her father chuckles and responds, "Oohay oodway antway ootway idkay appnay ooyay? Ooday ooyay inkthay ooyay are indlay ergbay ildrenchay?" Angelou writes that hearing her father speak Pig Latin "didn't startle me so much as it angered. It was simply another case of the trickiness of adults where children were concerned. Another case in point of the Grownups' Betrayal" (*Caged Bird*, 49).

For the young Marguerite Johnson, fresh from Stamps, Arkansas, "St. Louis was a foreign country." "In my mind," writes Angelou, "I only stayed in St. Louis a few weeks" (*Caged Bird*, 58). In St. Louis, Marguerite endures the most shattering experience of her childhood when she is raped by her mother's boyfriend, Mr. Freeman. The experience is a brutal one and necessitates the child's hospitalization:

> Then there was the pain. A breaking and entering when even the senses are torn apart. The act of rape on an eight-year-old is a

matter of the needle giving because the camel can't. The child
gives, because the body can, and the mind of the violator cannot.
        I thought I had died. (*Caged Bird*, 65)

She feels physical and psychological pain as a result of the rape and guilt from
exposing Freeman, who meets a violent death at the hands of "persons
unknown," but presumably Marguerite's tough St. Louis uncles (*Caged Bird*,
71–72). The rape precipitates a period of intense identity crisis for
Marguerite, who, after Freeman's death, stops speaking to everyone but her
brother, Bailey: "Instinctively, or somehow, I knew that because I loved him
so much I'd never hurt him, but if I talked to anyone else that person might
die too" (*Caged Bird*, 73). As a result of Freeman's death, Marguerite becomes
a voluntary mute. Although this temporary solution suits Marguerite, her St.
Louis family grows weary of her muteness, which they interpret as insolent
sullenness: "For a while I was punished for being so uppity that I wouldn't
speak; and then came the thrashings by any relative who felt himself
offended" (*Caged Bird*, 73). Marguerite loses much of her innocence during
this "perilous passage," which cuts her childhood painfully short. She feels
betrayed by adults in general, and she withdraws from their way of life into
a world of silence. Although Marguerite longs to be free from her guilt,
sadness, and the feeling that she is different from others, she cannot extricate
herself from the burdens inflicted by her environment.

Soon Marguerite and Bailey find themselves on the train going back
to Stamps, which provides the obscurity the eight-year-old craves "without
will or consciousness." Not knowing the exact origin of Marguerite's
unwillingness to talk, the blacks of Stamps sympathize with her, as she was
known for being "tender-hearted." "Southern Negroes used that term to
mean sensitive and tended to look upon a person with that affliction as
being a little sick or in delicate health. So I was not so much forgiven as I
was understood" (*Caged Bird*, 77). And because the sickness is acknowledged, the healing can begin. Marguerite Johnson returns to Stamps (the
source of her strength) to begin rebuilding the identity shattered by her
enforced migration and subsequent rape.

After a year of voluntary muteness, Marguerite "met, or rather got to
know" Bertha Flowers, "the aristocrat of Black Stamps." This represents another
important turning point in the development of the autobiographer's consciousness. Angelou writes of Flowers as "the lady who threw my first life line," and the
portrait she paints shows her high regard for the woman (*Caged Bird*, 77).

She had the grace of control to appear warm in the coldest

weather, and on the Arkansas summer days it seemed she had a private breeze which swirled around. Her skin was rich black that would have peeled like a plum if snagged, but no one would have thought of getting close enough to Mrs. Flowers to ruffle her dress, let alone snag her skin. She didn't encourage familiarity. She wore gloves too.

The action was so graceful and inclusively benign. (*Caged Bird*, 77–78)

From Flowers, Marguerite receives her "lessons in living."

She said that I must always be intolerant of ignorance but under-standing of illiteracy. That some people, unable to go to school, were more educated and even more intelligent than college professors. She encouraged me to listen carefully to what country people called motherwit. That in those homely sayings was couched the collective wisdom of generations. (*Caged Bird*, 83)

The value of Flowers's benign maternal influence should not be underesti-mated. Her model of black gentility takes root in the young girl's conscious-ness, and she remains for the mature narrator "the measure of what a human being can be" (*Caged Bird*, 78). Flowers makes tea cookies for Marguerite, reads aloud to her from *A Tale of Two Cities*, and teaches her to recite poetry. Flowers fulfills the role of teacher and healer, providing the traumatized youngster with a process through which to tap internal creative resources for self-healing: These "lessons in living" constitute part of the extensive prepa-ration Marguerite receives for life as a mature black woman. Marguerite needs the values and beliefs these "lessons" contain in order to anchor her identity. The knowledge and wisdom passed down through generations supplement what she reads in books. She *needs* the strength that this knowl-edge imparts, and from this knowledge she gains power.

The patterns established in *Caged Bird* continue in Angelou's subse-quent autobiographies, *Gather Together in My Name* (1974), *Singin' and Swingin' and Gettin' Merry Like Christmas* (1976), *The Heart of a Woman* (1980), and *All God's Children Need Traveling Shoes* (1986). The narrator adapts to her situation creatively, replenishing her sense of self in difficult circumstances, discovering her sexuality, and learning to play the role of nurturer-protector. Because of the loving protection, encouragement, and direction provided to Marguerite by her mother, her grandmother, and Flowers, she is better able to survive later confrontations with white society.

A specific encounter with racial violence motivates Momma to send her grandchildren to California. When whites force Marguerite's brother to help recover the sexually mutilated body of a lynching victim accused of "messing with" a white woman, Bailey begins to ask disturbing questions that his grandmother and uncle are not prepared to answer:

> His experience raised the question of worth and values, of aggressive inferiority and aggressive arrogance. Could Uncle Willie, a Black man, Southern, crippled moreover, hope to answer the questions, both asked and unuttered? Would Momma, who knew the ways of the whites and wiles of the Blacks, try to answer her grandson, whose very life depended on his not truly understanding the enigma? Most assuredly not. (*Caged Bird*, 168)

The enigma, of course, is the dialectical relationship between white hatred and black fear, which governed racial relationships in Stamps. Mrs. Henderson tried to protect Bailey and Marguerite by limiting their knowledge and by forbidding their discussion of certain topics (including "white people" and "doing it"), but the effectiveness of this method waned as her grandchildren approached young adulthood (*Caged Bird*, 30). Eventually, the two would unravel the enigma for themselves, based on observation and evidence.

Recognizing her inability to shelter her adolescent grandson and protect him from the routine racial violence that befell blacks in Stamps, Arkansas, Mrs. Henderson prays and begins making plans to relocate the children with their parents in California. Looking back on this experience in *Gather Together in My Name*, the autobiographer allows her grandmother to express a point of view she withholds in *I Know Why the Caged Bird Sings*. She says, "I never did want you children to go to California. Too fast that life up yonder. But then, you all's their children, and I didn't want nothing to happen to you, while you're in my care. Jew was getting a little too big for his britches." Mrs. Henderson views California as a land of opportunity for Bailey and Marguerite, "a place where lynchings were unheard of and a bright young Negro boy could go places. And even his sister might find a niche for herself."

Maya Angelou's celebration of self derives essentially from her celebration of the black women who nurtured her. She reveres not only the qualities of the individual women but also the tradition in which they participated and the way in which they prepared her, as best they could, to cope with the realities of being black and female. In *I Know Why the Caged Bird Sings*,

Momma conforms to the Jungian archetype of the Great Mother, protecting, nurturing, sheltering; Marguerite's own mother, Vivian Baxter, presents another representation of this same archetype. In "the transition from mother to grandmother," Jung wrote, "the archetype is elevated to higher rank." So it is with Marguerite's transition from childhood to motherhood; she is both initiated and reborn, becoming herself the carrier of the archetype.

In California, Marguerite comes under the primary care of her mother, a woman of great personal power, resourcefulness, and hypnotic beauty. "To describe my mother," writes Angelou, "would be to write about a hurricane in its perfect power. Or the climbing, falling colors of the rainbow. People she accepted paddled their own canoes, pulled their own weight, put their own shoulders to their own plows, and pushed like hell" (*Caged Bird*, 49). From her mother, Marguerite learns increased self-reliance; she grows out of the passive stage and begins to think for herself, asserting herself through action, and forging an identity and testing the perimeters of her cage through brief encounters with exploratory flight.

The motif of flight captures the spirit of Marguerite's adventurous attempts to transcend the limitations and restrictions imposed on her. Caught between her father's indifference and his jealous girlfriend when she goes to visit them in Southern California one summer, Marguerite runs away and lives for about a month in an abandoned junkyard with a financially independent and racially mixed group of youthful runaways. This experience has a positive effect in Marguerite's identity-building process:

> The unquestioning acceptance by my peers had dislodged the familiar insecurity. Odd that homeless children, the silt of war frenzy, could initiate me into the [brotherhood of man]. After hunting down unbroken bottles and selling them with a white girl from Missouri, a Mexican girl from Los Angeles, and a Black girl from Oklahoma, I was never again to sense myself so solidly outside the human race. (*Caged Bird*, 216)

Another positive identity-building experience occurs in the world of work. Marguerite is determined to become a "conductorette" on the San Francisco streetcars, even though no blacks have been hired previously. She visits the Market Street Railway Office with "the frequency of a person on salary" until she is hired, breaking the color barrier previously imposed against blacks and achieving a degree of independence (*Caged Bird*, 228).

The most significant area of challenge facing Marguerite is also the most intimate—that of self-image and sexuality. Considered less than attractive and not very well developed physically, Marguerite begins to harbor fears of being a lesbian after reading Radclyffe Hall's *Well of Loneliness*. Her heavy voice, large hands and feet, undeveloped breasts, and smooth armpits all seem clear indicators. A talk with her mother does nothing to alleviate her fear. Ironically, this irrational fear of lesbianism leads to Marguerite's pregnancy. What she needs, she decides, is "a boyfriend. A boyfriend would clarify my position to the world and, even more important, to myself. A boyfriend's acceptance would guide me into that strange and exotic land of frills and femininity." But in her social group, there are "no takers": "The boys of my age and social group were captivated by the yellow- or light-brown-skinned girls, with hairy legs and smooth little lips, whose hair 'hung down like horses' manes.' And even those sought-after girls were asked to 'give it up or tell where it is' " (*Caged Bird*, 238). Women deemed unattractive, Angelou writes, are "called upon to be generous" only if pretty girls are unavailable. Aware of this fact, Marguerite, like "Linda" in the Harriet Brent Jacobs narrative, plans the seduction of a handsome young man who lives in her neighborhood. Finding herself pregnant after the act (her first truly voluntary encounter with sex), she suffers feelings of "fear, guilt, self-revulsion" (*Caged Bird*, 241). She successfully conceals her pregnancy from her family for over eight months, managing to finish high school before revealing her secret to her mother.

The narrative itself ends, not with the birth of Guy, but with a poignant lesson taught by Marguerite's own mother. Though Marguerite could create a baby, she was herself still dependent on the protection and guidance of her mother. She lacked confidence in handling her child, her "total possession." "Mother handled him easily with the casual confidence of a baby nurse, but I dreaded being forced to change his diapers. Wasn't I famous for my awkwardness? Suppose I let him slip, or put my fingers on that throbbing pulse on top of his head?" (*Caged Bird*, 245).

One night, Marguerite's mother brings the three-week-old baby in to sleep with Marguerite, who protests vigorously, fearing that she will be "sure to roll over and crush out his life or break those fragile bones" (*Caged Bird*, 245). But her mother is insistent. In the night, she awakes to her mother's brisk but whispered command, ordering her to wake up but not to move. When she wakes up, she sees the infant sleeping peacefully by her side. "See," says her mother, "you don't have to think about doing the right thing. If you're for the right thing, then you do it without thinking" (*Caged Bird*, 246). Liliane Arensberg suggests that "Vivian Baxter, as a confident and compassionate mother lovingly bending over her daughter's bed . . . consummates Maya's growing sense of herself as an adult, life-giving woman."

As George Kent argues, *Caged Bird* "makes its public and political statements largely through generalizing statements which broaden individual characters into types: Grandmother Bailey into the Southern mother; Maya into the young black woman, etc."

Through her depiction of this nocturnal scene, Maya Angelou asserts her identity as both mother and daughter, as well as her relation to the maternal archetype. Her own mother, Vivian, still in the role of teacher-protector, is "elevated to a higher rank," becoming herself the grandmother or "Great Mother." Momma, of course, is elevated still higher. So having a baby was "the right thing to do" in that it opened new avenues of identity, not only for Marguerite, but for her mother and grandmother as well. Even though she was a young woman of only seventeen years who could not recognize the maternal instincts and imperatives that operated within her consciousness, she did, in fact, possess the necessary resources to raise and nurture her son. Through motherhood, she discovered new possibilities in her relationship with her mother and grandmother. In the words of Sidonie Smith, Marguerite "has succeeded in freeing herself from the natural and social bars imprisoning her in the cage of her own diminished self-image by assuming control of her life and fully accepting her black womanhood." And like her archetypal models, she would support her own child with ingenuity and inventiveness.

Maya Angelou has said that she is one of "a generation of women writers, writing in desperation to identify themselves and their times, to provide encouragement and direction" and to have a say in the definition of "what's really happening" (*ODU*). For her, the writing of autobiography is a conscious assertion of identity, as well as the presentation of an alternate version of reality seen from the point of view of the black female experience. Near the end of *I Know Why the Caged Bird Sings*, Angelou summarizes that point of view:

> The Black female is assaulted in her tender years by all those common forces of nature at the same time that she is caught in the tri-partite crossfire of masculine prejudice, white illogical hate and Black lack of power.
>
> The fact that the adult American Negro female emerges a formidable character is often met with amazement, distaste, and even belligerence. It is seldom accepted as an inevitable outcome of the struggle won by survivors and deserves respect if not enthusiastic acceptance. (*Caged Bird*, 231)

Like Era Bell Thompson, Maya Angelou speaks with the triple consciousness of the *American Daughter*. And she speaks, as do many other black
autobiographers, both male and female, as a survivor. She knows why she
has survived and what the source of her strength has been. She has chosen
to honor that source even as she celebrates the emergence of her indeed
"formidable character."

FRANÇOISE LIONNET

Con Artists and Storytellers: Maya Angelou's Problematic Sense of Audience

The story, though allegorical, is also historical; . . . and it is as reasonable to represent one kind of imprisonment by another, as it is to represent anything that really exists by that which exists not.

—Daniel Defoe, *Robinson Crusoe's Preface*

My books. They had been my elevators out of the midden.

—Maya Angelou; *Gather Together in My Name*

As a literary foremother, Zora Neale Hurston meant a great deal to Maya Angelou the autobiographer. Urged by her editor to start work on a multivolume project about her life, Hurston said that she really did not "*want*" to write an autobiography, admitting that "it is too hard to reveal one's inner self." Like Hurston, Angelou affirms that she "really got roped into writing *The Caged Bird*," challenged by an editor who dared her to succeed in the difficult task of writing "an autobiography as *literature*." That she wrote it as literature is the specific aspect of her work on which I shall focus in this chapter. Because the autobiographical project was a response to external pressures, it is in many ways directed to a white audience, but at the same time, it succeeds in gesturing toward the black community, which shares a long tradition among oppressed peoples of understanding duplicitous uses of language for survival. Thus a passage of *I Know Why the Caged Bird Sings* encapsulates the questions of "truth" and

From *Autobiographical Voices: Race, Gender, Self-Portraiture.* © 1989 by Cornell University.

referentiality as well as Angelou's problematic sense of audience. In that passage, Angelou alludes to her grandmother's secretive and cautious ways with language:

> Knowing Momma, I knew that I never knew Momma. Her African-bush secretiveness and suspiciousness had been compounded by slavery and confirmed by centuries of promises made and promises broken. We have a saying among Black Americans which describes Momma's caution. "If you ask a Negro where he's been, he'll tell you where he's going." To understand this important information, it is necessary to know who uses this *tactic* and on whom it works. *If an unaware person* is told a part of the truth (it is imperative that the answer embody truth), he is satisfied that his query has been answered. *If an aware person* (*one who himself uses the stratagem*) is given an answer which is truthful but bears only slightly if at all on the question, he knows that the information he seeks is of a private nature and will not be handed to him willingly. Thus direct denial, lying and the revelation of personal affairs are avoided. [164–65; my italics]

For Momma, the "signifying" of truths and untruths varies according to the status of her interlocutors, and it is in this differentiation between the "unaware" interlocutor and the "aware" that we can begin to understand Angelou's conception of "autobiographical" narration and the double audience she addresses in her writings: an audience split along racial and gender lines but also—and this is the important point here—split between those interlocutors, on the one hand, who share with the narrator an unquestioned sense of community and those, on the other hand, who have a relationship of power over that narrator.

Clearly, for Angelou, writing an autobiography has little to do with "the revelation of personal affairs," and like Hurston, she does not "reveal [her] inner self." Indeed, the passage about Momma can be read as an important example of the "self-situating" power of literary texts. Momma's caution functions as an explicit warning to the reader, who is thus challenged to take note of the double-voiced nature of Angelou's text. Her narrator alternates between a constative and a performative use of language, simultaneously addressing a white and a black audience, "image making" (CT 1) and instructing, using allegory to talk about history and myths to refer to reality, thus undermining the institutions that generate this alienated form of consciousness. Here, Angelou provides us with a model for reading and interpreting her narratives, just as Hurston had in her discussions of form and content, truth and hyperbole.

But unlike Hurston, whom we could see as strongly connected to other women in a network of friendly relationships, as well as to rich and solid folk traditions she helps to reclaim—that of "conjure women," for example—Angelou's narrator is a much more picaresque heroine, a modern-day Moll Flanders, who learns to survive by her wits. In that respect, she too is related to a black folk tradition, but one that is perhaps perceived as more "male": the shiftless trickster or con man, who relies on his ability to tell a good "story" to get out of sticky situations (Brer Rabbit, for instance). The narrator's mother also fits into this tradition. She is a consummate "business woman," runs her rooming house with a fist of steel, has "a roster of conquests" (*IK* 186) that testify to her independent nature. She is a Jill-of-all-trades who, by the fourth volume of the narrative, is said to have been "a surgical nurse, a realtor, had a barber's license and owned a hotel" (*HW* 28). The relationship between Maya and her mother has puzzled critics who have tried to approach the "autobiography" from the perspective of a "metaphysics of matrilinearism." I prefer to see in the descriptions of Vivian Baxter's life and character the model of a streetwise, self-confident, "finger-snapping" woman (cf. *IK* 54). It is against this maternal persona and role model that Maya the narrator keeps measuring her accomplishments, only to find herself lacking. Her mother is so competent that she can only feel inadequate when she tries to emulate Vivian's indomitable individualism.

An example of Maya's imitative strategy is her attempt at running a whorehouse on the outskirts of San Diego. (*GT* chaps. 13–15). This episode ends, after her efforts at outsmarting the tough lesbian whores who "work" for her prove unsuccessful, in her bewildered flight back to her grandmother's store in Arkansas. As the narrative develops, Maya gradually acquires her own survival techniques. These are, in a metaphoric way, closely linked to the development of her skills as "singer," "dancer," and "storyteller." In one of her San Francisco nightclub acts, for instance, she adopts the stage role of Scheherazade and succeeds, she says, because "I convinced myself that I was dancing to save my life" (*SS* 60). Her stated frame of reference is fiction and literature, and her style parodies that of such fictional autobiographies as *Moll Flanders*.

In this chapter, while focusing on Angelou's double-voiced technique of storytelling, I would like to emphasize three points. The chapter's first section shows how the narrator's love of books, always and everywhere, manages to pull her "out of the midden" (*GT* 90). As Tzvetan Todorov has said, "The desire to write does not come from life but from other writings." Books are Angelou's "first life line" after the traumatic events of her childhood (*IK* 77) and will continue to inspire her throughout her career. During her travels, for example, it is often through the prism of literature that she discovers and appreciates the peoples and places she visits: Verona through Shakespeare, Paris through Maupassant, London through Dickens. It thus seems appropriate, when analyzing her text, to use the literary paradigms she so cleverly manipulates. My second point concerns her use of the religious tradition: she inverts its messages, creating in the process nothing less than a feminist response to Augustine's *Confessions*. Finally, the third section shows how her problematic sense of audience is translated textually by an astute use of various embedded instances of alienated and nonalienated forms of human communication deriving from her folk traditions.

The Picaresque Heroine

Angelou's style owes as much to eighteenth- and nineteenth-century English narratives—those of Swift, Defoe, and Dickens in particular—as it does to the black vernacular. It is truly a crossroads of influences and, at its best, weaves all these strands into a pattern in which, though they have become indistinguishable from one another, they give depth and detail to the narrative. George E. Kent has shown that "two areas of black life" subtend the development of Angelou's narrative, "the religious and the blues traditions." Her grandmother represents the religious influence: black fundamentalism, the Christian Methodist Episcopal church. Her mother, on the other hand, stands for the "blues-street" tradition, the fast life. I agree with Kent's analysis but also believe there is a third term to add to this comparison: the literary tradition, all the fictional works the narrator reads avidly. This third tradition is represented figuratively in the text by two other strong women, Bertha Flowers and Martha Flowers (*IK* 77; *SS* 115). The text constructs these characters as fictional, boldly giving them almost identical names and stating that *flowers* is a recognizable slang word for "monthlies," or menstruation, in the black prostitutes' subculture (*GT* 39). When the narrator learns this "special" meaning of *flowers* from the two lesbian whores, she shows embarrassment and immediately resorts to "words" to conceal her feelings, to cope with her discomfort: "I knew that words, despite the old saying, never fail. And *my reading had given me words to spare*. I could and often did to myself or my baby, recite whole passages of Shakespeare, Paul Lawrence Dunbar poems, Kipling's 'If,' Countee Cullen,

Langston Hughes, Longfellows's [*sic*] *Hiawatha*, Arna Bontemps. *Surely I had enough words to cover a moment's discomfort*. I had enough for hours if need be" (*GT* 40; my italics).

The flow of words is meant to cover a momentary discomfort, a discomfort due to an allusion to "flowers," which thus connotes an implicit comparison between women's creative and procreative powers. The juxtaposition between the slang word and "literary" words points back to the narrator's rediscovery of human language after her deflowering at the age of eight. It is thanks to the help of "Bertha Flowers," who teaches her to recite poetry, that she begins to talk again after a year of sensory numbness and dumbness, following the rape trial. This juxtaposition also points forward to her friendship with "Martha Flowers," "a great soprano" and a member of the *Porgy and Bess* touring company, who will share her European experiences. Language and menstruation are thus brought into implicit parallel as flow, voice, words, songs all connote by association the fluid movements of music or text. There is a creative tension between Angelou's Nietzschean need to be free to "write with blood" and the narrative control she exerts on plot development. What this tension denotes is her attempt to come to terms with the paradoxes and contradictions inherent in the concept of female creativity.

Indeed, the comparison between intellectual production and pregnancy, creativity and procreation, has been a commonplace of Western discourse since Socrates, who practiced intellectual *maieusis* on his students. What seems to be implied in Angelou's text is that menstruation is a far better paradigm for creativity, a paradigm Marie Cardinal will use with considerable effect in *The Words to Say It*. Are we to infer that Angelou is implying a conflict between writing and mothering? I would suggest not, in view of the role assigned to her mother, Vivian Baxter. Full of energy and self-confidence, she represents creativity in the "rhythm and blues" tradition, and Angelou uses images of liquids to describe her: "As I scrambled around the foot of the success ladder, Mother's life flowed radiant. Fluorescent-tipped waves on incoming tides" (*GT* 104).

The mother's energy flows unchecked and unselfconsciously. She has raw power, and her style is improvised like the ebb and flow of jazz. If this flow of creative rhythms is in counterpoint to the actual mothering of a real child, it is interesting to note again that Angelou the author dedicates her first volume to her son. Perhaps this is a perfect example of the ambivalence that occupies the center of all feminist problematics about writing: to produce the book, the woman must follow rhythms of creativity which may be in conflict with the mothering/nurturing role. To be sure, one can see

Vivian Baxter as a nonnurturing, highly competitive, and goal-oriented mother. Yet she is the one who teaches Maya to trust her body, to follow her maternal instincts when her son Guy is born. *I Know Why the Caged Bird Sings* ends in the physical experience of giving birth to Guy. "Famous for [her] awkwardness," the narrator "was afraid to touch him." But Vivian coaxes her into sleeping with the baby, although at first she "lay on the edge of the bed, stiff with fear, and vowed not to sleep all night long" (245). Eventually she relaxes and sleeps with her arm curled and the baby touching her side. This experience teaches Maya the same lesson that Milkman, the hero of Toni Morrison's *Song of Solomon*, learns facing death, that "if you surrendered to the air, you could *ride* it."

Vivian puts it in a less poetic, more pragmatic way, teaching Maya that her body is a friend she can trust: "See, you don't have to think about doing the right thing. If you're for the right thing, then you do it without thinking" (246). What this remark implies is that the conflict between productive and reproductive roles is a false problem, a myth created by false anxieties; nonetheless it is a myth internalized by women writers, perhaps because there are as yet so few "creative mothers," like Vivian Baxter, who can show us how to "surrender to the air" *not* just in order to face death but so as to do "the right thing . . . without thinking," without being petrified by fear and guilt in the face of life, which is always change, flux, flow, tide, rhythm—like the music Vivian Baxter loves.

To the extent that Angelou feels strongly that a mother can never be fully independent—psychologically detached, that is—she constantly wrestles with this conflict. Her text embodies these tensions in its structure. During her year in Europe, she keeps having pangs of anxiety about her son, although she enjoys "every minute" of freedom: "Uncomfortable thoughts kept me awake. I had left my son to go gallivanting in strange countries and had enjoyed every minute except the times when I had thought about him" (*SS* 230). Hysterical from guilt and anxiety after her son becomes sick, she pays a useless visit to a psychiatrist, for whom, she imagines, she is only "another case of Negro paranoia" (235). Finally, she follows the advice of a friend and *writes* down her blessings: " I can hear / I can speak . . . I can dance / I can sing . . . I can write" (236). She regains her self-confidence, and her son simultaneously recovers: "Before my eyes a physical and mental metamorphosis began, as gradually and as inexorably as a seasonal change" (237). To write is to give herself the permission not to feel guilty. To write is to love her son in a life-affirming way. The third volume ends on this image of rebirth for both mother and son: she writes and he "names" himself, as we shall see presently. There is no real conflict:

it was only a societal myth about maternal neglect, an internalization of false dichotomies between mothering and smothering or mothering and working.

Angelou attempts to solve the conflict textually by creating metaphors that point to a reality beyond this form of deadly dualism. She creates a mythology of the "creative mother" so that other mothers writing do not have to "feel like a motherless child" (as the spiritual says) when attempting to be creative. For Nikki Giovanni, another contemporary black autobiographer, to "feel like a motherless child" is to be without a mythology of our own because we have "underestimated our strength." The power to create mythology is a characteristic of the "honkies" that Black women should imitate, she says. "the honkie is the best mythologist in creation. He's had practice because his whole wrap [*sic*] is to protect himself from his environment."

Clearly stated here is the quintessential Western dichotomy between nature and culture. Learning to "ride the air," however, would mean learning to be nurtured by nature—as Colette knew well—learning to take pleasure in the materiality of the world (our children), as well as the materiality of the word (our writing), as Angelou discovers. We are not very far from Roland Barthes's statements in *The Pleasure of the Text*:

> If it were possible to imagine an aesthetic of textual pleasure, it would have to include *writing aloud* [*l'écriture à haute voix*]. . . . its aim is not the clarity of messages, the theater of emotions; what it searches for (in a perspective of bliss [jouissance]) are the pulsional incidents, the language lined with flesh, a text where we can hear the grain of the throat, the patina of consonants, the voluptuousness of vowels, a whole carnal stereophony: the articulation of the body, of the tongue, not that of meaning, of language. A certain art of singing can give an idea of this vocal writing.

This "vocal writing" is familiar to Vivian who "sang the heavy blues . . . [and] talked with her whole body" (*IK* 54), and to Bertha Flowers, who advises Maya: "Words mean more than what is set down on paper. It takes the human voice to infuse them with the shades of deeper meaning" (*IK* 82). It is also familiar to anyone who has ever told stories to a small child, stories that infuse words with meaning and let the child hear "the grain of the voice," as Barthes would say. Children who are learning to use language enjoy the density of words in precisely that playful way.

Angelou's own playfulness with words is evident in her choice of names for the characters. The names of the narrator, her brother, her mother, her son, and her lovers all bear interesting indications of a fictional and metaphoric use of language, closely resembling Defoe's in *Moll Flanders*. Maya Angelou, as she explains, is the stage name of Marguerite Johnson (*marguerite* being the French word for a flower, the daisy). Maya, she writes, is a name created for her in childhood when her brother started calling her first "my sister," then "my," "mya," and finally "Maya" (*IK* 57). Angelou is a corruption of her first husband's name, Angelos. Tosh Angelos is a Greek who shares her love of jazz (i.e., black) music and English (i.e., white) literature, but their marriage fails because "he wrapped us in a cocoon of safety" (*SS* 27), which was like another cage, a shield, a veil against reality. After her divorce, she finds a job as a dancer in a bar: "If men wanted to buy my drinks, I would accept and tell them [the truth]. . . . That, along with imaginative dancing, would erase the taint of criminality. *Art* would be my *shield* and honesty my spear" (*SS* 58; italics mine).

The narrator abandons one kind of shield—marriage—but adopts a new one—art and dance. Now, in the Hindustani language, *māyā* is the word for "veil," and in Vedantic philosophy it is synonymous with the power to produce illusions and appearances. The Goddess Mahāmāyā personifies the world of illusion, and she is the power that creates phenomena. Might the author want to imply that the narrative is fiction and illusion, creations of Angelou, the author? That, like God, she has the power to (re)create the life story of the narrator, to show that she is an "angel," but in appearance only? That she "sings" like an angel, perhaps? And dances, like Salome, a "Dance of the Seven Veils" (*SS* 45), creating a multilayered artistic illusion? The text clearly allows for all these interpretations. Furthermore, if "Maya" is a creator and a goddess, she is invested with powers comparable to those of the "conjure women" of black tradition, and we would thus be justified in reinscribing this text within that tradition. I do not intend to do this here, but I do want to point out that this possibility exists, especially when we consider that the Greek word *angelos, -ou* means "messenger." Maya thus figures as the creator, Angelou as her messenger, the one who brings her forth while remaining veiled (*maya angelou* means the veil of the messenger: an interesting combination of Indo-European roots).

Ironically, Vivian Baxter's name points to an eighteenth-century figure with whose writings Defoe was familiar, the Reverend Richard Baxter, whose preaching style and "technique of persuasion," writes Ian Watt, "depended almost entirely on the simplest of rhetorical devices, repetition." Defoe and Angelou both rely heavily on the same device. In her texts repetition is most striking in the short summaries or recapitulations of past events that stud the narrative and serve as reminders to the reader before the onset of new developments. These are more and more frequent in the third and fourth volumes, becoming a leitmotiv, like the choral responses of church prayer and music, which are meant to create familiarity and audience participation. This style of conscious repetition harks back to the advice Baxter gives as a preacher. Discussing Baxter and the influence he has had on Defoe, Ian Watt quotes the eighteenth century preacher: "If we speak anything briefly, they feel not what we say. Nay, I find if we do not purposely dress out the matter into such a length of words, and use some repetition of it, that they may hear it inculcated on them again, we do but overrun their understandings, and they presently lose us."

All preachers, and those in the black church especially, use this technique. Angelou follows Baxter's advice on a purely textual level: her narrative mimics and parodies this style. On metaphoric and symbolic levels, however, she constructs an interesting inversion of this paradigm: Vivian Baxter, fast living, impatient, with no interest in details and repetitions ("Vivian Baxter could and would deal with grand schemes and large plots, but please, pray God, spare her the details." [*SS*, 101]), is the female character she most admires and openly tries to emulate, as daughters emulate mothers. Vivian Baxter is a figurative inversion of her eighteenth century namesake—the preacher—as her "blues-street" life makes clear. So, on the one hand, we have a religious style that allows us to insert Angelou's work back into the black *religious* context. On the other hand, we have a textual figure, Vivian, who is a model for the narrator and who embodies the free style of improvisation (with variation on and repetition of a single basic pattern) in black *music*: jazz and the blues. The link between these two poles is the literary tradition, which relays Richard Baxter, by means of Defoe's *Moll Flanders*, to the twentieth-century black female writer. The biological mother, Vivian Baxter, has a fictional counterpart in Moll, whose "autobiography" could be seen as the matrix that allows Angelou to produce and reproduce her own narrative discourse. As a central and polysemic narrative figure, Vivian embodies all the traditions whose combined influences are evident in Angelou's textual production.

Furthermore, the anxieties Maya feels before her mother seem to metaphorize the author's relation to the British narrative tradition: meeting her mother in St. Louis, Maya is stunned by Vivian's beauty and presence. Her light skin, straight hair, and talented dancing make her unreal to her children. "I could never put my finger on her realness" (*IK* 57), and she is "like a pretty kite that floated just above my head," (54) says Maya. She is an unattainable ideal, distant and out of reach for her "ugly" daughter. I would suggest that we can read in the descriptions of this too beautiful, almost white mother, the same "anxiety of authorship" that Angelou the writer may feel before her literary precursors, such as Daniel Defoe, for example, whose *Moll Flanders* she nonetheless tries to emulate. This eighteenth century narrative, closer in language to many southern idioms than those are to contemporary standard English, offers a sympathetic yet inescapably alienating reading of an individualistic "heroine." Vivian Baxter is such an individualist, and in *Gather Together in My Name*, the narrator does attempt to adopt her mother's life-style. But in sharing ideals of beauty and independence which are beyond reach, the daughter only alienates herself. Similarly, the English literary tradition has a beauty and a power that attract Angelou the writer, yet must leave her feeling inadequate before her precursor's discursive models of staunch individualism.

Angelou gives other clues to help the reader understand her naming technique: her son's name in the second volume is Guy. Then in the third volume, he becomes "Clyde," without explanation. We could see this as one example of the kind of "casual attitude to . . . writing," as Ian Watt puts it, which goes far toward explaining the "inconsistencies in matters of detail which are very common in all [Defoe's] works." Except that in Angelou's case, the matter of her son's name is hardly a "detail." At the end of the third volume, we are given the explanation that he himself has just decided to change his name to Guy. Clyde, he says, is "an O.K. name for a river, but my name is Guy" (238). At no point does the narrative explain or suggest why he was Guy throughout the second volume. What we can infer from the name Clyde however (the Clyde River of Scotland), is the idea of flowing waters, metaphoric female creation and procreation. Changing his name to Guy, this fatherless son appropriates the absent father's prerogative of naming and chooses a first name that is unmistakably "masculine": he thus sets himself apart from the female creative principle. As Janheinz Jahn says in his study of African culture: "The new-born child becomes a muntu only when the father or the 'sorcerer' gives him a *name* and *pronounces* it. Before this the little body is a kintu, a thing; if it dies it is not even mourned. . . . A creature . . . which has its place in the community of men is produced, not by act of birth, but by the word-seed: it is designated." Thus Clyde becomes a true member of the community after he has assumed the responsibility of naming himself. It marks the beginning of his separation and emancipation from the maternal realm. He is nine years old, and his show of independence connotes another separation, as in the act of birth, after a nine-month gestation. The child of her "immaculate pregnancy" (*IK* 245), he has now become a true "muntu" and designated himself as such: Guy, a guy, a man who rejects the erasure of his African past in much the same way that Malcolm X did by changing his name.

The names given to Maya's lovers and husbands suggest a duplicitous use of language and a conscious effort of fictional narration. *Tosh* in Scottish, means trim (and in black slang, to get or give "some trim" means to get laid [cf. *IK* 240]), as well as neat and proper. Tosh Angelos is a very proper and protective husband until marriage turns him into a louse. On the cruise ship that takes the opera company from Italy to Egypt, Maya meets the ship's doctor whose "eyes smoldered wonderful promises" (*SS* 201). He too is Greek: Geracimos Vlachos. But he says, "I am called Maki." He wants to marry her in order to emigrate to the United States, where he will be able to "make money" (214) practicing medicine. She flatly refuses. In the next volume, she marries a black South African freedom fighter. "His name was Vusumzi Make (pronounced Mahkay)" (*HW* 104). He turns out to be pretentious and overbearing. In Cairo she soon becomes disillusioned with this fake "African King," who furnishes their apartment in "Louis XVI brocaded sofa and chairs . . . French antique furniture . . . Oriental rugs," (*HW* 214). Instead of experiencing the "African" way of life, she is burdened with all the external signs of European monarchy. The words *make* (Old English) and *maki* (Old Norse) are cognates: they both mean mate, consort, spouse. It is quite clear that these three characters are facets of the same type and that Angelou is playfully suggesting ironic similarities among them.

The theme of similarity within difference in their names seems to point to a philosophy of life at once similar and different from Moll's (and Vivian Baxter's): the economic individualism of Moll would have dictated that she marry Maki, the doctor, since his M.D. degree could be turned into real currency, real wealth. Also, Moll would have taken advantage of Make's lavish life-style, but Maya only finds it distasteful and alienating. Defoe is "not ashamed to make economic self-interest his major premise about human life," says Watt. Angelou's premise is more *engagé* and more modern. Like Defoe, she uses what Watt calls "an episodic but life-like plot sequence," but her aim is always to return to the familiar and nurturing domain of books and literature. Like Moll, Angelou's narrator has definite ambitions, but whereas Moll wants to become a gentlewoman, Maya wants immortality and fame. She wants to join the "elite group of published writers" (*HW* 85): "I decided that one day I would be included in the family legend. . . . my name would be among the most illustrious. . . . I had written a juicy melodrama in which I was to be the star" (*GT* 28). Defoe writes with great sympathy for women's restricted roles in society, and Moll is a good example of a woman "smart enough" not to allow herself to be involuntarily restricted by a feminine role. Angelou's narrator struggles against similar social codes, and eventually finds the courage to stand her ground and define her territory, but it is the territory of a "too smart" woman (*GT* 166): libraries, books, and writing. In Cairo, she becomes a journalist (as Defoe was), and takes refuge in the newsroom of the *Arab Observer* and in its "library with hundreds of books in English" (HW 231). She achieves a measure of emancipation thanks to her intellectual talents and her love of books. It is quite an accomplishment for the little girl from Stamps, who grew up in the red dirt of the American South, "where children become bald from malnutrition" (*SS* 110). Her checkered existence finally comes to a resting point in Accra, where she lands a job as administrative assistant at the University of Ghana.

Language and Silence

The title of Maya Angelou's first volume, *I Know Why the Caged Bird Sings*, introduces the major metaphors that will run through all four of her books: imprisonment and singing. *In Black Autobiography in America*, Stephen Butterfield compares this work with those of Richard Wright and Frederick Douglass. The male writers, he says, tend to portray their lives of struggle against the white oppressor and their efforts to destroy the "cage" of racism and slavery, "But, unlike *Black Boy* and *The Life and Times*, the subject of *I Know Why the Caged Bird Sings* is not really the struggle of the bird; it is the exploration of the cage, the gradual discovery of its boundaries, the loosening of certain bars that she can slip through when the keepers' backs are turned.

Indeed Maya's "struggle" is of a different nature from that of the males: more personal and less public or social. There are no direct or violent confrontations with intense racial overtones. Her sense of humor is in sharp contrast to the seriousness of a Richard Wright. But I would suggest that, as the title of the volume implies, her subject is much more than the "exploration" or representation of this circumscribed domain. It is, rather, the investigation of the process through which the "bird" learns how to sing and the reasons why she does so in the face of adversity. To discuss the how and the why of the song, however, requires us to do a careful analysis of the textual layers and of their structuring moments.

For example, the store where Maya and her brother live, "her favorite place to be" (13), the center of activity in Stamps and the source of food and surprises, is an important structuring image, whereas the rape trial is a central and structuring moment of the first volume. The store full of treasures is like a book that contains unexpected pleasures for the reader ("Alone and empty in the mornings, it looked like an unopened present from a stranger. Opening the front doors was pulling the ribbon off the unexpected gift" [13]). The only place she calls "home" (*GT* 63), the store is a metaphor for the storehouse of memory, which can be opened—as the "cage" will be opened—by the ribbon of language. It is a refuge like the libraries and the books she loves (and indeed she will seek refuge in a library after her rape). For Marie-Therese Humbert too the village store will function as a protective matrix, as a safe and enclosed space where the narrator can feel restored and reborn.

The way in which Angelou's text presents the events leading both to her rape and to the trial provides an interesting context to the whole notion of familial rape vs. social violation. The trial scene is the subject of chapter 13, but it is already symbolically implied in the opening scene of the book, where the experience of being on display—in church—is powerfully rendered. This opening scene is a classic example of the theme of woman-as-spectacle, woman unwillingly displaying herself. Here, it is a little girl thrust before a community of people gathered to worship God the Father. She had been looking forward to this day, dreaming that she was going to "look like a movie star" when she recited her poem in church: "What you looking at me for? / I didn't come to stay . . ." But on that Easter morning, she does not metamorphose into "one of the sweet little white girls who were everybody's dream of what was right with the world" (1). Instead, she is painfully aware of the gap between that dream and her actual physical appearance: she is wearing a dress that is "a plain ugly cut-down from a white woman's once-was-purple throwaway" (2); her "skinny legs" and skin that "look[s] dirty like mud" seem to be the focus of everyone's gaze. Not surprisingly, she loses all her aplomb, forgets her lines, hears only the "wiggling and giggling" (1) of the other children, runs out of church: "I stumbled and started to say something, or maybe to scream, but a green persimmon, or it could have been a lemon caught me between the legs and squeezed. I tasted the sour on my tongue and felt it in the back of my mouth. Then before I reached the door, the sting was burning down my legs and into my Sunday socks" (3). As she runs back home "peeing and crying," all she can think about is that (as the popular superstition goes) she must *not* hold back the flow of urine or "it would probably run right back up to my head and my poor head would burst like dropped watermelon, and all the brains and spit and tongue and eyes would roll all over the place" (3). The problem is that she will surely "get a whipping" for losing mental and physical control and be mercilessly teased by the "nasty children" of the congregation. Her performance anxiety leads to complete failure, and failure results in harsh punishment imposed by family (the whipping) and society (the laughter of her peers).

This scene encapsulates all the elements that have become identified with the ambiguities of female performance: having to live up to an idealized image; feeling imprisoned in a body that does not correspond to the idealized image; dreaming of escaping from that "cage"; dealing with the problematics of public speech when "other things [are] more important," (1) such as the feeling of giving-oneself-away-as-spectacle (an "ugly" spectacle at that) and the literal numbness and dumbness that ensues. The flow of involuntary excretions is perceived as both releasing and threatening: if she holds it back, she may "die from a busted head"; (3) if she lets it flow, she will surely be punished. To write or not to write is another facet of the same predicament. Until abolition de jure, but until much later de facto, it was a punishable crime to teach a black to read or write; yet we also believe that a talented person may be "driven to a numb and bleeding madness" if creativity is constantly stifled and finds no outlet. The bottom line remains painful: whatever her choices, the consequences are going to be difficult. In this case, she runs away from the public eye, choking back tears and laughter, her lines unspoken, her pride wounded. Her body has had the upper hand, its physical release from tension manifested in this uncontrolled urge to urinate.

This opening scene squarely pits the mind against the body, the mind biting the red dust of Arkansas because the body is such a great liability. It is particularly significant that this episode, chronologically out of sequence in the narrative, should set the tone for the story. For this is clearly the tale of a woman who learns to "let the words flow," to perform in public and sing "gloriously," and to find the positive links between body and mind that will allow her to break free of the cage of prejudice and self-hatred. As discussed before, the book ends on another physical experience, the birth of her son, which teaches her to trust her body's language and knowledge, to make it the source and the model of her creativity. This trajectory is a familiar one in many women writers' autobiographies. The positive links that Angelou finds are literature and music.

Initially, however, she is literally brainwashed into silence by religion, family, and society. Grandmother Henderson is the primary agent—and model—of this silence. During cotton-picking season, she would get up everyday at four o'clock and "creak down to her knees, and chant in a sleep-filled voice: 'Our Father, thank you for letting me see this New Day. . . . Guide my feet this day along the straight and narrow, and help me *put a bridle on my tongue*,'"(5; my italics). Saying too much or saying the wrong thing is akin to being impudent, and "the impudent child was detested by God" (22).

The consistent self-control that Momma can exert in stressful encounters (cf. 24–27) is in sharp contrast to Maya's frequent loss of control in church. There is another instance of hysterical laughter and uncontrolled urinating in chapter 6, and these episodes are severely punished. The hysteria, however, comes right after the narrator has been commenting on her increasing capacity for tuning out the world and wrapping herself in a cocoon of silence and private daydreams: "Turning off or tuning out people was my highly developed art. The custom of letting obedient children be seen but not heard was so agreeable to me that I went one step further: Obedient children should not see or hear if they chose not to do so" (34).

This is the first ominous hint we have of the state of catatonic indifference she will fall into after the rape trial. Raped by her mother's neglected lover, she identifies with her rapist, whose densely physical presence had released in the lonely child a sense of belonging, of affiliation and security. Yet her trust is betrayed by the man she wanted to love as a father. Her body has suffered excruciating pain, but that in itself is nothing new for a child used to repeated corporal punishment. Her imaginary world of language and literature is stolen by the intrusion of phallic power. Her family, as a whole, fails her. Yet the "rape" is not over. She also has to confront society in the courtroom, and that encounter reduces her to total silence. It is during the trial that she finally internalizes the religious teachings of her childhood completely and consequently begins to perceive herself as evil: "I had sold myself to the Devil and there could be no escape" (73). The defendant's lawyer attempts to put the blame on her, and the child becomes convinced that she is responsible for the rape: "I didn't want to lie, but the lawyer wouldn't let me think, so *I used silence as a retreat* " (70; my italics). The child quickly learns how to decode the social system in order not to be victimized any further. She has no choice but to lie for survival's sake. On the familial and social level, the rapist has been punished, justice has been done. On a personal level, however, Maya's ordeal is just beginning: having sworn on the Bible to say the truth, she is now much more traumatized by the memory of the lie and by the belief that she is responsible for the man's death.

She begins to see herself, through society's eyes, as an ambiguous victim. She gets the message that she must, on some level, have done something wrong. Since the rapist is responsible for making her lie, he must be evil. Because of him, evil invades her too, she is hopelessly contaminated by those troublesome bodily fluids, which are polluting and taboo: "Obviously I had forfeited my place in heaven forever, and I was as gutless as the doll I had ripped to pieces ages ago. . . . *I could feel the evilness flowing through my body and waiting, pent up, to rush off my tongue if I tried to open my mouth*. I clamped my teeth shut, I'd hold it in. If it escaped, wouldn't it flood the world and all the innocent people?" (72; my italics). Language is a form of "evilness," waiting to escape from her inner self like those fluids and involuntary excretions that can be hard to control (urine or semen) or simply embarrassing ("flowers," or menstruation). Language is evil, polluting, uncontrollable, and most of all the source of undeserved and incomprehensible punishments. The little girl is thus in possession of another deadly secret: that every word she utters may allow her inner and evil reality to escape and to hurt or kill others. She has no choice but to remove herself from the community by refusing language:

> Just my breath, carrying my words out, might poison people and they'd curl up and die like the black fat slugs that only pretended.
>   I had to stop talking.
>   I discovered that to achieve perfect personal silence all I had to do was to attach myself leechlike to sound. . . . I simply stood still—*in the midst of the riot of sound. After a minute or two, silence would rush into the room from its hiding place because I had eaten all the sounds* (73; my italics).

Her isolation and alienation are complete. She achieves control over yet other bodily functions, her tongue, her breath. She closes off all her orifices, paradoxically, by letting the outside world of sounds rush in, so that the inner reality of evil is prevented from rushing out. She achieves "perfect personal silence" by being totally open, or *disponible*, to the external world while keeping her inner world repressed or suppressed.

The sequence of textual events Angelou establishes draws a close parallel between the experience of rape and the child's internalization of societal and religious standards. First, her body is appropriated by the father figure precisely on Saturday, the day she would normally have exercised her freedom to read, to "breath[e] in the world" of literature (64). Then, in the courtroom, she is given a reflection of herself as evil, just as in the opening scene of the book she saw herself mirrored in the eyes of the church community as a shameful and "black ugly dream" (2) who was "sucking in air to breath out shame" (1). Now she sees herself as a sinful and dirty vessel. Her secret and imaginary world has been violated, contaminated, and she can no longer escape there. Performance anxiety made her speechless in church. Now she discovers that language can perform, create reality, that language *is* powerful performance because it can kill. Mr. Freeman dies, and Maya metaphorically cuts off her own tongue.

In the Greek legend of Philomela, Tereus, and Procne, it is Tereus the rapist who, after violating Philomela, rips out her tongue in order to prevent her from telling the truth to her sister Procne, Tereus's wife. Philomela then sends to her sister a piece of embroidery on which she has woven her story. Maya's self-inflicted punishment is similar to Philomela's. But it is as a result of her own absorption of patriarchal, social, and religious discourses that she stifles herself. She has become a docile and benumbed element of the oppressive system that controls her life, until the discovery of literature allows her to weave her own story. It is clear from her own remarks that Angelou the author identifies with Philomela: when she first becomes a showgirl and a dancer in San Francisco, she is attracted to a drummer who befriends her but loves only his wife Philomena, about whom he says: "—pretty name, ain't it? She can tell a story that would break your heart. Or else she can make you split your sides" (*SS* 58). Angelou's own narrative is a tragicomic tale of growing up black and female in America. She creates an allegory of the feminine condition which cuts across historical, social, and racial lines, using laughter and compassion to defuse the implicit violence of her subject matter.

We may recall that in the *Confessions*, Augustine discusses his access to human language. ("I ceased to be an infant unable to talk, and was now a boy with the power of speech [non enim eram infans. . . . sed iam puer loquens eram]" as a function of his initiation into the "stormy or tempestuous life of human society [procellosam societatem]." His acquisition of the power of speech as well as his schooling in rhetoric are paralleled with the "fornications" he began to engage in, meaning "lying and cheating," as well as other "perversions." Ultimately, his progress to God must include a gradual silencing of his tongue, a quieting of the "storm" of language. It is the example of Bishop Ambrose which teaches him a nondiscursive spirituality of silence ("his voice was silent and his tongue was still"). That is why his "autobiography" ends with an exegetic reading of Genesis, a reading that puts the narrative chapters under erasure and eliminates all further "personal" or "literary" use of language by the author. Augustine becomes filled with the otherness of God and transcends his corporeality as he reaches a spiritual resting point in the Word of God, and in the text of Genesis. From then on, his use of language is confined to its ontological purposes: words are signifiers used to convey the transcendental signified, God.

Angelou's narrator also wants "to achieve perfect personal silence" as a means of redemption from the "evilness flowing through [her] body." That is why she quiets her tongue and thus removes herself from human society. But she cannot find peace in God because she had already "sworn on the Bible that everything [she] said would be the truth, the whole truth, so help

[her] God" (*IK* 71). And the God she knows is not a warm, loving black father; rather she imagines him looking like the policeman who announces to her family the death of Mr. Freeman: "Had they found out about the lie? . . . The man in our living room was taller than the sky and whiter than my image of God. He just didn't have the beard" (71). So she creeps into a cocoon of numbness and becomes almost catatonic, all her senses dulled: she hears people's voices as though muffled, cannot perceive colors very well, and forgets names. Meanwhile, her brother Bailey is becoming adept at using his "silver tongue" to shape words and "two-pronged sentences" (76) of sarcasm and jokes that enchant the rural community of Stamps, where they have both returned after the trial. Bailey is becoming the consumate con artist while the girl is sinking deeper into silence.

It is after a year in Stamps that she meets Mrs. Bertha Flowers, a very dark-skinned woman, whose color "was a rich black" (78). She is a maternal and nurturing figure like Momma, but her aristocratic demeanor and formal education make her an instant role model for Maya, the imaginative reader of English novels. This woman has a positive self-image and makes Maya "proud to be a Negro, just by being herself" (79). As a narrative figure, she is the opposite of the tall white godlike policeman, and she becomes Maya's savior, a sort of tribal deity who helps her reevaluate her position within the community as well as the community's virtues. Maya begins to compare the "uneducated" speech patterns of her grandmother unfavorably to Mrs. Flowers's perfect diction and elocution. The child begins to notice the "texture" of the human voice and simultaneously opens up to human language as Mrs. Flowers encourages her to read aloud and to try "to make a sentence sound in as many different ways as possible" (82). But she also teaches Maya that illiteracy is not ignorance and that in the "mother wit" of country people is "couched the collective wisdom of generations" (83). Thus, from the start, Maya is forestalled from a destructive temptation to hierar-chize different cultural models or to devalue the "primitive" folk attitudes of her rural background—an insight which Angelou the writer surely owes to her familiarity with Hurston's work.

Mrs. Flowers recites *A Tale of Two Cities* and Maya hears poetry "for the first time" (84) in her life:

> "It was the best of times and the worst of times. . . ." Her voice slid in and curved down through and over the words. She was nearly singing. I wanted to look at the pages. Were they the same that I had read? Or were there notes, music, lined on the pages, as in a hymn book? Her sounds began cascading gently. I knew

from listening to a thousand preachers that she was nearing the end of her reading, *and I hadn't really heard, heard to understand, a single word.* [84; my italics]

In contrast to the noise and "riot of sound" that make her deaf to the world and to herself, the narrator now discovers "vocal writing": the materiality of language, the self-referential nature of the poetic word, "the patina of consonants, the voluptuousness of vowels" as Barthes would suggest. She hears the sounds but does not understand their meaning, because meaning is not important. Language becomes an arbitrary system of signs not grounded in external reality, especially not in the transcendent meaningful reality of God but rather in the pure, playful immanence of sounds. The sensual joy of literature favors a process of ecstasis and self-dispossession as Maya escapes through imagination:

I have tried often to search behind the sophistication of years for the enchantment I so easily found in those gifts. The essence escapes but its aura remains. To be allowed, no, invited, into the private lives of strangers, and to share their joys and fears, was a chance to exchange the Southern bitter wormwood for a cup of mead with Beowulf or a hot cup of tea and milk with Oliver Twist. When I said aloud, "It is a far, far better thing that I do, than I have ever done . . ." tears of love filled my eyes at my *selflessness.* [84; my italics]

Augustine too finds "selflessness" in reading: it is the process of reading which allows him to absorb in his human, historical, linear dimension the timelessness of eternal substance, the plenitude of intercourse and communion with God, and thus to return to his transcendent origins. His narrative and decentered use of language makes way for a selfless and silent disappearance into God's otherness which becomes his ideal self. And we may also recall here Nietzsche's warnings about "selflessness," which reading can favor, although it is also the source of great happiness: "Come to me pleasant, brilliant, clever books." For Augustine, "selflessness" is deference to God; for Nietzsche, it is the alienation by our cultural selves of our creatural, animal, and biocentric drives.

Reading, for Maya, is also depersonalizing, but this depersonalization returns her instead to the *collectively human* dimensions she had forsaken, with language, in her attempt to shield herself from the wrath of God the Father. Reading enables her to enter into a human dialogue with Mrs.

Flowers, to discover a loving and nurturing intellectual relationship. She loses her *self* but merges with a community of *others*. Bertha Flowers is an ideal other but *not* a mirroring presence: she mediates and guides Maya's entry into a multiplicity of "private lives," which can only enlarge and enrich the girl's point of view, as they become her frames of reference, her lifelines to adulthood. It is worth noting that the literary texts Maya actually mentions correspond to the two secular poles discussed in this chapter, the folk tradition and literary discourse. Some critics read *Beowulf* as a medieval folktale, and *Oliver Twist* is a fictional autobiographical narrative. In this and many other such instances of situational self-reflexivity, the narrative signals to us the frame of reference within which it attempts to situate itself. It thus encodes models of reading appropriate to its messages and intrinsic to its structure, offering to the attentive reader the key paradigms needed for interpretative analysis.

Another such instance of situational self-reflexivity, this one within the religious mode, occurs when Maya starts having "secret crawl[s] through neighborhood churches" (*SS*, 28), in search of a way to get back in touch with a heritage and a territory that are gradually eroding under Tosh's white influence. She visits a black fundamentalist Baptist church and the text for the sermon is from the Old Testament: "Dry Bones in the Valley." The preacher is a master of his craft: "He told the story simply at first, weaving a quiet web around us all, binding us into the wonder of faith and the power of God" (31). Hypnotized by his style, she joins in the dancing and singing trances and is "reborn" as she surrenders to the power of the community. The teaching of this particular sermon, as she describes it, is a metaphor for the process of autobiography and anamnesis: "I knew of no teaching more positive than the legend which said that will and faith caused a *dismembered skeleton*, dry on the desert floor, to knit back together and walk" (*SS* 31; my italics). To re-member and piece together the past in the hope of achieving a degree of self-integration within language which will miraculously redeem her, save her from death and emptiness, indeed give her immortality, is the acknowledged project of writing for Maya. This "legend" of the Old Testament is a powerful way for her to get back in touch with her vernacular tradition after her more "cerebral" excursus into "high" art and literature.

If, living with Tosh, she begins to miss her "religious" tradition, with Make and in his political milieu she will miss "literature." This movement back and forth between religion and literature is dialectical only in appearance, for in both traditions she manages to extract the means of communication, the techniques of storytelling, which help her learn and refine her craft as a writer. She rejects the "white God" of religion but retrieves the cultural heritage of the black church, the sermons and the music, the gospel songs and spirituals, which are so close to the secular blues. When she starts going to church secretly, it is the music that attracts her at first: "The spirituals and gospel songs were sweeter than sugar" (28). This contact with the culture of her slave ancestors keeps her firmly anchored in the reality of her past, putting into perspective the "cerebral exercises and intellectual exchange" (*SS* 29) that were the basis of her relationship to Tosh. This episode is another allegorical representation within the "autobiographical" text of the history of black people in America. Religious gatherings were forbidden to slaves. Here, Tosh is violently opposed to religion. The slaves would still gather secretly to sing and chant and pray for "freedom" (usually in an after-life) and to ritualistically glorify death as a release from the ills of this world. The narrator's and Tosh's relationship thus takes on mythic dimensions as it symbolizes an aspect of race (or master-slave) relations during preabolition days. Religion, like literacy, was considered a potentially subversive instrument in the hands of the slaves, and the masters needed to prevent, or severely repress, any hint of resistance or disobedience. Hence the "secret meetings in the woods to praise God ('For where two or three are gathered together in my name, there am I in the midst of them')" as the narrator recalls her great-grandmother, the former slave, teaching her (*SS* 28). Her secret church visits echo and connote that historical past.

Revival services and sermons are a *locus classicus* of black autobiographical narratives, and the treatment they receive varies according to the degree of alienation the narrator feels toward the evangelism of the black church. Not all black writers share Angelou's belief in the positive elements of black religion. Richard Wright is bitterly opposed to religious rhetoric, believing that it generates hypocrisy, sadism, cruelty, and hatred. Langston Hughes and James Weldon Johnson do not share her emotional response to revivalism. Johnson, for example, has a patronizing and humorous attitude toward the simple faith of southern blacks. Participating in a revival service, he falls asleep, and when someone shakes him, he pretends to be in a trance, and wakes up fully only to recount a "vision" and thus avoid blame. His distance and detachment are in contrast to Maya's surrender to the electrifying atmosphere of the Baptist church. As narrator, she handles the scene with irony and humor; but it is a wry commentary, after the fact, on her capacity for losing herself in the folk process of religious revival, for undergoing an emotional "rebirth."

Structurally, this episode of "rebirth" in the third volume, is a counterpoint to the narrative segment dealing with poetry and Mrs. Flowers in the first volume. Initially, Maya is reborn when she reenters the community of speaking humans via the medium of literature. Here, by contrast, we have a "religious" rebirth in the traditional revival mode: it is in fact a return to her black folk background. She succeeds in avoiding conflict between the various traditions as she adopts from each one the elements that are truly a part of "popular" or "vernacular" culture, be it folk tales or folk poems, (fictional) personal narratives, gospels, spirituals, or blues. The experience of rebirth could thus be seen as an exorcism from the self of those "polluting" thoughts and beliefs that lead to the devaluing of the collective wisdom and "mother wit" of her black heritage. With Tosh, the white atheist, it is the dryness of her overly refined life-style which begins to weigh on her: "After watching the multicolored people in church dressed in their gay Sunday finery and praising their Maker with loud voices and sensual movements, Tosh and my house looked very pale. Van Gogh and Klee posters which would please me a day later seemed irrelevant. The scatter rugs, placed so artfully the day before, appeared pretentious" (SS 29). Clearly, "the multicolored people" are so not just because of their "Sunday finery" but because the skin color of "black" people runs the gamut from the "fresh-butter color" of her mother (IK 49) to the "rich black . . . plum" of Mrs. Flowers (78), with all the inter-mediate variations: the "brown moon" of Momma's face (26), the "dark-chocolate" skin of her best friend, Louise (118): "Butter-colored, honey-brown, lemon- and olive-skinned. Chocolate and plum-blue, peaches-and-cream. Cream. Nutmeg. Cinnamon. I wondered why my people described our colors in terms of *something good to eat* " (GT 14; my italics). In variety and heterogeneity there is a sensual pleasure upon which her talent feeds (much as Augustine tells of "feeding" on God ["fruens te" 4:1]). Marriage to Tosh is a lonely and marginalizing experience, like her year of silence. By contrast, whenever she is integrated in a group of heterogeneous—though marginal—individuals, she feels truly comfort-able. It is thus clear that the search for community and audience informs the whole process of narration for Angelou.

The month she spends hiding in a junkyard at the age of sixteen provides the first such experience of real community: a "collage of Negro, Mexican and white" (IK 214) homeless, outcast children become her "family." Liliane K. Arenberg has pointed out that "of signal importance is that these children disprove the racial prejudice—and its concurrent death fantasies—of her earlier experiences." She sleeps in a wrecked car, spends the day scavenging, and learns to survive against the odds. Instead of being acted upon, she increasingly gains control by acquiring useful skills: "During the month that I spent in the yard, I learned to drive . . . to curse and to dance" (215). Her brief stay in this small utopia—ironically referred to as Brobdingnag—gives her the self-confidence to accept the perniciousness of the real world while learning to shield herself from it and to use it to her advantage: "Odd that the homeless children, the silt of war frenzy, could initiate me into the brotherhood of man. After hunting down unbroken bottles and selling them with a white girl from Missouri, a Mexican girl from Los Angeles and a Black girl from Oklahoma, I was never again to sense myself so solidly outside the pale of the human race. The lack of criticism evidenced by our ad hoc community influenced me, and set a tone of tolerance for my life" (*IK* 216). This "ad hoc community" of multicolored children teaches her peace. Meanwhile the bulk of the adults are literally and figuratively engaged in war (World War II). Her experience of being unquestioningly accepted changes her completely, "dislodge[s] the familiar insecurity" (216) of displacement and dis-ease which had reached its apex when she was stabbed by Dolores, her father's girlfriend. Textually, she manages to encode a similar variety and diversity because she draws on so many traditions and weaves them into a narrative that integrates as many styles and influences as the "multicolored people" of the church gathering and the junkyard do. We are truly in the realm of *bricolage* here: biological miscegenation, social "junk" or "silt," and textual braiding, or *métissage*, of traditions.

Con Artists and Storytellers

In his discussion of Homer's *Odyssey*, Tzvetan Todorov distinguishes among three properties of speech: speech-as-action, or *parole-action*, speech-as-narrative, or p*arole-récit*, and feigned speech, or *parole feinte*. The last, he says, belongs simultaneously to both of the first two categories because it frees the sign from the referent (as in a *récit* or tale) with the express purpose of performing an act conveying information that can affect reality (as in speech-as-action). Feigned speech, then, is always performative.

In talking about the "tactics" and "stratagems" black narrators use to avoid dealing directly with "truth," Angelou stresses the performative aspect of Momma's cautious means of communication. We have seen how she signifies upon this tradition in her use of fictional narrative devices and in her naming, but Angelou also makes use of vernacular traditions that represent a purely constative case of "speech-as-narrative." This is a mode of oral narrative that can be divided into three categories: "poetic" speech (toasts and jokes), ghost stories, and fantasy.

First, the poetry of Maya's maternal uncles. They represent the urban traditions; they like to gossip, tell jokes, and roughhouse. Theirs, however, is

a totally gratuitous and playful love of words: "Uncle Tommy . . . strung ordi-
nary sentences together and they came out sounding either like the most
profane curses or like comical poetry" (*IK* 56). The hearer is completely free
to adduce his own meaning from Uncle Tommy's droll statements. He is a deft
and natural comedian, whose purpose is only to entertain and thereby to reinforce an existing sense of community. The Baxter clan is a tightly knit, highly
competitive group in which each individual must pull his own weight and do
so with ease and aplomb. They have a high tolerance for variety and difference,
so long as this difference does not reflect negatively on their strong sense of
family. Here *parole-récit* is a humorous art and discourse, playful pleasure.

Second, the popular oral tradition of ghost stories, which help pass the
time on long winter nights. The storytellers usually try "to best each other
in telling lurid tales of ghosts and hants, banshees and juju, voodoo and other
anti-life stories" (*IK* 133). Audience and performers share a common fascination for evoking the unknown, for conjuring the eerie. Again, the sense of
community is intact. The purpose of these ghost stories is commonly understood: to frighten and entertain, to reinforce rural superstitions or old
African beliefs, while the whole group shares sweet potatoes and peanuts
slowly roasted under coals or ashes. In an episode of chapter 22 the visitor
who comes to spend the stormy evening with them shares their dinner and
impersonates his dead wife as he tells a ghoulish tale of her apparitions in the
night. Like the parasite who entertains his hosts, he gets nourishment and
pays it back with words. Of special interest in the staging of that episode is
the intermingling of literature and folklore. Maya and Bailey are keeping
warm by the potbellied stove while reading: he is immersed in *Huckleberry
Finn* and she is rereading *Jane Eyre*. The arrival of the visitor interrupts that
activity but the children remain suspended out of time as the ghost story
inserts itself into their consciousness, becoming superimposed on the fantasy
worlds of Twain and Brontë, worlds that happen to appeal to the same
emotions: fascination with the unknown and escapism.

Third, fantasy, which is Maya's forte. When Momma takes her to a
bigoted dentist, Maya imagines a triumphant confrontation between them,
her toothache abating as she dreams of her grandmother obliterating the
evil Dr. Lincoln. In the embedded story that she recounts to herself to alleviate the pain, the most significant distortion of reality is in the speech
patterns of Momma: "Her tongue had thinned and the words rolled off
well enunciated. Enunciated and sharp like little claps of thunder" (*IK* 161).
She fantasizes that the dentist, on the other hand, stutters, drools, and has
a very humble voice. Momma is larger than life and can even "afford to *slip
into the vernacular* because she ha[s] such eloquent command of English"

(161; my italics). In other words, to use the vernacular is a conscious choice the writer can allow herself after she has shown her ability to articulate her point of view in the "King's English."

In this instance of alienated, imaginary discourse (wishful thinking and feelings of impotence before an all too powerful and degrading social system), the fundamental dis-ease of this marginal character reveals itself. The narrator's conscious remarks about levels of language indicates that mastery of the master's English is the sine qua non of any subversive intent in a fictive utterance. Her fantasy, a counterpoint to the later episode in the dead car junkyard, is like a science fiction tale. It does not claim to have a direct bearing on daily reality, yet it satirizes the social structures that generate this alienated discourse, thus providing a powerful comment on reality. Its message is directed to Maya's initial, original community, the one that is powerless, and peripheral to the larger social sphere where Dr. Lincolns gravitate: yet, she implies, her community could wield mythic force (like Momma) if only it cared to appropriate (the master's) language.

As is becoming clear, the narrator learns many different styles of human communication from her extended family's tale telling, escapist tales that are antilife (like ghost stories) or triumphant (like her fantasy world in which villains are dispatched). But escapist tales involve no risks, and the story is a pleasurable (if sometimes scary) experience for both narrator and narratee(s). The didactic intent, if it exists, is of secondary importance. The primary consideration is the art of entertaining an audience whose presence and feedback are unproblematic.

But what happens when the storyteller becomes alienated from this initial community? Language then becomes a means of obtaining what is not willingly given, that is, attention, justice, reparation, and so on. And indeed it would seem that for Angelou, the process of writing is a way of articulating those particular alienations and the demands that ensue. To judge by her use of standard English (rather than dialectal speech patterns), it would seem that she aims her book at a primarily "white" audience of urbanized and educated readers. She does use some slang and colloquialisms, but her grammar is almost always standard, as is her spelling. Discussing her schooling in San Francisco, she says: "In the classroom we all learned past participles, but in the streets and in our homes the Blacks learned to drop *s*'s from plurals and suffixes from past-tense verbs. We were alert to the gap separating the written word from the colloquial. *We learned to slide out of one language and into another without being conscious of the effort*" (IK 191; my italics).

The "written word" is directed toward an audience that may not have the patience to decode the vernacular. Angelou, the "messenger," thus acts as translator. More important, however, Angelou self-consciously makes a distinction between written and oral which implies that mastery of the written language is the prerequisite to mastery over one's fate. Just as she had realized, with Mrs. Flowers, that "language is man's way of communicating with his fellow man and it is language alone which separates him from the lower animals" (*IK* 82), she now asserts that education and the ability to write correctly are tools in the hands of the oppressed, tools that must be honed and sharpened, the better to serve their purpose of communication. Since her stance, as indicated before, is clearly one of *engagement*, she thus assumes a responsibilty which can be fulfilled only if the "written word" is an instrument of social change. It is clear that she sees language as a tool that helps shape destiny. She is interested in its performative as well as its purely sensual aspects. Thus when her brother Bailey becomes estranged from his family and gets into drugs, gangs, and pimping, she notes: "His language had changed. He was forever dropping slangy terms into his sentences like dumplings in a pot" (*IK* 217), whereas he had been apt at manipulating speech patterns: "The double entendres, the two-pronged sentences, slid over his tongue to dart rapier-like into anything that happened to be in the way" (*IK* 76). He could still, when arguing with his mother, be a master of sharp wit: "Bailey looped his language around his tongue and issued it out to Mother in alum drops" (*IK* 219). But when trying to articulate, under stress, his love/hate relationship to ruthless Vivian, who pushes her children out of the nest, Bailey exerts control over his feelings by resorting to careful, almost painful efforts of language: "he chose his words with the precision of a Sunday school teacher" (*IK* 223).

Maya too makes great efforts to please her mother. She drops her southern euphemisms (cf. *IK* 234). She tries to become self-sufficient and worldly and acquires the difficult art of "dexterous lying" (229) in order to obtain what she wants. In one case, she wants a job as streetcar conductor; she wants to be the first black San Francisco "conductorette." As she goes to apply for the job, she must write a resume: "Sitting at a side table my mind and I wove a cat's ladder of near truths and total lies. I kept my face blank (an old art) and wrote quickly the fable of Marguerite Johnson, aged nineteen, former companion and driver for Mrs. Annie Henderson (a White Lady) in Stamps, Arkansas" (*IK* 229). She does get the job and acquires new status in her mother's eyes. It is hard-earned status, for between Bailey and Vivian, the expert verbal duelists, she is either a neutral third and excluded middle or a mediating confidante in their dialogue of deaf ears. Her normal tendency being to avoid confrontation, she prefers to give up territory and remain silent. As she explains, she does not dare compete with, or interfere in, Vivian's vast capacity to enjoy life and to fly into legendary rages: "Her tongue was sharper than the creases in zoot pants and I knew better than to try to best her. I said nothing" (*GT* 83).

In order to handle her own family, the narrator learns from a position of weakness how to swerve and to survive. This knowledge prepares her for life in white society, where the safest strategy is to wear masks: "Never let white folks know what you really think. If you're sad, laugh. If you're bleeding inside, dance" (*GT* 86). This training in adaptive behavior is an apprenticeship in dissimulation, a lesson in how to become a trickster, a manipulator of signs, a con artist and a writer. The trickster is like the fool, the one who draws attention to the king's nakedness and satirizes the accepted norms of a social order. In a pragmatic sense, though, for the satire or social critique to be effective it must be disguised, guileful, or artful, but not so deceitful as to be completely misunderstood, not so deceptive as to make us miss its "point." Of paramount importance, then, is the sense of an audience whose attention must be captured and retained. As a liminal figure, caught between her mother and brother, who are "entangled in the Oedipal skein" (*IK* 218), the narrator finds her ability to make herself heard severely curtailed. Her newfound sense of self-certainty and community after the junkyard experience collapses on itself as she reenters family life. She cannot share that experience, tell that tale, because her primary audience is indifferent and impatient. Busy Vivian has no time for details and increasingly slick Bailey is orbiting a different planet, no longer the brother she knew: "He may have been glad to see me, but he didn't act much like it. When I tried to tell him of my adventures and misadventures, he responded with a casual indifference which *stilled the tale on my lips*" (*IK* 217). Having a story to tell and the confidence to do so is not enough. Interaction with a real or virtual hearer is an integral part of the storytelling situation. At the end of the first volume, the narrator has found her voice, literally (with Mrs. Flowers) and figuratively (she now has a message to transmit). But she has no audience, or more precisely, her audience's indifference forces her into self-imposed silence. This is the familiar position of the spokesperson who feels that s/he is preaching to those who don't want to (can't) hear and who, consequently, either gives up, tries to find alternate means of reaching an audience, or resorts to various violent and confrontational tactics.

Of these alternatives, however, the only one possible for the artist is to seek means of expression which will convey her point of view without provoking blinding fear, disbelief, utter revulsion, and the concurrent tuning out of the audience. Perhaps it was Billie Holiday, the blues singer, who best exemplified that dilemma when she recalled her first rehearsals of the song "Strange Fruit," from Lewis Allan's story of a lynching: "I worked like the devil on it because I was never sure . . . I could get across to a plush night-club audience the things that it meant to me." When there is no shared experience between singer and audience, the impact of the song can only be weighed hypothetically. Translation of the content into a form of expression that appeals to the subjective desires of the audience and facilitates their entry into the world of the other is hard work for the performer and becomes inseparable from her message.

As singer, dancer, and performer, Maya Angelou has an acute sense of audience interaction. She thus stages her own alienated relationship to her hypothetical reader, knowing full well that the reader must be "conned" into believing that she has a privileged relation to an autobiographical "truth," which the rhetorical features of her style explicitly problematize. This double bind determines her narrative choices of events and metaphors. In the narrative segment that describes her initial attempts at tale telling within the confines of her own indifferent family, we clearly see her giving up. At the other extreme, when she and Bailey come back south to live in the store after the St. Louis episode, the sense of community is unquestioned. All of Stamps would come to the store to be entertained with stories of their trip north, enabling Bailey to sharpen his "silver tongue" at the expense of the naive country folk. His audience is clearly defined and eager to lend its ears, even if he is shown to be considerably alienated from the rural people toward whom he directs his sarcasms. His experience of the urban North has estranged him from this initial community. Congruence between teller and listener need not be perfect if the teller has sufficient firsthand knowledge of the listener's general frame of reference and can tailor his discourse to (partially) fit that frame.

These linguistic skills differ only in degree from those of the successful and affluent gamblers (or numbers men), the real con men, their mother's friends. Foremost among them is Daddy Clidell, who introduces Maya to the colorful characters of the black underground and teaches her the fine art of swindling to keep her from ever becoming "anybody's mark" (*IK* 187). From Clidell's tales emerges a single pattern: the more stupid the con man acts, the more likely he is to win over his arrogant white "mark." This kind of ingenuity gives the con man hero status in the ghetto, where the ability to turn "the crumbs from his country's table. . . [into] a Lucullan feast" (190) is the most admired of skills. This skill rests on the culture-hero's ability to take control of a situation and assume certain risks while appearing to relinquish all authority. In other words, it involves a carefully planned strategem of deception, feigning, and role playing. We have already seen that the outcome of the rape trial had depended on Maya's ability to do just that: to decode the social system and respond to it in a deceitful way that put her in control. Her lie, or *parole feinte*, brought her to her mother's arms, "her desired destination" (71), while putting her at risk in the eyes of God. For the con artist, the aim is to spin a tale—*parole feinte*—with the express purpose of swindling the mark and profiting by it. The risk involved is in the eyes of the law: the punishment may be prison if the swindler is caught. In both cases, control puts the protagonist at risk with respect to the symbolic (religious or social) order and hence bears tragic or heroic dimensions. To have lied was deeply disturbing for Maya, the child raised in a fundamentalist milieu, and that was the religious tragedy of her success in the courtroom. What she now learns from these smart tricksters is the poetic justice of fighting back with tall tales and becoming wealthy in the bargain. Only then does she see the possibility of becoming the heroine of such triumphant tales.

At the end of her fourth volume, Angelou recounts a tale of Brer Rabbit: how he succeeded in winning his freedom from the angry farmer by pretending to be more afraid of the thorny briar patch than of the farmer's cooking pot. She identifies completely with Brer Rabbit, feeling just as free, standing in the library of the newsroom where she has earned the right to work and write for a living, despite Vusumzi Make's pompous initial objections. She has safeguarded his sense of honor by a ritualistic and complex appeal to his desire for power, control, and authority. In this instance, Maya is the fool and Make, the mark: all previous and implicit racial connotations in the tale of Brer Rabbit undergo a radical transformation. On the level of signifiers, the only remaining element of the tale is that power and control are best defined by an authoritative use of language. Power resides in the narrative figure, Maya, who can best reach out to the other, Make, and articulate his desires in terms of *her* needs. This is a technique that the narrative text shows Maya learning from many sources: her oral tradition as well as her newly acquired skills as a dancer and performer. What this suggests in terms of audience interaction is that Angelou's narrator, like Brer Rabbit, often seems to be telling us just what we want to hear, as "unaware persons" deserving only "a part of the truth." Once we understand her "tactics" and "stratagems," however, it becomes clear that for her, writing is a way of claiming her territory from forces that refuse to grant it, a way of telling us "not where she has been, but where she is going." Her technique, then would correspond exactly to what Michel de Certeau has termed "the practice of everyday life": an art of storytelling like the one Homer and the Greeks practiced and the con artists of today continue to perfect. It is a way of operating within a system of power which allows the "weak" to seize victories over the "strong" by employing "tactics" known to the Greeks under the name of *mētis*. It is a form of intelligence and savoir faire, a resourcefulness and an opportunism that is the hallmark of those who will never be the masters of the terrain on which their daily struggles are fought but who develop in practice multiple and polyvalent means of survival that allow them to elude that power system successfully. The double-voiced nature of Angelou's text allows her to oppose an oppressive social system without risk of becoming a term within that system, since a part of her message—because it relies on indirect "signifying" practices—will always elude any direct attempt to inscribe it within the general frame of that dominant discourse. This elusiveness bespeaks a form of alienation differing only in degree from Momma's "secretiveness and suspiciousness" and inherent in all survival strategies.

Indeed, in the briar patch Brer Rabbit is free to claim his space in the communal warren, whereas in the library, Angelou relentlessly explores the constantly changing boundaries of alienated human communication. We have the distinct feeling that she would like (us) to believe that her tale is a triumphant one but cannot quite convince herself of it. Hers is a *parole feinte* that mourns the loss of the illusory possibility of pure *parole-recit*, of direct and unmediated communication with interlocutors who share the same referential and mythic world as she does. In other words, she mourns the disappearance of a mirage, the mirage that is Africa for the children of the colonialist diaspora.

FRED LEE HORD

Someplace to Be a Black Girl

If growing up is painful for the Southern black girl, being aware of her displacement is the rust on the razor that threatens the throat.

The Black female is assaulted in her tender years by all those common forces of nature at the same time that she is caught in the tripartite crossfire of masculine prejudice, white illogical hate and Black lack of power. The fact that the adult American Negro female emerges a formidable character is often met with amazement, distaste and even belligerence. It is seldom accepted as an inevitable outcome of the struggle won by survivors.

These two statements from Maya Angelou's *I Know Why the Caged Bird Sings* reflect the dilemma of Ms. Angelou's girlhood and the way that she forged out of that dilemma. The first part of a series, this autobiographical installment traces her development from a girl of three in Stamps, Arkansas to a woman of almost seventeen with a baby boy in San Francisco, California. And it is the early development of a black female "Invictus" who is becoming the master of her fate and the captain of her soul by the end of this phase of her life. She is discovering who she is in spite of the forms of masculine prejudice, white illogical hate and black lack of power with which she has been besieged. The most critical masculine prejudice with which she was confronted was that in the eyes of black boys—eyes persuaded by young minds already affected by the colonizer's definitions that hourglass figures

From *Reconstructing Memory: Black Literary Criticism.* © 1991 by Fred Lee Hord, Ph.D.

were the only ones with which to pass the time of day, and that fair skin, straight hair, a slender nose and thin lips were requisites for beauty. And though she is not yet in favor with her own eyes by the time she brings two more male eyes into the world, she is not obsessed with looking like white girls. The illogical hate of whites was ripe in Stamps and real in San Francisco, but she has refused to accommodate the power reverberations of that hate. Albeit she lived with black lack of power, it has not possessed her being. She has accepted neither whites controlling the lives of African-Americans nor African-Americans surrendering theirs. Thus, from a narrow crack in that small southern town and an ostensibly wider one in that large western city—St. Louis, Los Angeles and Mexico in between—she wedged a space, someplace to be a black girl. Marguerite Johnson—even though the painful process of maturation for a black girl in the South was intensified by her awareness that she had been assigned a place of no place—inevitably created a "place to be somebody," for she was a survivor.

To discover how Marguerite created someplace to be a black girl, we shall examine how she took the book world she gained access to and super-imposed it on the overlapping yet distant black and white worlds in Stamps. Further, we shall analyze how she increasingly expanded the world she inte-grated from those first three by using the expanding space of societal permis-sion and societal contact in her experience after Stamps. Marguerite "always but ever and ever, thought that life was just one great risk for the living," and so took risks, disguised and open ones, in order to be. The freedom of the book world was too sweet not to transfer to the breathing ones.

Although Marguerite had already located the book world in print, it was Mrs. Bertha Flowers who set it securely on the axis of human communi-cation. With the real world run by whites—a world with scarce black-white contact, much less communication—Mrs. Flowers' revelation that books could be rounded into a Third World provided a place much more livable than Stamps. Marguerite explains the meaning of the secret world furnished by Mrs. Flowers:

> To be allowed, no, invited, into the private lives of strangers and
> to share their joys and fears, was chance to exchange the
> Southern bitter wormwood for a cup of mead with Beowolf or a
> hot cup of tea and milk with Oliver Twist.

The book world was a world of integration, where you were the con-fidant of all the denizens—in whose skins, regardless of color, you could move inside and breathe free. Yes, the black Dunbar, Hughes, Johnson and

DuBois lived in that world, but so did the white Shakespeare, Kipling, Poe, Butler, Thackeray, and Henley. She saved her "young and loyal passion for the black writers, but she discovered ways to enjoy the company of white writers who related to her real world. It "was Shakespeare who said, 'When in disgrace with fortune and men's eyes'," a condition she identified with when she thought about her plight in Stamps, a young castaway without parents in a freedom-stifling, small southern town. The statement also fit her estimate of herself in the eyes of people, especially young black boys. Shakespeare sympathized with the "black, ugly dream" that was her existence, and so became her "first white love." She rationalized her courtship "by saying that after all he had been dead so long it couldn't matter to anyone any more." The "beautiful sad lines" of "Annabel Lee" appertained to the sadness of her life "stalled by the South and Southern Black lifestyle." And whether it was the comic strips, cowboy books or Horatio Alger, she craved another space, a place to be a happy black girl. The freedom of the cowboys, "the strong heroes who always conquered in the end," and the penniless shoeshine boys who, with goodness and perseverance, became rich, rich men and gave baskets of goodies to the poor on holidays, became more real than the people in her haltingly moving space. Tiny Tim was her favorite on "Sunday as he eluded the evil men and bounded back from each seeming defeat as sweet and gentle as ever." As she daydreamed herself into fortune and the grace of men's eyes, she identified with "the little princesses who were mistaken for maids, and the long-lost children mistaken for waifs." Marguerite refused to restrict her life to the world of the cotton fields; like her father, Bailey Sr., she had "aspirations of grandeur." And it was this survivor spirit that impelled her to turn her mind fast enough to occupy a less confining globe.

Marguerite Johnson banished segregation in her book world, and she wanted no part of her culture that she associated with powerlessness in the world of book learning. Considered stuck-up by her schoolmates, she took pride in the school principal's proper English and tailored her speech accordingly, speech free of what she considered the rough edges of a "Southern accent" or "common slang." In fact, one of her most traumatic experiences was graduation from the eighth grade at Lafayette County Training School. The long anticipated event was ruined by a combination of the white arrogance of the commencement speaker, Mr. Donleavy, and the apparent acceptance by African-Americans in the audience that they could only aspire to be great athletes. Education was supposed to be the exit out of the stultifying South, and now a white man was saying that they should try to emulate only the "Jesse Owenses and Joe Louises." Enraged by the presumptuousness and rebutting each sentence, she wondered "what school official in the white-goddom of Little Rock had the right to decide that these two men must be our only heroes." Further, she willed instant death to the black owner of the first Amen, hoping that he/she would choke on the word. She also considered the recitation of "Invictus" by Elouise, the daughter of the Baptist minister, impertinent, and was aggravated by Henry Reed's valedictory address, "To Be or Not to Be." If according to Mr. Donleavy—who represented all whites—African-Americans could not be, and Whites were the masters of their fate and the captain of their souls, then commencement was just another exercise in futility. "We were maids and farmers, handymen and washerwomen, and anything higher that we aspired to was farcical and presumptuous." If education was not a way out of the strictures of the Stamps in this country, then democracy was a sham, and all the people, black and white, who were regarded as contributors to that cause, had lived in vain. It would have been preferable for everyone to have died than continue to play out this "ancient tragedy" of while power and black impotence. Marguerite summarizes the feelings that characterized her attitude about being denied self-determination:

> It was awful to be Negro and have no control over my life. It was brutal to be young and already trained to sit quietly and listen to charges brought against my color with no chance of defense.

It was only when Henry Reed, class valedictorian, began to lead the class and then the black audience in the Negro National Anthem—which had been snuck from its customary place to remove the risk of offending the speaker and his white companion—that Marguerite sensed the strength and the pride of black people. Although she had sung the words thousands of times, she "had never heard it before . . . never thought they (words) had anything to do with me." And so black writers assumed a new dimension. They were not only kindred souls in the free book world, but they enlarged the space in the real one by expanding the spirit until one felt the very power. For the first time, the Anthem carried as much a freedom message as had Patrick Henry's words, "I know not what course others may take, but as for me, give me liberty or give me death." For the first time, Marguerite recognized how black writers not only made possible an alternative world, but pushed the boundaries outward in her actual world:

> Oh, Black known and unknown poets, how often have your auctioned pains sustained us? Who will compute the lonely

nights made less lonely by your songs, or the empty pots made less tragic by your tales?

Perhaps, for Marguerite, who could abide no indication of weakness in her people, this was the most useful lesson of those eight years. Mr. Donleavy had unwittingly helped her to demystify her ideas about the power of education for powerless African-Americans, but a racial and literary ancestor had afforded her the strength to resist his dehumanization. Only the strong survive!

Now that we have established some measurement of Marguerite's book world, we need to investigate her ideas of the two living worlds— black and white—that she wished to coincide with the paper one. We need to ascertain what qualities in both worlds were so undesirable that she felt compelled to fit another world on them to oppose her dehumanization. First, however, it is important that we know how she did identify with the black world in Stamps. Marguerite's strongest identification with black people was with their independence, their desire and ability to be free from the control of whites. Although she commiserated with their abject conditions in Stamps, she wanted them to abide their poverty with a straight spine.

All of the black people that she admired possessed some degree of freedom from whites. Momma Johnson, her grandmother, owned a store which whites patronized, owned land and houses, and "had more money than all the powhitetrash." In fact, she lent money to whites, including the dentist, during the Depression. Marguerite "knew that there were a number of white folks in town that owed her favors." So Momma was a black woman to look up to, who not only was "the only Negro woman in Stamps referred to once as Mrs."—though by error—but who also asserted herself and won strange victories over both poor white girls and a rich white man—the dentist.

In the store, Momma sidestepped servility with the "powhitetrash girls" by anticipating their needs and thus obviating their orders. Outside the store on one memorable occasion, she was heckled by the girls but stood her ground quietly with the moan-song of old black Christian warriors in her throat even when they subjected her to the indignity of indignities—having one of their gang expose her genitals by doing a handstand without under-wear. Even though Marguerite could not fathom why her grandmother did not come inside to avoid such humiliation, she realized, after the ordeal, that "whatever the contest had been out front, . . . Momma had won."

Momma also won the bout with Dentist Lincoln, who had never treated a black patient. She pleaded with him to extract two of Marguerite's teeth, reminding him that she had once lent him money, but he refused, saying that he would rather stick his "hand in a dog's mouth than a nigger's." Marguerite remembered how she had been dismissed by Momma, and how she had imagined a scene between Momma and the dentist and his nurse. In that scene, Momma, with "well enunciated" words, castigated the dentist, ordered him out of Stamps, relegated him to a veterinarian, and refused to waste the energy to kill him. When leaving, "she waved her handkerchief at the nurse and turned her into a crocus sack of chicken feed."

Mr. McElroy and Mrs. Flowers were two mysterious black adults whom Marguerite admired because they also seemed to control their own lives. Mr. McElroy was the only black man that she "knew, except for the school principal and the visiting teachers, who wore matching pants and jackets. . . . A man who owned his land and the big many-windowed house with a porch that clung to its sides all around the house. An independent Black man." Mrs. Flowers, patron saint who had helped her retrieve her dignity with books and thus her ability to speak after she had been silenced by the rape of her stepfather, "was the aristocrat of Black Stamps." The rape rendered her powerless and reduced her beneath dignity. She could not speak until she regained her dignity; she could not regain her dignity until she recovered her power. Mrs. Flowers was the agent of her empowerment and epitomized dignity:

> Like women in English novels who walked the moors (whatever they were) with their loyal dogs racing at a respectful distance. Like the women who sat in front of roaring fireplaces, drinking tea incessantly from silver trays full of scones and crumpets. Women who walked over the 'heath' and read morocco-bound books and had two last names divided by a hyphen.

If this sounds like a young black girl in whiteface, we must remember that Marguerite's book world was a ready replacement for what often appeared to be a subjugated culture—black life in Stamps. Unwittingly, she drew her living models from the face of power, although both her hate of white dehumanization and her visceral belonging to the people that sometimes made her "a proud member of the wonderful, beautiful Negro race" insisted that the owner of the face be black.

Joe Louis, the Brown Bomber, wore a black face, and held the fists of almost all black people in his hands when he stepped into the ring to not only defend his heavyweight championship but his people. Marguerite was one of his people, one of the black ritual participants in the late Thirties on the nights of the Louis fights. She remembered how the community gathered and wailed on the radio to bring the news of another Louis victory—a black victory. And it wasn't only Carnera on the canvass; it was all white people. And then Marguerite was proud to belong to her people, because Joe Louis was the "champion of the world. A Black boy. Some Black mother's son . . . the strongest man in the world." So Marguerite belonged to the strongest people in the world, at least for a while.

Marguerite carried other black heroes on the shoulders of her mind when they seemed to live free of white clutches. When Bailey Sr., her father, came to Stamps, she was "so proud of him it was hard to wait for the gossip to get around that he was in town." Why? He spoke "proper English, like the school principal, and even better. . . . Every one could tell from the way he talked and from the car (De Soto) and clothes that he was rich and maybe had a castle out in California." Marguerite needed exemplars of what she considered freedom to believe in the possibility of her own. Although, as we shall see, she became more secure in her identity as her real world expanded beyond Stamps, she was thrilled by the fact that her uncles in St. Louis whipped whites as well as African-Americans and that the black underground men in San Francisco made fortunes from "the wealthy bigoted whites, and in every case . . . used the victims' prejudice against them."

If independence in the black world of Stamps was the most important quality contributing to Marguerite's identification with black people, subordination was so unbearable that she could not keep full residency in that world. She allied emotionally with her community, with their ordeals in cotton fields, in "rivers of blood," and with white noses in the sky. But, it was the fire of black reaction that she wanted; "no more water, the fire next time." Part of her early rejection of southern black culture—her avoiding the common slang and her wanting others to think that she had to be forced to eat black cuisine—was because she associated those things with the powerlessness of black people.

No matter which blacks in Stamps exhibited what Marguerite deemed approval of white dehumanization or characteristics that she related to black powerlessness, she disclaimed their behavior. She made no exceptions. Even her grandmother and her crippled son, Uncle Willie, whom she loved dearly, chafed her when they seemed to tolerate white humiliation. Momma warmed her under her wings in many ways—for which Marguerite was always grateful—but she did not understand why Momma permitted the "powhite-trash" girls to be disrespectful to her in her own store, using her first name. And until Marguerite was quieted by her and convinced by her smiling face that somehow the girls had lost that pitched battle of humiliation outside the store, she was enraged that Momma, who owned the land that the girls lived

on, allowed them to afront her with a display of nakedness. She describes
the aftermath:

> I burst. A firecracker July-the-Fourth burst. How could Momma
> call them Miz? The mean nasty things . . .What did she prove?
> And then if they were dirty, mean and impudent, why did
> Momma have to call them Miz?

Marguerite wanted to shoot the girls with "the 410, our sawed-off
shotgun behind the screen door." And until she had been dismissed by her
grandmother from the private office of the insulting Dr. Lincoln—a
dismissal that she construed as a sign that her grandmother was going to
bless out the white dentist—Marguerite had been angry with Momma for
describing "herself as if she had no last name to the young while nurse" who
answered the back door and closed it firmly in their faces. Her handicapped
Uncle Willie managed no more sympathy when he tolerated the "powhitetrash" children's calling him by his first name, and he mortified her by
obeying their orders "in his limping dip-straight-dip fashion."

Outside her family, Marguerite was no more understanding of African-
Americans following Southern protocol or sympathetic to their efforts to
wrest meaning from life if they seemed accommodative to whites. Although
Marguerite was an integral part of Southern black rituals and a firsthand
witness to the atrocities that shaped those rituals, she expected the miracle of
the spirit to raise the living bones. During the perturbations of the graduation exercises mentioned earlier, she castigated all African-Americans who
did not appear to be incensed by the racism of Donleavy's remarks. And
although she sympathized with the cotton pickers who stopped at Momma's
store for physical and spiritual sustenance, "had seen the fingers cut by the
mean little cotton bolls, and . . . had witnessed the backs and shoulders and
arms and legs resisting any further demands," she insisted that they rise:

> I thought them all hateful to have allowed themselves to be
> worked like oxen, and even more shameful to try to pretend that
> things were not as bad as they were. When they leaned too hard
> on the partly glass candy counter, I wanted to tell them shortly to
> stand up and 'assume the posture of a man.'

And although Marguerite was taken to the annual revivals by Momma,
and interpreted the happiness on the black faces and their verbal participa-
tions in the sermons of the evangelists as satisfaction "that they were going

to be the only inhabitants of that land of milk and honey, except of course a few white folks like John Brown," she watched them after the benediction, and thought that "outside and on the way home, the people played in their magic as children poke in mud pies, reluctant to tell themselves that the game was over."

Marguerite never accepted the occlusions of her place as a black girl in the white South. In thought, word and deed, she pushed against them, making soft spots and then fissures. When "the used-to-be sheriff" rode up to the store late one day and warned Momma to hide Uncle Willie, because the Klan would be by later to avenge the behavior of "a crazy nigger (who) messed with a white lady today," Marguerite pledged that not even St. Peter would secure a testimony from her that the act had been kind. She detested "his confidence that my uncle and every other Black man who heard of the Klan's coming ride would scurry under their houses to hide in chicken drop-pings." When the "powhitetrash children," who did not obey the customary laws of being respectful, "took liberties in my store that I would never dare," she pinched them, "partly out of angry frustration." Marguerite's experiences in St. Louis with "the numbers runners, gamblers, lottery takers and whiskey salesmen" waiting in the living room of her mother's mother for favors, and with the Syrian brothers at Louie's tavern competing for her mother's atten-tion because she approximated white beauty standards, were sources of new models of black female strength for her return to Stamps as well as of rein-forced mystification about her appearance. And so she was more likely than ever to resist the violations of her space as a human being, although she was only able to shift her center of gravity regarding her beauty from white to high yellow. Thus later in Stamps, when she worked in the kitchen of a while woman, Mrs. Viola Cullinan, who insisted on abbreviating her name to Mary, Marguerite reacted to being "called out of her name" by dropping Mrs. Cullinan's favorite dishware, "a casserole shaped like a fish and the green glass coffee cups." Yet, when watching a Kay Francis movie from the Negro balcony, she not only dismissed the obsequious behavior of Kay's black maid and chauffeur as beneath her dignity, but she answered the white laughter at such behavior with her own, reveling in the fact of "white folks" not knowing that the woman they were adoring could be my mother's twin, except that she was white and my mother was prettier."

Marguerite used the expanded possibilities of the world after Stamps to further enlarge her world. In Stamps, she had to create a world of freedom—a place to be a black girl—in her book world, in her identification with Blacks who seemed independent of white strictures, in her refusal to identify with Blacks who stayed in their white-determined places, and in her resistance to white dictation and dehumanization. In San Francisco, for "a thirteen-year old Black girl, stalled by the South and Southern Black life style, the city was a state of beauty and a state of freedom." And yet, in spite of a Miss Kirwin, a brilliant teacher at George Washington High School who, as Mrs. Flowers, acknowledged her place in the world "for just being Marguerite Johnson;" and a month-long experience in a junkyard car home with whites, as well as Mexicans and other Blacks—which demonstrated the possibilities of human harmony with places and spaces enough for everyone—she saw the unmistakable evidence of racism:

> San Francisco would have sworn on the Golden Gate Bridge that racism was missing from the heart of their air-conditioned city. But they would have been sadly mistaken.

Not only were there stories of racism that went the rounds, but there were the realities. Marguerite imbibed the stories of her stepfather's friends about the prejudices of wealthy, bigoted whites being exploited by black con men as tonic for the more subtle Northern symptoms of the disease. But concrete racism could only be tempered by concrete resistance. And so, when at fifteen, she decided to pursue the career of a streetcar operator, only to be informed by her mother that colored people were not accepted on streetcars, Marguerite once again found it necessary to stretch her tall resistance to make room for her spirit. After initially forgiving the white receptionist at Market Street Railway Company for protecting the bastion of white supremacy with the niceties of ritualistic circumventions, even accepting "her as a fellow victim of the same puppeteer" who denied her and her people places to be somebody, she was awakened from her meditation that "the miserable little encounter had nothing to do with me, the me of me, any more than it had to do with that silly clerk" by the "Southern nasal accent (and) usual hard eyes of white contempt" of the conductorette on her way home. Marguerite brought her South up North, where it belonged, realizing that racism was no respecter of geography:

> All lies, all comfortable lies. The receptionist was not innocent and neither was I. The whole charade we had played out in that crummy waiting room had directly to do with me, Black, and her, white.

Marguerite Johnson persisted in her resistance to the thumbnail place of black girls in the South, in the anywhere. She became "the first Negro on the San Francisco streetcars." She could not like the "fate to live the poorest, roughest life;" she could not "bear the heavy burden of Blackness" that required her to balance dehumanization on even the back of the mind; she had "to be or not to be." Marguerite, in her book world that she opposed to the white world, in her black world that she opposed to the hue man world, survived and began to center her marginalized status, moving toward the myths of black identity and black ethos. She was a poet of the spirit who knew that internal rhyme was as beautiful as end rhyme, perhaps one and the same. As she said at twelve:

> If we were a people much given to revealing secrets, we might raise monuments and sacrifices to the memories of our poets, but slavery cured us of that weakness. It may be enough, however, to have it said that we survive in exact relationship to the dedication of our poets (including preachers, musicians and blues singers).

Include Marguerite!

MARY VERMILLION

Reembodying the Self: Representations of Rape in Incidents in the Life of a Slave Girl and I Know Why the Caged Bird Sings

A study of a woman's written record of her own rape can illustrate the dual consciousness which Susan Stanford Friedman identifies as a primary characteristic of female life-writing. According to Friedman, a woman's alienation from her culturally defined self motivates the creation of an alternate self in her autobiography. Because patriarchal cultural definitions of a woman center on her body and sexual status, the rape victim not only becomes painfully aware of her culturally defined self, but she also confronts a hideous paradox as she tries to construct an alternate self. In trying to perceive herself as whole and untouched, the rape victim runs the risk of fragmenting her identity, of excluding her body from what she considers as the rest of her self. Such negation of her body is a natural continuation of the actual rape: the victim tells herself that *she* was not there during the rape—it was not *she* whom he raped. Unanswerable questions then loom. If she was not there, then who was? Who is this "she," this "self" who exists bodiless?

The rape victim's uncertainties about her own subjectivity stem in part from a long tradition in Western patriarchal thought—what Elizabeth Spelman terms "somatophobia," fear of and disdain for the body. Spelman demonstrates that patriarchal thinkers from Plato onward have channeled most of this disdain toward the female body. I will briefly examine the partnership of misogyny and somatophobia in Shakespeare's *The Rape of Lucrece*

From *Biography* 15:3. © 1992 by the Biographical Research Center, University of Hawaii.

because his poem influenced the two autobiographers whom I examine in the second and third parts of this essay. Maya Angelou specifically refers to the poem, and it shaped the novels of seduction that Harriet Jacobs critiques in her autobiography. Shakespeare describes the raped Lucrece as privileging her innocent mind over her violated body: "Though my gross blood be stain'd with this abuse, / Immaculate and spotless is my mind." Stephanie Jed describes how somatophobia springs from such a Platonic duality between body and mind: "Implicit in every construct of a chaste or integral mind is the splitting off of the body as the region of all potential contamination." The dire but logical consequences of this splitting off emerge when Lucrece views her violated body through patriarchy's eyes. Perceiving her body as her husband's damaged property, she gives the following rationale for killing herself:

> My honor I'll bequeath unto the knife
> That wounds my body so dishonored.
> 'Tis honor to deprive dishonor'd life,
> The one will live, the other being dead.
> So of shame's ashes shall my fame be bred,
> For in my death I murther shameful scorn:
> My shame so dead, mine honor is new born.

Informing Lucrece's deadly resolution are somatophobia and two other key aspects of patriarchal ideology: the identification of the female with her body and the equation of female "honor" and chastity. The destruction of Lucrece's body perpetuates these patriarchal conceptions of womanhood.

The woman who records her own rape must—if she does not wish to do with her pen what Lucrece does with her sword—close the distance between her body and whatever her society posits as a woman's integral self (i.e., sexual reputation, mind, soul, desire, or will). She must reclaim her body. While this written reclamation is difficult for any woman, it presents a special problem for the black woman because of the meanings that hegemonic white cultures have assigned to her body. According to Spelman, somatophobia supports both sexist and racist thinking because these hegemonic cultures have posited women as more body-like than men and blacks as more body-like than whites. Within these two hierarchical relationships, the black woman is implicitly perceived as the most body-like, and this perception fosters her oppression in somatophobic societies. Numerous scholars have demonstrated that both the institution of slavery and antebellum writing constructed the black woman as the sum total of her bodily labour and suffering. Antebellum writers—including abolitionists and black males—depicted the black woman as breeder, wet nurse, field laborer. and most significant, as sexually exploited victim. So pervasive were these images of the black woman's body that the National Association of Colored Women's Clubs, founded in 1896, targeted for its most vehement attacks negative stereotypes of black women's sexuality. Angela Davis and bell hooks illustrate how these nineteenth-century stereotypes inform twentieth-century racist images of the black woman as promiscuous and bestial. Because of this long history of negative stereotypes, the black woman who records her own rape faces the arduous task of reaffirming her sexual autonomy without perpetuating the racist myths that associate her with illicit sexuality. She must recover and celebrate her body without reinforcing racist perceptions of her as mere body.

This task is, of course, also a crucial project for contemporary black feminists. Reviewing Spike Lee's film, *She's Gotta Have It* (1986)—in which a black woman, Nola Darling, is raped—hooks writes:

> She [Darling] has had sex throughout the film; what she has not had is a sense of self that would enable her to be fully autonomous and sexually assertive, independent and liberated. . . . A new image, the one we have yet to see in film, is the desiring black woman who prevails, who triumphs, not desexualized, not alone, who is 'together' in every sense of the word.

How two black women who have suffered rape (or its threat) begin to construct this "new image" will be my focus as I examine Harriet Jacobs's and Maya Angelou's autobiographies.

≈≈≈≈≈≈≈

Jacobs, in *Incidents in the Life of a Slave Girl* (1861), adopts the pseudonym Linda Brent and describes how, as a young enslaved girl, she coped with the threat of rape from her master, Dr. Flint. In order to escape this threat, as well as slavery itself, Brent deliberately chooses to have sexual relations with another white man, Mr. Sands. Many critics have argued that Jacobs's narration of these events echoes and subverts various components of nineteenth-century sentimental discourse—particularly the seduction plot and the basic tenets of "true womanhood" (piety, purity, submissiveness, and domesticity). In my examination of these subversions, I will focus on how

Jacobs critiques somatophobia and degrading images of the black female body. Brent's decision to have sexual relations with Sands marks a turning point in Jacobs's reembodying strategies. Before this point, she obscures her own corporeality in order to counter negative stereotypes about black women, and after this point, she begins constructing new positive images of the black female body.

For over one hundred years preceding Jacobs's writing of her autobiography, sentimental novelists portrayed both raped and seduced heroines as believing, like Shakespeare's Lucrece, that their sexual activities sever their integral selves from their bodies. In Susanna Rowson's *Charlotte Temple* (1791), for instance, when the eponymous heroine leaves her paternal home with her seducer, she mourns, "It seemed like the separation of soul and body." Sentimental heroines who undergo such a separation (i.e., lose their "sexual purity")—be it by their own choice or not—face a bout of madness or muteness usually followed by a slow, painful death. Inscribing the "fallen" woman's body as damaged male property, the sentimental novel identifies the female with her body and promotes somatophobia. Furthermore, in dishing out the same "punishment" to both raped and seduced heroines, the sentimental novel as a literary mode obscures seduction's crucial difference from rape: seduction requires a contest of wills while rape requires the mastery of one will over another. In disguising this difference, the sentimental novel erases female volition. Jacobs, I believe, must have recognized that such an erasure reinforced the slaveholder's negation of the enslaved woman's will. In order to reclaim her own volition, she appropriates the sentimental novel's obfuscation of rape and seduction. By portraying in the language of seduction her former master's legally sanctioned threat to rape her, Jacobs refutes his idea that she was his property, "subject to his will in all things."

Jacobs further accentuates her own volition by depicting the unequal contest between Brent's and Flint's bodies as an equal contest of words. Observing that Jacobs's autobiography contains more reconstructed dialogue than any male-authored slave narrative, William Andrews maintains that Brent and Flint's dialogues pivot on arguments of the slave woman's rights to define herself. I want to argue that Jacobs also uses dialogue to challenge the hegemonic culture's perception of her as mere body. Flint tries to control Brent by whispering foul words into her ear, and Jacobs writes that he "*peopled*" my young mind with unclean images, such as only a vile monster could think of" (27, emphasis added). With the choice of the word "peopled," Jacobs merely hints that Flint would like to "people" his plantation through Brent's body. She portrays the sexual threat that Flint poses as a predominantly psychological/spiritual one and thus lessens her reader's tendency to associate her body with illicit sexuality. Jacobs continues to mystify her former master's physical power and legal right to rape her by confining it to verbal expressions. She primarily depicts his economic mastery over Brent not as his ability to overpower her physically, but as his power to perpetuate her slavery in his last will and testament. Jacobs further confines Flint's power to words as she portrays him sending Brent letters, making speeches, and, ironically, promising to make her a lady, a category from which black women were excluded by the white planter culture. Even after Brent runs away, it is Flint's words, and not his body, that threaten her. In her first hiding place the sight of Flint gives her a "gleam of satisfaction" (100), but the sound of his voice "chills her blood" (103). Brent's differing reactions to Flint highlight Jacobs's primary strategy in recording his threat to her body. As Flint's body nears Brent's, as he enters the house she hides in, Jacobs describes him as a mere voice. In recording Flint's attempts to disembody her, she disembodies him.

In thus obscuring the corporeality of Flint's threat of rape, Jacobs minimizes her own body and thereby strikes a blow against the racist stereotype of the black woman as sexually exploited victim. The pen with which she strikes, however, is double-edged, and like Lucrece's dagger, annihilates her own body. In the early part of her autobiography, Jacobs, like Lucrece, privileges an interior self over her body and nearly erases its presence in her text.

Brent's decision to have sexual relations with Sands, however, begins Jacobs's rewriting of her body into her life story. Most feminist readers of Jacobs's narrative interpret her discussion of this incident as her most powerful rejection of sentimental discourse and "true womanhood." I want to emphasize that Jacobs's reversals of the seduction plot's conventions also enable her to reject the body/mind duality that promotes somatophobia. When Flint asks if she loves the father of her unborn child, she retorts, "I am thankful that I do not despise him" (59). Unlike the stock seduced maiden, Brent has no uncontrollable passion for Sands. Reasoning that he will buy and free her and the children they have, Brent exerts her own will to escape Flint's. "It seems," she states, "less degrading to give one's self, than to submit to compulsion. There is something akin to freedom in having a lover who has no control over you except that which he gains by kindness and attachment" (56). Mary Helen Washington calls this declaration "the clearest statement of . . . the need for control over one's female body." Jacobs, I believe, seizes this control by insisting upon a connection between her sexuality and autonomy: "I knew what I did, and I did it with deliberate calculation" (55). By thus emphasizing that Brent willed her sexual activity, Jacobs critiques the somatophobic sentimental convention that severs a unchaste woman's body from her integral self, and she inscribes Brent's union with Sands as a union of her own body and will.

After Brent escapes Flint's plantation, his pursuit of her is so rigorous that she is forced to hide for seven years in a crawl space in her grandmother's attic. Of these years in hiding Andrews writes that "her disembodied presence in patriarchal society lets her become for the first time Dr. Flint's manipulator instead of his tool." While I acknowledge this power shift, I want to further explore Andrews's use of the word "disembodiment." Confined to a coffin-like space and temporarily losing the use of her limbs, Brent is indeed disembodied in her situation. Yet it is, I maintain, in describing this very disembodiment that Jacobs embodies herself in her text. Her descriptions of Brent's physical sufferings in the attic reinforce the bond between her body and her will. Jacobs engages a pattern of first cataloging Brent's physical ills, and then comparing them favorably to her state as a slave:

> I was eager to look on their [her children's] faces; but there was no hole, no crack through which I could peep. This continued darkness was oppressive. It seemed horrible to sit or lie in a cramped position day after day, without one gleam of light. Yet I would have chosen this, rather than my lot as a slave. (114)

Here Brent's physical suffering accentuates not only her ability to choose but also the reason behind her choice—her children's freedom.

Jacobs also emphasizes this connection between Brent's will, body, and children by juxtaposing her agony in hiding with the pain of the slave mother whose children have been sold (122). This recurrent figure who has lost both her will and the fruit of her body represents the completely disembodied black woman. She is Jacobs's anti-type and has no wish to continue her life. "Why *don't* God kill me?" asks one (16). "I've got nothing to live for now," says another (70). In Chapter 13, "The Church and Slavery," Jacobs uses the disembodied slave mother to demonstrate how the somatophobic privileging of an interior self over the body disembodies the black race. In this scene the childless woman not only voices her suffering and loss, but Jacobs also minutely records her physical torment. The woman stands and beats her breast, then sits down, "quivering in every limb." The white constable who presides over the Methodist class meeting disregards her longing for her sold children, her physical suffering, and the many enslaved people who weep in sympathy with her. He stifles a laugh and says, "Sister, pray to the Lord that every dispensation of his divine will may be sanctified to the good of your poor needy soul" (70). This "spiritual" advice disembodies the woman and her friends, leaving them only their singing voices: "Ole Satan's church is here below. / Up to God's free church I hope to go" (71). While these words disparage the white constable, they also confirm his privileging of soul over body. Critiquing the slaveholder's religion within her rewriting of the seduction plot, Jacobs juxtaposes the "Christian" slaveholder's devaluation of the black body with the sentimental novel's devaluation of the female body and thereby unveils the somatophobia in both discourses.

She further contests both of these disembodying discourses with her descriptions of Brent's activities in her attic hideaway. It is in this part of the text that Brent—tearful, hysterical, and sleepless—most resembles the sentimental heroine. Brent's crawling exercises, her drilling of peepholes, her sewing, reading, and letter writing oddly mimic domestic industriousness. During the second winter, in which cold stiffens her tongue, Brent's muteness and delirium echoes that of a "fallen" and dying sentimental heroine. Jacobs thus parallels Brent's attic with the private space that usually confines the sentimental heroine: the kitchen, the parlor, the upstairs chamber, the deathbed, and the grave. Jane Tompkins calls such female space "the closet of the heart," and observes that sentimental fiction "shares with the evangelical reform movement a theory of power that stipulates that all true action is not material, but spiritual." Jacobs challenges this stipulation by emphasizing the drastic material change that Brent works from within her "closet of the heart." As Valerie Smith observes, Brent "uses to her advantage all the power of the voyeur." She prevents her own capture by embroiling Flint in an elaborate plot to deflect his attention, and she meets with Sands to secure his promise to free her children. In her hiding place she not only has a mystical vision of her children, but she actually succeeds in gaining their freedom from slavery.

This uniting of spiritual and material action reenacts Jacobs's earlier textual union of Brent's body and will, and it situates her maternity as a powerful symbol of her autonomy. In her autobiography, Jacobs transforms her body from a site of sexual oppression to a source of freedom—freedom from slavery for herself and her children and freedom from somatophobic racist ideologies that demean the black female body. With one of Brent's early experiences in the North, however, Jacobs suggests that her maternity is not the only cause for celebrating her body. Brent sees portraits of her friend Fanny's children and remarks, "I had never seen any paintings of colored people before, and they seemed to me beautiful" (162). With this statement, Jacobs subtly indicates that her readers must likewise see the black race anew. Jacobs's autobiography, like Fanny's portraits, insists that the value and worth of the black female body exists outside of its functions in a patriarchal slaveholding society.

≈≈≈≈≈≈

Important differences obviously exist between Jacobs's antebellum autobiography and Maya Angelou's twentieth-century record of her rape at age
eight in *I Know Why the Caged Bird Sings* (1969). One important difference is
the way in which somatophobia manifests itself in their texts. Because Angelou
does not have to contend with the nineteenth-century patriarchal ideology of
"true womanhood," she is freer to portray her rape, her body, and her sexuality.
Yet Jacobs describes herself as beautiful and sexually desirable, while Angelou,
as a child and young adult, sees herself as ugly. Jacobs posits somatophobia
outside herself and critiques it as part of slaveholding culture while Angelou
portrays her younger self internalizing and finally challenging the somatophobia inherent in twentieth-century racist conceptions of the black female
body. Despite these differences, Angelou's text contains reembodying strategies similar to those of Jacobs. Both women contest somatophobia by questioning religious ideologies rewriting white literary traditions, and celebrating
their bodies and motherhood as symbols of their political struggles. In order
to challenge racist stereotypes that associate black women with illicit sexuality,
both writers obscure their corporeality in the early part of their texts by trans-
forming the suffering connected with rape into a metaphor for the suffering of
their race. In Jacobs's text rape is a metaphor for the severed body and will of
the slave, and Angelou similarly uses her rapist's violation of her body and will
to explore the oppression of her black community.

Angelou first connects her rape with the suffering of the poor. "The act
of rape on an eight-year-old body," she writes, "is a matter of the needle
giving because the camel can't." In this description, Angelou subtly links her
rapist with the wealthy man whom Jesus warned would have a difficult time
getting into heaven, and she reinforces this link by alluding to Jesus's words
in her ironic description of a black revival congregation's sentiments: "The
Lord loved the poor and hated those cast high in the world. Hadn't He
Himself said it would be easier for a camel to go through the eye of a needle
than for a rich man to enter heaven?" (108). As she continues to imagine the
congregation's thoughts, Angelou makes the connection between her rape
and the plight of the poor in class society more racially explicit, and, like
Jacobs, she also demonstrates that privileging a future world over the present
perpetuates black oppression:

> They [the congregation] basked in the righteousness of the poor
> and the exclusiveness of the downtrodden. Let the whitefolks
> have their money and power and segregation and sarcasm and

big houses and schools and lawns like carpets, and books, and mostly—mostly—let them have their whiteness. (110)

With the image of the camel and the needle, Angelou transforms her rape into a symbol of the racism and somatophobia that afflict Maya and her race throughout much of *Caged Bird*.

Rape in Angelou's text, however, primarily represents the black girl's difficulties in controlling, understanding, and respecting both her body and her words in a somatophobic society that sees "sweet little white girls" as "everybody's dream of what was right with the world" (l). Angelou connects white definitions of beauty with rape by linking Maya's rape with her first sight of her mother, Vivian Baxter. Angelou's description of Vivian echoes that of the ghost-like whites who baffle young Maya. Vivian has "even white teeth and her fresh-butter color looked see-through clean" (49). Maya and her brother, Bailey, later determine that Vivian resembles a white movie star. Angelou writes that her mother's beauty "literally assailed" Maya and twice observes that she was "struck dumb" (49–50). This assault by her mother's beauty anticipates the physical assault by Mr. Freeman, her mother's boyfriend, and Maya's muteness upon meeting her mother foreshadows her silence after the rape. With this parallel Angelou indicates that both rape and the dominant white culture's definitions of beauty disempower the black woman's body and self-expression.

Angelou further demonstrates the intimate connection between the violation of Maya's body and the devaluation of her words by depicting her self-imposed silence after Freeman's rape trial. Freeman's pleading looks in the courtroom, along with Maya's own shame, compel her to lie, and after she learns that her uncles have murdered Freeman, she believes that her courtroom lie is responsible for his death. Angelou describes the emotions that silence Maya:

> I could feel the evilness flowing through my body and waiting, pent up, to rush off my tongue if I tried to open my mouth. I clamped my teeth shut, I'd hold it in. If it escaped, wouldn't it flood the world and all the innocent people? (72)

Angelou's use of flood imagery in this crucial passage enables her to link Maya's inability to control her body and her words. Throughout the text Maya's failure to keep her bodily functions "pent up" signals the domination of her body by others. The autobiography's opening scene merges her inability to control her appearance, words, and bodily functions. Wanting to look like a "sweet little white girl," Maya is embarrassed about her own appearance and cannot remember the words of the Easter poem she recites. With her escape from the church, Angelou implicitly associates Maya's inability to rule her bladder with her inability to speak:

> I stumbled and started to say something, or maybe to scream, but a green persimmon, or it could have been a lemon, caught me between the legs and squeezed. I tasted the sour on my tongue and felt it in the back of my mouth. Then before I reached the door, the sting was burning down my legs and into my Sunday socks. I tried to hold, to squeeze it back, to keep it from speeding. (3)

Maya's squeezing back in this passage anticipates her stopping the flood of her words after the rape, and Angelou also connects this opening scene of urination with one of Freeman's means of silencing Maya. After ejaculating on a mattress, he tells her that she has wet the bed, and with this lie, he denies her knowledge about her own body and confounds her ability to make a coherent story out of his actions.

This inability to create a story about her body pervades the remainder of *Caged Bird* as Maya struggles to cope with her emerging womanhood. Angelou, however, is not content to let the mute, sexually abused, wishing-to-be-white Maya represent the black female body in her text. Instead, she begins to reembody Maya by critiquing her admiration for white literary discourse. An early point at which Angelou foregrounds this critique is in Maya's meeting with Mrs. Bertha Flowers. Presenting this older black woman as the direct opposite of young Maya, Angelou stresses that Flowers magnificently rules both her words and her body. Indeed Flowers's bodily control seems almost supernatural: "She had the grace of control to appear warm in the coldest weather, and on the Arkansas summer days it seemed she had a private breeze which swirled around, cooling her" (77). She makes Maya proud to be black, and Maya claims that Flowers is more beautiful and "just as refined as whitefolks in movies and books" (79). Although Maya begins to respect and admire the black female body, white heroines still provide her standard for beauty, and Angelou pokes fun at the literary discourse that whitens Maya's view of Bertha Flowers and womanhood:

> She [Flowers] appealed to me because she was like people I had never met personally. Like women in English novels who walked the moors (whatever they were) with their loyal dogs racing at a respectful distance. Like the women who sat in front of roaring

fireplaces, drinking tea incessantly from silver trays full of scones and crumpets. Women who walked over the 'heath' and read morocco-bound books. (79)

This humorous passage demonstrates that Maya's self-perception remains dangerously regulated by white culture. Angelou treats such regulation less comically when Flowers breaks Maya's self-imposed silence by asking her to read aloud. The first words Maya speaks after her long spell of muteness are those of Charles Dickens.

Angelou dramatizes the danger that a borrowed voice poses to Maya in her description of Maya's relationship with Viola Cullinan. Maya makes fun of this white woman, whose kitchen she briefly works in, until she discovers that Cullinan's husband has two daughters by a black woman. Then Maya—in a gesture of sisterhood and empathy that is never returned by Cullinan—pities her employer and decides to write a "tragic ballad" "on being white, fat, old and without children" (91). Such a ballad would, of course, completely exclude Maya's own experience: black, thin, young, and (near the end of her autobiography) with child. Through Maya's speculation that Cullinan walks around with no organs and drinks alcohol to keep herself "embalmed," Angelou implies that Maya's potential poetic identification with Cullinan nearly negates her own body. Cullinan's empty insides echo Maya's own perception of herself after the rape as a "gutless doll" she had earlier ripped to pieces (72).

Angelou's most complex and subtle examination of Maya's attachment to white literary discourse occurs when she lists as one of her accomplishments the memorization of Shakespeare's *The Rape of Lucrece*. Christine Froula maintains that Maya's feat of memory suggests the potential erasure of black female reality by white male literary discourse. More specifically, I believe, Angelou's reference to *Lucrece* subtly indicates that Maya's propensity for the verbal and the literary leads her to ignore her own corporeality. After their rapes both Maya and Lucrece turn to representations of suffering women. Maya reads about Lucrece, and Lucrece, finding a painting of the fall of Troy, views Hecuba's mourning the destruction of her city and husband, King Priam. Unlike Lucrece, Maya seeks strength not from pictorial representations of female bodies, but from print, and this preference for the verbal over the pictorial suggests her tendency to privilege literature over her own physical reality. Lucrece decides to speak for the mute sufferers in the painting, and Shakespeare writes, "She lends them words, and she their looks doth borrow." Maya's situation is an inversion of Lucrece's lending of words and borrowing of looks. The once mute Maya can borrow Lucrece's words, but she must somehow lend these words her own "looks" if she does not wish Shakespeare's equation of Lucrece's virtue and whiteness to degrade her own blackness. In remembering *The Rape of Lucrece* Maya must also remember or reconstruct her own body.

One of the ways that she accomplishes this is by celebrating the bodies of other black women. In the only story Maya creates within *Caged Bird*, she augments her grandmother's physical and verbal powers. After a white dentist refuses to treat Maya because she is black, Maya imagines her grandmother ten feet tall, arms doubling in length. As this fantasy grandmother orders the dentist out of town and commands him to quit practicing dentistry, her words, too, metamorphose: "Her tongue had thinned and the words rolled off well enunciated. Well enunciated and sharp like little claps of thunder" (161). With Maya's brief fantasy, Angelou demonstrates how her own autobiography functions. Maya's story, which empowers her grandmother's body and speech, attacks the dentist's derogatory behavior; Angelou's autobiography, which celebrates Maya's body and words, critiques the rape and racial oppression she suffers.

Maya finds, however, that her body and words exist uneasily together. While in the early part of the narrative Maya depends heavily on literature, in the text's final San Francisco section, all words, particularly those packaged as literature, fail to account for her adolescent body's changes. Reading Radclyffe Hall's *The Well of Loneliness* (1928) leads Maya to mistakenly interpret these changes as signals that she is becoming a lesbian. When Maya confronts her mother with this fear, Angelou further demonstrates the inability of the verbal to explain the physical. Vivian's requiring Maya to read aloud the dictionary definition of the word "vulva" echoes strangely Flowers's asking Maya to read aloud from Dickens. Unlike Dickens's prose, however, Noah Webster's and Vivian's words lose their soothing power as soon as Maya is confronted with a stronger physical reality—her own admiration for her girlfriend's fully developed breasts. This scene in which Maya shifts her attention from words to bodies paves the way for Angelou's concluding celebration of the black female body.

Seeking physical rather than verbal knowledge of her sexuality, Maya determines to have sex with one of "the most eligible young men in the neighborhood" (239). Their encounter, which "is unredeemed by shared tenderness" (240), leaves sixteen-year-old Maya pregnant and alone. The young man quits talking to her in her fourth month, and Maya's brother, who is overseas, advises her not to tell her parents until she graduates from high school. Yet it would be wrong to see Maya's motherhood as "a tragic way to end the book and begin life as an adult." While Angelou portrays the pain and confusion resulting from Maya's pregnancy, she places a far greater emphasis on her newfound autonomy. Even Maya's naive style of seduction accentuates her feminist stance. She asks the young man, "Would you like to have a sexual intercourse with me?" (239). In posing this straightforward question, Maya claims control of her body and her identity for the first time in the text. Just as Jacobs describes Brent's union with Sands as a union of her body and will, Angelou celebrates Maya's encounter with the young man. She accentuates Maya's reclamation of her body and volition by ironically alluding to the violation she suffered as an eight year old. "Thanks to Mr. Freeman nine years before," asserts Angelou, "I had had no pain of entry to endure" (240).

By detailing how the pregnant Maya copes with her isolation, Angelou pays further tribute to Maya's increased autonomy and acceptance of her own body. Beginning to reject the literary myths that led her to deny her own agency, Maya accepts complete responsibility for her pregnancy: "For eons, it seemed, I had accepted my plight as the hapless, put-upon victim of fate and the Furies, but this time I had to face the fact that I had brought my new catastrophe upon myself" (241). This acceptance of responsibility also leads Maya to a greater acceptance of her own body's powers:

> I had a baby. He was beautiful and mine. Totally mine. No one
> had bought him for me. No one had helped me endure the sickly
> gray months. I had had help in the child's conception, but no one
> could deny that I had had an immaculate pregnancy. (245)

Angelou's use of the word "immaculate" not only challenges racist stereotypes that associate black women with illicit sexuality, but it also suggests that Maya has shed her earlier conceptions of her body as "dirty like mud" (2) and "shit-colored" (17). Because the eight-year-old Maya perceives her own mother as looking like the "Virgin Mary" (57), the word "immaculate" also indicates that the teenage Maya begins to see in herself the power and beauty she sees in Vivian.

Maya's lack of confidence in her body briefly returns, however, in the autobiography's final paragraphs. Vivian's suggestion that Maya sleep with her child accentuates her worry that she is too clumsy to handle a baby. Vivian banishes this fear by waking Maya and showing her the baby sleeping under a tent that Maya unconsciously formed with her body and a blanket. "See," Vivian whispers, "you don't have to think about doing the right thing. If you're for the right thing then you do it without thinking" (246). Presenting the mother/child bond as a symbol of Maya's newfound autonomy, this closing scene reverses her earlier privileging of the verbal over the physical and celebrates the harmonious interaction of her body and will.

≈≈≈≈≈≈≈

Rape can destroy a woman's autonomy and self-image, yet Jacobs and Angelou transform this potentially destructive event into an opportunity to celebrate their resistance to somatophobia and negative stereotypes about the black female body. An early scene in *Caged Bird* serves as a synecdoche for the reembodiment both Angelou and Jacobs accomplish in recording their experiences of rape. Three "powhitetrash" girls ape the posture and singing of Maya's grandmother, yet she emerges victorious and beautiful from this degradation and calms the enraged Maya. Afterwards Maya rakes away the girls' footprints in the lawn and creates a new pattern: "a large heart with lots of hearts growing smaller inside, and piercing from the outside rim to the smallest heart was an arrow" (27). These connected hearts, which represent the bond between Maya and her grandmother, encapsulate Angelou's and Jacobs's celebration of black motherhood as a sign of personal autonomy. In the grandmother's triumph over the white girls who mock and caricature her body, and in young Maya's erasure of their footprints, I see Angelou's and Jacobs's refutation of negative stereotypes about their bodies. Maya's newly raked pattern resembles their autobiographies—their writings (or rightings) of the black female body outside of dominant cultural definitions.

JAMES BERTOLINO

Maya Angelou Is Three Writers:
I Know Why the Caged Bird Sings

After reading Maya Angelou's autobiographical volume *I Know Why the Caged Bird Sings*, I find myself thinking of her as three different writers. The first is a writer of extraordinary imagination and verbal originality, well worth reading for her artistic effects, her style. The second writer is one who bears honest witness to her own development as a sensitive, highly intelligent human being, probing deeply into powerful childhood experiences, examining how wounds can bring the gift of awareness. The third is a socially conscious writer whose portrayal of the pain, frustration and waste caused by racial prejudice is stunning and persuasive. Reading any of these three "writers" can be a rewarding experience, but do they together create something that is greater than the sum of its parts? The answer is, of course, yes, but before discussing how these identifiable elements enhance each other, let's look at them separately.

When Angelou was a child in the town of Stamps, Arkansas she fell in love with William Shakespeare. It's remarkable for any child under the age of ten to be seriously involved with Shakespeare, but for a black child in a small, southern community, it was a phenomenon. While her ears were full of the rich inventiveness of black colloquial speech, her mind was engaged by the fine-tuned lines of Shakespeare, W.E.B. DuBois and Paul Lawrence Dunbar.

Her own writing, no matter how masterfully controlled, seems ever ready to embrace unexpected bursts of imagery and sound that seem encrusted with life—language that stretches syntax and breaks free: "The

From *Censored Books: Critical Viewpoints.* © 1993 by The Scarecrow Press.

sounds of tag beat through the trees while the top branches waved in contrapuntal rhythms. I lay on a moment of green grass and telescoped the children's game to my vision. The girls ran about wild, now here, now there, never here, never was, they seemed to have no more direction than a splattered egg" (115).

What is perhaps most distinctive about Maya Angelou's writing is its consummate felicity. She not only writes with unflinching honesty about her most painful moments, she crafts language that will enact the reality: you feel the textures, smell the odors, shiver with the chill of stunned awareness.

While she was recognized early as a gifted child, she was physically different from her peers as well. Tall and skinny, by age sixteen she was six feet with a body "shaped like a cucumber." Her parents were both beautiful and, at least in her father's case, quite vain. Her only brother, Bailey (a year older), whom she treasured above all else, was also a beautiful child. "Where I was big, elbowy and grating, he was small, graceful and smooth. . . . His hair fell down in black curls, and my head was covered with black steel wool" (17).

As a young child Maya, or Marguerite, was so unhappy about her appearance she fantasized a personal myth: ". . . a cruel fairy stepmother, who was understandably jealous of my beauty, had turned me into a too-big Negro girl, with nappy black hair, broad feet and a space between her teeth that would hold a number-two pencil" (2). As she approached her teens, her Uncle Tommy often told her, ". . . don't worry 'cause you ain't pretty. Plenty pretty women I seen digging ditches or worse. You smart. I swear to God, I rather you have a good mind than a cute behind" (56).

Her personal development did become focussed on her mental abilities, and her creative talents. She apparently was wise enough to take her uncle's advice, though as she matured she also managed to turn her physical limitations to her advantage. She trained her deep, theatrical voice, took dance lessons, and became well-known for her commanding presence on the stage and, later, television.

A key event in her development was being taken in as a protege by a Mrs. Flowers, the only black woman in Stamps with aristocratic bearing. She encouraged Maya to memorize and recite poetry, insisting that ". . . words mean more than what is set down on paper. It takes a human voice to infuse them with the shades of deeper meaning" (82). Maya was about nine years old at the time, and had already suffered through an intense emotional period when she would not, or could not, speak—a reaction to having been molested and raped when she was eight.

From the age of three Maya and her brother had been raised by her grandmother ("Momma") and her crippled Uncle Willie in Stamps. Her mother and father were separated and pursuing their respective lives free of the children. Maya, Bailey and Uncle Willie helped Momma run the only black-owned general store in the region. Maya learned to be responsible, and while she was a superior student in school, at home she was learning many practical lessons, and how to understand and deal with different kinds of people. She also respected her elders. Her grandmother's world "was bordered on all sides with work, duty, religion and 'her place.' I don't think she ever knew that a deep-brooding love hung over everything she touched" (47).

When she was eight, she and her brother were taken to their mother in St. Louis, where they entered a world peopled by gamblers, numbers runners and men named Hard-hitting Jimmy, Two Gun, Sweet Man and Poker Pete. When Maya saw her mother for the first time in five years, she "knew immediately" why her mother had sent them away. "She was too beautiful to have children" (50).

A man named Mr. Freeman lived with her mother, and supported the family, while mother brought in a little extra by "cutting poker games in gambling parlors" (58). Maya felt Mr. Freeman was a little pathetic when he sat up late waiting for her mother. He, like the men on the streets and in the saloons, was "hypnotized by the beautiful lady who talked with her whole body" (54). Maya felt as sorry for him as for "a litter of pigs born in our back-yard sty in Arkansas. We fattened the pigs all year long for the slaughter on the first good frost, and even as I suffered for the cute little wiggly things, I knew how much I was going to enjoy the fresh sausage and headcheese they could give only with their deaths" (60).

Maya had never had a father around, and when Mr. Freeman held and stroked her in a gentle way, she felt that for the first time she had a real father. Even when he became sexually aroused, her combination of innocence and hunger for loving attention kept her from becoming alarmed. One morning, after Mr. Freeman had been up most of the night waiting for her mother, and neither mother nor her brother were home, he turned up the radio to drown-out her cries and raped her. He threatened to kill her precious Bailey if she told anyone.

Angelou's description of her molestation and rape is probably the most valuable part of her remarkable book. We live in a time when the issue of child abuse has almost become an obsession in our society, and it's important that such a story be told honestly, without sensationalism, yet with enough palpable detail and enough insight so we, the readers, might begin to understand. Her language resonates with the New Testament at the same time it strikes us with its psychological insight and stark details: "A breaking and entering when even the senses are torn apart. The act of rape on an eight-year-old body is a matter of the needle giving because the camel can't. The child gives, because the body can, and the mind of the violator cannot" (65).

Mr. Freeman was convicted of his crime; however, his lawyer got him released on some technicality, and before the day was over Mr. Freeman was dead. The policeman who delivered the news said it looked like he'd been kicked to death (probably by Maya's uncles, though the responsible parties were never found). For many years Maya felt guilt and remorse over Mr. Freeman's death, for the fact that her words had convinced the court. For though he'd ravaged her horribly, he'd nonetheless been the closest thing she'd had to a real father. And though Mr. Freeman "had surely done something very wrong . . . I was convinced that I had helped him do it" (70).

While the Negro section of St. Louis in the 1930s "had all the finesse of a gold-rush town" (51) it still was a place where black people had power and often led the kind of lives they preferred. When Maya and Bailey were sent back to Arkansas, after less than a year with their mother in St. Louis, they were again faced with the depressing reality of overt racial oppression. "The idea came to me that my people may be a race of masochists and that not only was it our fate to live the poorest, roughest life but that we liked it like that" (102).

When Maya was very young—her first years in Stamps—people thought it odd that she spoke without a southern accent. She had her own ideas about that: "Wouldn't they be surprised when one day I woke out of my black ugly dream, and my real hair, which was long and blond, would take the place of the kinky mass that Momma wouldn't let me straighten? My light blue eyes were going to hypnotize them" (2).

It wasn't long, however, before she began to be critical of white people rather than envious: "I couldn't understand whites and where they got the right to spend money so lavishly. Of course, I knew God was white too, but no one could have made me believe he was prejudiced" (40). One "terrible Christmas," when she was about seven, her vain father sent her his photograph, and her mother sent "a doll with blue eyes and rosy cheeks and yellow hair painted on her head" (43). Maya went outside into the cold Winter air, sat down and cried. She and her brother tore the stuffing out of the white doll the day after Christmas.

A few months later their father came to Stamps to take the children to St. Louis to live with their mother. At this point Maya was eight and Bailey nine. Being black had already become a source of pride for them, and Maya was critical of her father. "He sounded more like a white man than a Negro. Maybe he was the only brown-skinned white man in the world. It would be just my luck that the only one would turn out to be my father" (48).

The irony is that one of the reasons Maya did so well as a student, and loved to read from so young an age, was because her parents had taught her to speak perfect English and to respect the great works of literature and all things associated with high white culture.

A pivotal moment for Maya Angelou came at her grade school graduation. A local white politician had been invited to give the commencement address and, after he'd detailed his plans for improving the educational opportunities for the white schools, he described how his second most important priority was to develop the athletic facilities in the black schools. "The white kids were going to have a chance to become Galileos and Madame Curies and Edisons and Gauguins, and our boys (the girls weren't even in on it) would try to be Jesse Owenses and Joe Louises" (151).

When the class valedictorian (he being the only student with higher grades than Maya) gave his address from Shakespeare, Maya couldn't believe her ears. "Hadn't he got the message? There was no 'nobler in the mind' for Negroes because the world didn't think we had minds, and they let us know it" (154). She determined that day to always have control over her life, despite her race (within a few years she would become the first black woman employee on the San Francisco trolley car system). When the program concluded with the Negro national anthem ("Lift Ev'ry Voice and Sing" by James Weldon Johnson and J. Rosamond Johnson) Maya again felt "a proud member of the wonderful, beautiful Negro race."

An experience that would set the tone for her adult life happened when she was fifteen, on vacation with her father in Los Angeles. After her father's girlfriend attacked her, cut her with a knife for coming between them, Maya ran away for a month, then rejoined her mother in San Francisco. After wandering aimlessly with no money, having no friends or family she could call, as night approached she found an automobile junkyard where she slipped into a fairly clean car and spent the night. When she awoke the next morning, the car windows framed Negro, Mexican and white faces, all staring in at her.

She had happened on a small society of homeless children and teenagers, one that had a system of rules for "citizenship." People of opposite sex could not share the same automobile for the night; no criminal activity was allowed, for fear of drawing the police. To provide the essentials for survival, the boys mowed lawns, ran errands for merchants and swept out pool halls. The girls collected bottles for the deposit, and worked weekends in diners. All the money was held communally. "After a month my thinking process had so changed that I was hardly recognizable to myself. The unquestioning acceptance by my peers had dislodged the familiar insecurity. . . . The lack of criticism evidenced by our ad hoc community influenced me, and set a tone for my life" (216).

The non-judgmental atmosphere of the junkyard community also became an effective model for her writing. All of her experiences became valid as markers on the path to self-awareness, no matter how troubling or apparently insignificant. Her powerful feelings about racial prejudice and her criticisms of white people were resolved in that social gathering where all the races, ages and both genders worked together for the good of the community. Finally, the brilliant glue that made it all cohere as literature, was her extraordinary writing style. That atmosphere of permission helped give her the courage to write the way that felt best, the way that excited her, and brought forward for comprehension the deep information that lay behind the formation of her personality.

I believe *I Know Why the Caged Bird Sings* is one of the essential books produced by our culture, and we should all read it, especially our children. Maya Angelou's generosity is beyond compare.

OPAL MOORE

Learning to Live: When the Bird Breaks from the Cage

I bring the dreaded disease. I encourage their children to open their hearts to the "dark" side. To know the fear in them. To know the rage. To know the repression that has lopped off their brains—
Toi Derricotte "From the Black Notebooks"

There is, it seems, a widespread movement afoot to assert the innocence of children even as we deny or sabotage that innocence. There is what appears to be a head-in-the-sand impulse to insist upon this innocence by simply refusing to acknowledge its non-existence. Never mind the "mean streets," never mind the high teen pregnancy rates and drug use, or the phenomenal school dropout rates, or spiraling teen suicide statistics—never mind these real dangers to childhood. There are agencies at work to shield these unprotected children from books that might reveal to them the workings of their own minds and hearts, books that engender the agony of thought and the fearfulness of hope. If we cannot protect children from experience, should we protect them from knowing?

I Know Why the Caged Bird Sings, the autobiography of Maya Angelou, is the story of one girl's growing up. But, like any literary masterpiece, the story of this one black girl declaring "I can" to a color-coded society that in innumerable ways had told her "you can't, you won't" transcends its author. It is an affirmation; it promises that life, if we have the courage to live it, will

From *Censored Books: Critical Viewpoints.* © 1993 by The Scarecrow Press.

be worth the struggle. A book of this description might seem good reading for junior high and high school students. According to People for the American Way, however, *Caged Bird* was the ninth "most frequently challenged book" in American schools (Graham 26, 1). *Caged Bird* elicits criticism for its honest depiction of rape, its exploration of the ugly spectre of racism in America, its recounting of the circumstances of Angelou's own out-of-wedlock teen pregnancy, and its humorous poking at the foibles of the institutional church. Arguments advocating that *Caged Bird* be banned from school reading lists reveal that the complainants, often parents, tend to regard any treatment of these kinds of subject matter in school as inappropriate—despite the fact that the realities and issues of sexuality and violence, in particular, are commonplace in contemporary teenage intercourse and discourse. The children, they imply, are too innocent for such depictions; they might be harmed by the truth.

This is a curious notion—that seriousness should be banned from the classroom while beyond the classroom, the irresponsible and sensational exploitation of sexual, violent, and profane materials is as routine as the daily dose of soap opera. The degradation of feeling caused by slurs directed against persons for their race/class/sex/sexual preference is one of the more difficult hurdles of youthful rites of passage. But it's not just bad TV or the meanness of children. More and more, society is serving an unappetizing fare on a child-sized plate—television screens, t-shirt sloganeers, and weak politicians admonish children to "say 'no' to drugs and drugpushers"; to be wary of strangers; to have safe sex; to report their own or other abusing parents, relatives or neighbors; to be wary of friends; to recognize the signs of alcoholism; to exercise self control in the absence of parental or societal controls; even to take their Halloween candy to the hospital to be x-rayed before consumption. In response to these complications in the landscape of childhood, parent groups, religious groups, and media have called for educators to "bring morality back into the classroom" while we "get back to basics" in a pristine atmosphere of moral non-complexity, outside of the context of the very real world that is squeezing in on that highly touted childhood innocence every single day.

Our teenagers are inundated with the discouragements of life. Ensconced in a literal world, they are shaping their life choices within the dichotomies of TV ads: Bud Light vs. "A mind is a terrible thing to waste." Life becomes a set of skewed and cynical oppositions: "good" vs. easy; yes vs. "catch me"; "right" vs. expediency.

In truth, what young readers seem most innocent of these days is not sex, murder, or profanity, but concepts of self empowerment, faith, struggle as quest, the nobility of intellectual inquiry, survival, and the nature and complexity of moral choice. *Caged Bird* offers these seemingly abstract (adult) concepts to a younger audience that needs to know that their lives are not inherited or predestined, that they can be participants in an exuberant struggle to subjugate traditions of ignorance and fear. Critics of this book might tend to overlook or devalue the necessity of such insights for the young.

Caged Bird's critics imply an immorality in the work based on the book's images. However, it is through Angelou's vivid depictions of human spiritual triumph *set against a backdrop* of human weakness and failing that the autobi-ography speaks dramatically about moral choice. Angelou paints a picture of some of the negative choices: white America choosing to oppress groups of people; choosing lynch law over justice; choosing intimidation over honor. She offers, however, "deep talk" on the possibility of positive choices: choosing life over death (despite the difficulty of that life); choosing courage over safety; choosing discipline over chaos; choosing voice over silence; choosing compas-sion over pity, over hatred, over habit; choosing work and planning and hope over useless recrimination and slovenly despair. The book's detractors seem unwilling to admit that morality is not edict (or an innate property of inno-cence), but the learned capacity for judgement, and that the necessity of moral choice arises only in the presence of the soul's imperfection.

Self empowerment, faith, struggle as quest, survival, intellectual curiosity, complexity of choice—these ideas are the underpinning of Maya Angelou's story. To explore these themes, the autobiography poses its own set of oppositions: Traditional society and values vs. contemporary society and its values; silence vs. self expression; literacy vs. the forces of oppression; the nature of generosity vs. the nature of cruelty; spirituality vs. ritual. Every episode of *Caged Bird*, engages these and other ideas in Maya Angelou's portrait of a young girl's struggle against adversity—a struggle against rape: rape of the body, the soul, the mind, the future, of expectation, of tender-ness—towards identity and self affirmation. If we cannot delete rape from our lives, should we delete it from a book about life?

Caged Bird opens with the poignant, halting voice of Marguerite Johnson, the young Maya Angelou, struggling for her own voice beneath the vapid doggerel of the yearly Easter pageant:

"What you lookin at me for?"
"I didn't come to stay. . . ."

These two lines prefigure the entire work. "What you lookin at me for . . ." is the painful question of every black girl made selfconscious and self doubting by a white world critical of her very existence. The claim that she "didn't come to stay" increases in irony as the entire work ultimately affirms the determination of Marguerite Johnson and, symbolically, all of the unsung survivors of the Middle Passage, to do that very thing—to stay. To stay is to affirm life and the possibility of redemption. To stay—despite the circumstance of our coming (slavery), despite the efforts to remove us (lynching) or make us invisible (segregation).

Angelou, in disarmingly picturesque and humorous scenes like this opening glimpse of her girl-self forgetting her lines and wetting her pants in her earliest effort at public speech, continually reminds us that we survive the painfulness of life by the tender stabilities of family and community. As she hurries from the church trying to beat the wetness coursing down her thighs, she hears the benedictory murmurs of the old church ladies saying, "Lord bless the child," and "Praise God."

This opening recitation lays a metaphorical foundation for the autobiography, and for our understanding of the trauma of rape that causes Marguerite to stifle her voice for seven years. In some ways, the rape of Marguerite provides the center and the bottom of this autobiographical statement.

Critics of the work charge that the scenes of seduction and rape are too graphically rendered:

> He (Mr. Freeman) took my hand and said, "Feel it." It was mushy and squirmy like the inside of a freshly killed chicken. Then he dragged me on top of his chest with his left arm, and his right hand was moving so fast and his heart was beating so hard that I was afraid that he would die. . . . Finally he was quiet, and then came the nice part. He held me so softly that I wished he wouldn't ever let me go. (61)

The seeming ambivalence of this portrait of the dynamics of interfamilial rape elicits distaste among those who prefer, if rape must be portrayed at all, for it to be painted with the hard edges of guilt and innocence. Yet, this portrait reflects the sensibilities of eight year old Marguerite Johnson—full of her barely understood longings and the vulnerability of ignorance:

> . . . Mama had drilled into my head: "Keep your legs closed, and don't let nobody see your pocketbook." (61)

Mrs. Baxter has given her daughter that oblique homespun wisdom designed to delay the inevitable. Such advice may forewarn, but does not forearm and, characteristic of the period, does not even entertain the unthinkable improbability of the rape of a child. Aside from this vague caution, and the knowledge that "lots of people did 'it' and they used their 'things' to accomplish the deed. . . ," Marguerite does not know how to understand or respond to the gentle, seemingly harmless Mr. Freeman because he is "family," he is an adult (not to be questioned), and he offers her what appears to be the tenderness she craves that had not been characteristic of her strict southern upbringing.

When asked why she included the rape in her autobiography, Angelou has said, "I wanted people to see that the man was not totally an ogre" (*Conversations*, 156). And it is this fact that poses one of the difficulties of rape and the inability of children, intellectually unprepared, to protect themselves. If the rapists were all terrible ogres and strangers in dark alleys, it would be easier to know when to run, when to scream, when to "say no." But the devastation of rape is subtle in its horror and betrayal which creates in Marguerite feelings of complicity in her own assault. When queried by Mr. Freeman's defense attorney about whether Mr. Freeman had ever touched her on occasions before the rape, Marguerite, recalling that first encounter, realizes immediately something about the nature of language, its inflexibility, its inability to render the whole truth, and the palpable danger of being misunderstood:

> I couldn't . . . tell them how he had loved me once for a few minutes and how he had held me close before he thought I had peed in my bed. My uncles would kill me and Grandmother Baxter would stop speaking, as she often did when she was angry. And all those people in the court would stone me as they had stoned the harlot in the Bible. And Mother, who thought I was such a good girl, would be so disappointed. But most important, there was Bailey. I had kept a big secret from him (70–71).

To protect herself, Marguerite lies: "Everyone in the court knew that the answer had to be No. Everyone except Mr. Freeman and me" (71).

Some schools that have chosen not to ban *Caged Bird* completely have compromised by deleting "those rape chapters." It should be clear, however, that this portrayal of rape is hardly titillating or "pornographic." It raises issues of trust, truth and lie, love, the naturalness of a child's craving for human contact, language and understanding, and the confusion engendered by the power disparities that necessarily exist between children and adults.

High school students should be given the opportunity to gain insight into these subtleties of human relationships and entertain the "moral" questions raised by the work: should Mr. Freeman have been forgiven for his crime? After all, he appears to be very sorry. When Marguerite awakens from the daze of trauma, Mr. Freeman is tenderly bathing her: "His hands shook" (66). Which is the greater crime, Mr. Freeman's rape of Marguerite, or Marguerite's lying about the nature of their relationship (which might be seen as having resulted in Mr. Freeman's death)? What should be the penalty for rape? Is the community's murderous action against Mr. Freeman's unthinkable crime merely a more expedient form of the state's statutes on capital punishment? Might we say he was "judged by a jury of his peers"? Which is the greater crime—if Marguerite had told the truth and Mr. Freeman had been acquitted, or Marguerite's lie, and Mr. Freeman's judgement by an outraged community? What *is* the truth? Didn't Marguerite actually tell the basic truth, based on her innocence, based on her inability to understand Mr. Freeman's motives? As Maya Angelou might say, "Those are questions, frightful questions, too intimate and obscenely probing" (*Black Women Writers*, 3) Yet, how can we deny young readers, expected to soon embark upon their own life-altering decision-making, the opportunity to engage in questions so relevant as these. How can we continue to forearm them solely with t-shirt slogans?

Caged Bird, in this scene so often deleted from classroom study, opens the door for discussion about the prevalent confusion between a young person's desire for affection and sexual invitation. Certainly, this is a valuable distinction to make, and one that young men and women are often unable to perceive or articulate. Angelou also reveals the manner by which an adult manipulates a child's desire for love as a thin camouflage for his own crude motives. A further complication to the neat assignment of blame is that Marguerite's lie is not prompted by a desire to harm Mr. Freeman, but out of her feelings of helplessness and dread. Yet, she perceives that the effect of that lie is profound—so profound that she decides to stop her own voice, both as penance for the death of Mr. Freeman and out of fear of the power of her words: ". . . a man was dead because I had lied" (72).

This dramatization of the ambiguity of truth and the fearfulness of an Old Testament justice raises questions of justice and the desirability of truth in a world strapped in fear, misunderstanding, and the inadequacy of language. The story reveals how violence can emerge out of the innocent routines of life; how betrayal can be camouflaged with blame; that adults are individual and multi-dimensional and flawed; but readers also see how Marguerite overcomes this difficult and alienating episode of her life.

However, the work's complexity is a gradual revelation. The rape must be read within the context of the entire work from the stammer of the opening scene, to the elegant Mrs. Flowers who restores Marguerite's confidence in her own voice (77–87) to the book's closing affirmation of the forgiving power of love and faith. Conversely, all of these moments should be understood against the ravaging of rape.

Marguerite's story is emblematic of the historic struggle of an entire people and, by extension, any person or group of people. The autobiography moves from survival to celebration of life and students who are permitted to witness Marguerite's suffering and ascendancy might gain in the nurturing of their own potential for compassion, optimism and courage.

This extended look at the scene most often censored by high school administrators and most often criticized by parents should reveal that Angelou's *Caged Bird*, though easily read, is no "easy" read. This is, perhaps, part of the reason for the objections of parents who may feel that the materials are "too sophisticated" for their children. We should be careful, as teachers, designers of curriculum, and concerned parents, not to fall into the false opposition of good vs. easy. What is easier for a student (or for a teacher) is not necessarily good. In this vein, those parents who are satisfied to have this work removed from required lists but offered on "suggested" lists should ask themselves whether they are giving their kids the kind of advice that was so useless to Maya Angelou: "keep your legs closed and don't let nobody see your pocketbook." Without the engagement of discussion, *Caged Bird* might do what parents fear most—raise important issues while leaving the young reader no avenue to discover his or her relationship to these ideas. Perhaps the parents are satisfied to have controversial works removed to the "suggested" list because they are convinced that their children will never read anything that is not required. If that is their hope, we have more to worry about than booklists.

If parents are concerned about anything, it should be the paucity of assigned readings in the junior high and high school classrooms, and the quality of the classroom teaching approach for this (and any other) worthwhile book. Educators have begun to address the importance of the preparation of teachers for the presentation of literature of the caliber of *Caged Bird* which is a challenge to students, but also to teachers who choose to bring this work into the classroom. *Caged Bird* establishes oppositions of place and time: Stamps, Arkansas vs. St. Louis and San Francisco; the 1930s of the book's opening vs. the slave origins of Jim Crow, which complicate images related to certain cultural aspects of African-American life including oral story traditions, traditional religious beliefs and practices, ideas regarding discipline and displays of affection, and other materials which bring rich-ness and complexity to the book, but that, without clarification, can invite misapprehension. For example, when Marguerite smashes Mrs. Cullinan's best pieces of "china from Virginia" by "accident," the scene is informative when supported by its parallels in traditional African-American folklore, by information regarding the significance of naming in traditional society, and the cultural significance of the slave state practice of depriving Africans of their true names and cultural past. The scene, though funny, should not be treated as mere comic relief, or as a meaningless act of revenge. Mrs. Cullinan, in insisting upon "re-naming" Marguerite Mary, is carrying forward that enslaving technique designed to subvert identity; she is testing what she believes is her prerogative as a white person—to establish who a black person will be, to call a black person by any name she chooses. She is "shock[ed] into recognition of [Marguerite's] personhood" (*Black Women Writers*, 9). She learns that her name game is a very dangerous power play that carries with it a serious risk.

With sufficient grounding, *I Know Why the Caged Bird Sings* can provide the kinds of insights into American history and culture, its values, practices, beliefs, lifestyles, and its seeming contradictions that inspired James Baldwin to describe the work, on its cover, as one that "liberates the reader into life simply because Maya Angelou confronts her own life with such a moving wonder, such a luminous dignity," and as ". . . a Biblical study of life in the midst of death." A book that has the potential to liberate the reader into life is one that deserves our intelligent consideration, not rash judgements made from narrow fearfulness. Such a work will not "teach students a lesson." It will demand an energetic, participatory reading. It will demand their seriousness. With the appropriate effort, this literary experi-ence can assist readers of any racial or economic group in meeting their own, often unarticulated doubts, questions, fears, and perhaps assist in their own search for dignity.

Chronology

1928   Maya Angelou is born Marguerite Johnson on April 4 in St. Louis, Missouri, the daughter of Bailey and Vivian Baxter Johnson.

1931   Her parents divorce; Angelou and her four-year-old brother are sent to live with their maternal grandmother, Annie Henderson, in Stamps, Arkansas.

1936   During a visit to her mother in St. Louis Angelou is raped by her mother's boyfriend. The man is beaten to death by her uncles and Angelou does not speak for almost five years. She returns to Stamps and discovers literature under the tutelage of an educated neighbor, Mrs. Flowers.

1940   Graduates from the eighth grade at the top of her class. Her mother, now a professional gambler, takes the children to live in San Francisco.

1940–44   Attends George Washington High School in San Francisco and takes dance and drama lessons at the California Labor School.

1945   While still in high school, becomes the first black woman streetcar conductor in San Francisco; graduates from Mission High School at age 16; one month later, gives birth to a son.

1946   Works as a cook for $75 per week at the Creole Cafe; with $200 she moves to San Diego.

1947   After becoming involved in prostitution as a madam, Angelou
            returns to Stamps. She upbraids a rude white store clerk; her
            grandmother, fearing reprisals from the Ku Klux Klan, sends
            her back to San Francisco.

1948   Joins a nightclub dance act; then works as a restaurant cook;
            spends several days as a prostitute, until her brother threatens
            violence if she continues.

1950   Marries Tosh Angelos; they divorce three years later.

1953   Angelou resumes her career as a dancer at the Purple Onion.

1954–55   Joins a twenty-two nation tour of *Porgy and Bess*, sponsored by
            the U.S. Department of State.

1955   Returns to care for her young son, Guy; becomes instructor of
            Modern Dance at the Rome Opera House and at Hambina
            Theatre, Tel Aviv.

1957   Appears in a play, *Calypso Heatwave*. Makes a commitment to
            become a writer and black civil rights activist; moves to Brooklyn
            and participates in the Harlem Writers Guild, a group that
            included John Henrik Clarke, Paule Marshall, James Baldwin,
            and social activist author John Killens.

1959–60   Succeeds Bayard Rustin as northern coordinator of Martin
            Luther King, Jr.'s, Southern Christian Leadership Conference.

1960   Appears in the Off-Broadway production of *The Blacks*; produces
            and performs Off-Broadway in Cabaret for Freedom, written
            with Godfrey Cambridge.

1961–62   Associate editor of the *Arab Observer*, an English-language news-
            paper in Cairo, Egypt.

1963-66   Assistant administrator of the School of Music and Drama at the
            University of Ghana's Institute of African Studies at Legon-

Accra, Ghana. Feature editor of the *African Review*; contributor to the Ghanian Broadcasting Company.

1964   Appears in *Mother Courage* at the University of Ghana.

1966   Appears in *Medea* and *The Least of These* in Hollywood; lecturer at the University of California, Los Angeles.

1970   Writer in residence at the University of Kansas; receives Yale University fellowship; *I Know Why the Caged Bird Sings* is published and nominated for a National Book Award.

1971   A volume of poetry, *Just Give Me a Cool Drink of Water 'fore I Diiie* is published and nominated for a Pulitzer Prize.

1972   Television narrator, interviewer, and host for African-American specials and theatre series.

1973   Receives a Tony Award nomination for her Broadway debut in *Look Away*. Marries Paul Du Feu in December; they divorce in 1981.

1974   *Gather Together in My Name* is published; directs the film *All Day Long*; appears in the adapted Sophocles play *Ajax* at the Mark Taper Forum; named distinguished visiting professor at Wake Forest University, Wichita State University, and California State University.

1975   A volume of poetry, *Oh Pray My Wings Are Gonna Fit Me Well*, is published; appointed by President Gerald R. Ford to the American Revolution Bicentennial Council; member of the National Commission on the Observance of International Women's Year; becomes member of the board of trustees of the American Film Institute; appointed Rockefeller Foundation scholar in Italy; receives honorary degrees from Smith College and Mills College.

1976   *Singin' and Swingin' and Gettin' Merry Like Christmas* is published; directs her play, *And I Still Rise*; named Woman of the Year in Communications; receives honorary degree from Lawrence University.

1977   Appears in the television film *Roots*, and receives an Emmy Award nomination for best supporting actress.

1978   *And I Still Rise* is published.

1981   *The Heart of a Woman* is published. Angelou receives a lifetime appointment as Reynolds Professor of American Studies, Wake Forest University.

1983   *Shaker, Why Don't You Sing*, a volume of poetry, is published. Angelou is named one of the Top 100 Most Influential Women by the *Ladies' Home Journal*; receives the Matrix Award.

1986   *All God's Children Need Traveling Shoes; Mrs. Flowers: A Moment of Friendship; Poems: Maya Angelou* are published.

1987   *Now Sheba Sings the Song* is published; receives the North Carolina Award in Literature.

1988   Directs Errol John's *Moon on a Rainbow Shawl* in London.

1990   A volume of poetry, *I Shall Not Be Moved*, is published.

1993   The inaugural poem *On the Pulse of Morning; Soul Looks Back in Wonder*, poems; and *Wouldn't Take Nothing for My Journey Now* are published. Angelou contributes poetry to the film *Poetic Justice*.

1994   *My Painted House, My Friendly Chicken, and Me* and *Phenomenal Women: Four Poems Celebrating Women* are published.

1995   *A Brave and Startling Truth* is published.

1996   *Kofi and His Magic*, a children's story, is published.

Contributors

HAROLD BLOOM is Sterling Professor of Humanities at Yale University and Professor of English at New York University. He is the author of *The Visionary Company*, *The Anxiety of Influence*, *Poetry and Repression*, and other volumes of literary criticism. His forthcoming study, *Freud, Transference and Authority*, considers all of Freud's major writings. A MacArthur Prize Fellow, Professor Bloom is general editor of five series of literary criticism published by Chelsea House.

SIDONIE ANN SMITH has written extensively on women's autobiography. Her works include two books: *Poetics of Women's Autobiography: Marginality and the Fictions of Self-Representation* and, co-edited with Julia Watson, a collection of essays, *De-Colonizing the Subject: The Politics of Gender in Women's Autobiography*.

GEORGE E. KENT was Professor of English at the University of Chicago and the author of *Blackness and the Adventure of Western Culture*.

MYRA K. MCMURRY received a Ph.D. from Emory University with a dissertation entitled *Self and World: the Problem of Proportion in the Novels of George Meredith*.

LILIANE K. ARENSBERG contributed to *First Person Female, American*, a supplement to the September 1977 issue of *American Notes & Queries*.

CHRISTINE FROULA is associate professor of English at Yale University. She has published books and essays on modern literature, contemporary theory, and feminist criticism including *Modernism's Body: Sex, Culture, and Joyce*.

KENETH KINNAMON is a professor of English and Chairman of the Department at the University of Arkansas. He has published *The Emergence of Richard Wright: A Study in Literature and Society*, a monograph on James Baldwin, and edited *James Baldwin: A Collection of Critical Essays*, and *New Essays on Native Son*. With Joseph Benson, Michel Fabre, and Craig Werner, he is co-editor of *A Richard Wright Bibliography*; and with Richard K. Barksdale, *Black Writers of America*.

JOANNE M. BRAXTON is Professor of American Studies and English at the College of William and Mary. She is the author of *Black Women Writing Autobiography: A Tradition Within a Tradition* and co-editor, with Andree N. McLaughlin, of *Wild Women in the Whirlwind: The Renaissance in Contemporary Afra-American Writing*.

FRANÇOISE LIONNET is Associate Professor of English at the University of Chicago and the author of *Blackness and the Adventure of Western Culture* and *Autobiographical Voices: Race, Gender, Self-Portraiture*. Her works include studies of Francophone and African-American women writers, French Caribbean and North African post-colonial literature, and issues of multi-cultural discourse.

FRED LEE HORD (MZEE LASANA OKPARA) is the author of *Reconstructing Memory: Black Literary Criticism*. He edited, with Jonathan Scott Lee, and wrote the introduction to *I Am Because We Are: Readings in Black Philosophy* and, with Pansye S. Atkinson, *African Americans: a Bibliography of Library Holdings at Frostburg State College*; and he is the author of a book of poems, *After Hours*.

MARY VERMILLION is Assistant Professor at Mt. Mercy College, in Cedar Rapids, Iowa. She has published articles on English literature, including *Buried Heroism: Critiques of Female Authorship in Southerne's Adaptation of Behn's Oroonoko*.

JAMES BERTOLINO has published eighteen books of poetry and numerous essays and articles. He has won awards for his poetry and for his activities in small press poetry books.

OPAL MOORE is professor of English at Radford University. She has published short stories, poetry, and essays about Black experience in America in various periodicals and collections. Her forthcoming books are *I Ain't No Stranger . . . I Been Here Before* and *Mildred D. Taylor: Moral Teacher*.

Bibliography

Benson, Carol. "Out of the Cage and Still Singing," *Writer's Digest* (January 1975): 18–20.

Bloom, Lynn Z. "Maya Angelou," *Dictionary of Literary Biography*, 38. Detroit: Gale, 1985. 3–12.

Buss, Helen M. "Reading for the Doubled Discourse of American Women's Autobiography," *Auto-Biography Studies*, 6:1 (Spring 1991): 95–108.

Butterfield, Stephen. *Black Autobiography in America*. Amherst: University of Massachusetts Press, 1974.

Chrisman, Robert. "*The Black Scholar* Interviews Maya Angelou," *Black Scholar* (January–February 1977): 44–52.

Cordell, Shirley J. "The Black Woman: A Focus on 'Strength of Character' in *I Know Why the Caged Bird Sings*," *Virginia English Bulletin*, 36:2 (Winter 1986): 36–39.

Cudjoe, Selwyn R. "Maya Angelou and the Autobiographical Statement," *Black Women Writers (1950–1980): A Critical Evaluation*. New York: Bantam, 1984. 6–24.

Demetrakopoulos, Stephanie A. "The Metaphysics of Matrilinearism in Women's Autobiography: Studies of Mead's *Blackberry Winter*, Hellman's *Pentimento*, Angelou's *I Know Why the Caged Bird Sings*, and Kingston's *The Woman Warrior*," in *Women's Autobiography: Essays in Criticism*. Ed. Estelle Jelinek. Bloomington: Indiana University Press, 1980. 180–205.

Elliot, Jeffrey, ed. *Conversations with Maya Angelou*. Jackson: University Press of Mississippi, 1989.

Estes-Hicks, Onita. "The Way We Were: Precious Memories of the Black Segregated South," *African American Review*, 27:1 (Spring 1993): 9–18.

Foster, Frances. "Parents and Children in Autobiography by Southern Afro-American Writers," *Home Ground: Southern Autobiography*. Ed. Bill J. Berry. Columbia: University of Missouri Press, 1992. 98–109.

Georgoudaki, Ekaterini. *Race, Gender, and Class Perspectives in the Works of Maya Angelou, Gwendolyn Brooks, Rita Dove, Nikki Giovanni, and Audre Lorde*. Thessaloniki: Aristotle University of Thessaloniki, 1991.

Gilbert, Susan. "Maya Angelou's *I Know Why the Caged Bird Sings*: Paths to Escape," *Mount Olive Review*, 1:1 (Spring 1987): 39–50.

Goodman, G., Jr. "Maya Angelou's Lonely Black Outlook," *The New York Times* (March 24, 1972): 28.

Gottlieb, Annie. "Growing Up and the Serious Business of Survival," *New York Times Book Review* (June 16, 1974): 16, 20.

Gruesser, John C. "Afro-American Travel Literature and Africanist Discourse," *Black American Literature Forum*, 24:1 (Spring 1990): 5–20.

Inge, Tonette Bond, ed. *Southern Women Writers: The New Generation*. Tuscaloosa: University of Alabama Press, 1990.

Kelly, Ernece B. [Review of *I Know Why the Caged Bird Sings*] *Harvard Educational Review* 40:4 (November 1970): 681–82.

Lionnet, Françoise. *Autobiographical Voices: Race, Gender, Self-Portraiture*. Ithaca: Cornell University Press, 1989. 130–68.

Lupton, Mary Jane. "Singing the Black Mother: Maya Angelou and Autobiographical Continuity," *Black American Literature Forum*, 24:2 (Summer 1990): 257–76.

MacKethan, Lucinda H. "Mother Wit: Humor in Afro-American Women's Autobiography," *Studies in American Humor*, 4:1–2 (Spring 1985): 51–61.

McPherson, Dolly. *Order Out of Chaos: The Autobiographical Works of Maya Angelou*. New York: Peter Lang, 1990.

———. "Defining the Self through Place and Culture: Maya Angelou's *I Know Why the Caged Bird Sings*," *MAWA Review*, 5:1 (June 1990): 12–14.

Megna-Wallace, Joanne. "Simone de Beauvoir and Maya Angelou: Birds of a Feather," *Simone de Beauvoir Studies* 6 (1986): 49–55.

Neubauer, Carol E. "Maya Angelou: Self and a Song of Freedom in the Southern Tradition," *Southern Women Writers: The New Generatioin*. Tuscaloosa: University of Alabama Press, 1990. 114–141.

———. "Displacement and Autobiographical Style in Maya Angelou's *The Heart of a Woman*," in *Black American Literature Forum*, 17:3 (Fall 1983): 123–29.

———. "An Interview with Maya Angelou," *Massachusetts Review*, 28:2 (Spring 1987): 286–92.

O'Neale, Sondra. "Reconstruction of the Composite Self: New Images of BlackWomen in Maya Angelou's Continuing Autobiography," *Black Women Writers (1950–1980): A Critical Evaluation*. Ed. Mari Evans. New York: Bantam, 1984. 25–36.

Premo, Cassie. "When the Difference Becomes Too Great: Images of the Self and Survival in a Postmodern World," *Genre* 16 (1995): 183–91.

Ramsey, Priscilla R. "Transcendence: The Poetry of Maya Angelou," *A Current Bibliography on African Affairs*, 17:2 (1984–85). 139–153.

Redmond, Eugene B. "Boldness of Language and Breadth: An Interview with Maya Angelou," *Black American Literature Forum*, 22:2 (Summer 1988): 156–57.

Saunders, James Robert. "Breaking Out of the Cage: The Autobiographical Writings of Maya Angelou," *The Hollins Critic*, 28:4 (October 1991): 1–11.

Tate, Claudia, ed. *Black Women Writers at Work*. New York: Continuum, 1983. 1–11.

Tawake, Sandra Kiser. "Multi-Ethnic Literature in the Classroom: Whose Standards?" *World Englishes: Journal of English as an International and Intranational Language*, 10:3 (Winter 1991): 335–40.

Wall, Cheryl. "Maya Angelou," *Women Writers Talking*. Ed. Janet Todd. New York: Holmes & Meier, 1983. 59–67.

Weller, Sheila. "Work in Progress/Maya Angelou," *Intellectual Digest* (June, 1973).

Acknowledgments

"The Song of the Caged Bird: Maya Angelou's Quest for Self-Acceptance" by Sidonie Ann Smith from *Southern Humanities Review*, 7:4 (Fall 1973). Copyright © 1973 by Auburn University.

"Maya Angelou's *I Know Why the Caged Bird Sings* and Black Autobiographical Tradition" by George E. Kent from *African American Autobiography: A Collection of Critical Essays*. Copyright © 1993 by Prentice-Hall. Reprinted with permission of the publisher. Article originally appeared in *Kansas Quarterly* 7 (1975): 72–78.

"Role Playing as Art in Maya Angelou's 'Caged Bird'" by Myra K. McMurry from *South Atlantic Bulletin*, 41:2 (May 1976). Copyright © 1976 by the South Atlantic Modern Language Association.

"Death as Metaphor of Self in *I Know Why the Caged Bird Sings*" by Liliane K. Arensberg from *CLA Journal*, 20:2 (December 1976). Copyright © 1976 by the College Language Association.

"The Daughter's Seduction: Sexual Violence and Literary History" by Christine Froula from *Signs*, 11:4 (Summer 1986). Copyright © 1986 by The University of Chicago Press. Reprinted with permission of the publisher and the author.

"Call and Response: Intertextuality in Two Autobiographical Works by Richard Wright and Maya Angelou" by Keneth Kinnamon from *Studies in Black American Literature, Vol. II: Belief vs. Theory in Black American Literary Criticism*, edited by Joe Weixlmann and Chester J. Fontenot. Copyright © 1986 by The Penkevill Publishing Co.

"Maya Angelou's *I Know Why the Caged Bird Sings*: Paths to Escape" by Susan Gilbert from *Mount Olive Review*, 1:1 (Spring 1987): 39–50. Copyright © 1987 by Mount Olive College.

"A Song of Transcendence: Maya Angelou" by Joanne M. Braxton from *Black Women*

Index